The economics of organised crime

This is the first book to use economic theory in the analysis of all the different aspects of organised crime: the origins, the internal organisation, market behaviour and deterrence policies. The theory of rent-seeking is adopted to help understand the origin of criminal organisations from a state of anarchy, while modern industrial organisation theory is used to explain the design of internal rules in the organised crime sector. The market behaviour of organised crime is analysed taking into account its double nature of competitive firm and of monopolist on rule-making. Finally, the 'crime and economics' approach is applied to the analysis of corruption that occurs when the organised crime sector and the government collude to exploit their monopoly on rule-making.

This book provides a careful balance between theoretical and institutional or empirical contributions. Each chapter outlines the normative results of the analysis in order to design more sophisticated deterrence policies.

Centro Interuniversitario di Studi Teorici per la Politica Economica

The Inter-University Centre for Theoretical Studies in Economic Policy (STEP) was founded jointly by the Departments of Economics of Bocconi University (Milan), the University of Bologna, and the University of Venice (Cà Foscari). STEP is also affiliated with CEPR. The aim of STEP is to support theoretical research on economic policy, and to promote academic exchange, both nationally and internationally, by organising seminars and conferences.

Department of Economics, Bologna University

The Department of Economics of Bologna University was established in 1982 and brought together in a single administrative structure the members of the former Institutes of Economics and Finance, of Public Policy and of Economic History, together with the Economic Geographers and the Economic Historians. Since its formation, the Department has always pursued a policy of strengthening its ties with local and national institutions as well as with international academic institutions and research centres.

The economics of organised crime

Edited by

GIANLUCA FIORENTINI

and

SAM PELTZMAN

CAMBRIDGE
UNIVERSITY PRESS

Published by the Press Syndicate of the University of Cambridge
The Pitt Building, Trumpington Street, Cambridge CB2 1RP
40 West 20th Street, New York, NY 10011–4211, USA
10 Stamford Road, Oakleigh, Melbourne 3166, Australia

First published 1995

Printed in Great Britain at the University Press, Cambridge

A catalogue record for this book is available from the British Library

Library of Congress cataloguing in publication data applied for

ISBN 0 521 47248 2 hardback

HV
6171
E36
1995

Contents

PART II   THE CRIMINAL ORGANISATION AS A FIRM

Figures

Tables

Foreword

For many years the Centre for Economic Policy Research (CEPR), the Centro Interuniversitario di Studi Teorici per la Politica Economica (STEP), and the Dipartimento di Scienze Economiche (DSE) dell'Università di Bologna have cooperated in organising conferences, seminars and other scientific meetings, both institutionally and through the individual participation of their members. This cooperation has also involved the Università Bocconi (Milano) and the Università di Venezia. Indeed, on the Italian side, the organisation of these activities gave rise in the late 1980s to the formation of the Italian Macroeconomic Policy Group, which produced, together with CEPR, a number of successful conference volumes: on the European Monetary System, on the prospects of a European Central Bank, and on the Italian experience with high public debt.

These scientific endeavours were generally focused on problems of macroeconomic policy in open economies. The subject matter of the conference that produced the papers collected in this volume falls outside the traditional definition of macroeconomic policy. Yet, besides its specific importance in theory and unfortunate relevance in practice, we feel that the economics of organised crime goes well beyond the realm of 'industrial organisation'. The importance of this sector of human activity involves the economies of some countries and their international relations in such a deep and pervasive way that it may even affect the economic performance and constrain the macro-economic policies of their entire economies. This is the reason why we believe that the subject fits very well within the line of themes on which the scientific cooperation among our institutions has developed through the years.

Normally we like the subjects of our intellectual efforts to become even more important in future. In this case, however, we hope that this book will contribute, by improving the understanding of economists and policy-makers, to make the problems analysed here less important in future for all our countries.

Giorgio Basevi
Director of STEP

Richard Portes
Director of CEPR

Stefano Zamagni
Director of the DSE

Acknowledgements

The conference reported in this volume was held at the Department of Economics of the Università degli Studi di Bologna. We should like first to thank the University for serving as the site of the conference and for its hospitality not only for the formal proceedings but also for the social events which provided such delightful settings for the continuation of discussions. We are grateful to the Department for providing administrative and organisational arrangements.

Financial and logistic support was provided generously by public foundations and private firms. We would especially mention: Assitalia, Bologna; Banca d'Italia, Roma; Camera di Commercio, Bologna; Cassa di Risparmio, Bologna; Consiglio Nazionale delle Ricerche, Roma; Fondazione ENI Enrico Mattei, Milano; Istituto Mobiliare Italiano, Roma; Lega Cooperative, Bologna; and Unipol, Bologna.

The conference was organised by CEPR and a local committee comprising Professors Giorgio Basevi, Gianluca Fiorentini and Stefano Zamagni. The programme committee comprised Professors Sam Peltzman and Giorgio Basevi (Co-Chairmen) and Professors Gary Becker, Isaac Ehrlich, Herschel Grossman, Tom Schelling, Nicholas Stern, Vito Tanzi and Stefano Zamagni.

Gianluca Fiorentini and Sam Peltzman

Conference participants

Annelise Anderson *Hoover Institution, Stanford University*
Pino Arlacchi *Università di Firenze*
Fabrizio Barca *Banca d'Italia*
Giorgio Basevi *Università di Bologna and CEPR*
William J. Baumol *Princeton University*
Luigi Campiglio *Università Cattolica del Sacro Cuore di Milano*
Marco Celentani *Universidad Carlos III, Madrid*
Frank A. Cowell *LSE*
Giovanni Dal Monte *Università di Napoli*
Michael Defeo *US Department of Justice*
Flavio Delbono *Università di Bologna and CEPR*
Vincenzo Denicolo *Università di Bologna*
Issac Ehrlich *State University of New York at Buffalo and Hong Kong University of Science and Technology*
Gianluca Fiorentini *Università di Firenze*
Diego Gambetta *Department of Applied Social Studies, Oxford*
Herschel I. Grossman *Brown University*
John R. Lott Jr *University of Pennsylvania*
Francis Lui *State University of New York at Buffalo*
Carla Marchese *Università di Torino*
Massimo Marrelli *Università di Napoli*
Riccardo Martina *Istituto Universitario Navale, Napoli*
Sam Peltzman *University of Chicago*
Michele Polo *Università Bocconi, Milano*
Peter Reuter *Rand Corporation*
Pier Luigi Sacco *Università di Firenze*
Ernesto Savona *Università di Trento*
Domenico Siniscalco *Università di Torino and Fondazione ENI Enrico Mattei, Milano*

Stergios Skaperdas *University of California, Irvine*
Vito Tanzi *IMF*
Piero Tedeschi *Università Bocconi, Milano*
Stefano Zamagni *Università di Bologna*

1   Introduction

GIANLUCA FIORENTINI and
SAM PELTZMAN

1   Overview

Most of the economists who involve themselves in the analysis of the activities of criminal organisations are led by a concern for what newspapers report about their continuous violations of the basic norms which have come to rule social life. However, such an interest also comes from the belief that some conceptual tools, theoretical results and empirical facts obtained by economists working on other issues can be put to work to reach a better understanding of their origins and activities.

Further, since economists as such hold no comparative advantage in the area of ethical reflection with respect to other scholars such as moral philosophers or theologians, the economists' most valuable contribution, at least because relatively scarce, should come from a positive analysis of the workings of criminal organisations, of their internal structure and of the constraints limiting their activities, with special reference to the constraints posed by the legal government. In this respect, we will show that economists interested in policy-making at large may also have something to learn from a closer analysis of how illegal markets and activities constrain the activities of a policy-maker when the latter intervenes on legal markets.

Even if economists may have some comparative advantage in the analysis of organised crime, they have done relatively little work in the area. This even if it is more than twenty years since 'crime and economics' became an established and autonomous area of research. However, most of the work following the contribution of Becker (1968) has been targeted on individual agents' allocative choice between legal and illegal activities in the face of different deterrence systems and different opportunity costs.[1] Moreover, extensions of the approach based on individuals' rational use of their scarce resources to areas where many scholars believe that social conditions are more relevant have been followed with some impatience.

This debate on the usefulness of economic models for understanding individuals' choices in non-traditional areas is centred on two basic themes. First, opinions differ about the heuristic possibilities of economic modelling based on rational choice, strictly understood. On one hand there are the economists of American tradition – especially those from Chicago – who are in general more confident about such possibilities. On the other hand, most European economists are definitely reluctant to adopt the usual economists' tools outside their traditional areas of research. This because of the widespread impression that individuals' behaviours in those areas cannot really be understood using the economic model of rational choice. Hence, the conclusion that individuals' behaviours in illegal activities – not being rational in the economic sense – are to be left to a sociological analysis of pathologies and deviations.

This reluctance to apply standard economic analysis to illegal activities has also been justified on the basis of an alleged imperialism of the economic approach which aims to provide exhaustive explanations of individuals' choices in performing illegal activities. However, from a direct reading of most works in the literature on crime and economics, one would find that the economic approach limits itself to emphasising the potential effects of economic variables such as disposable incomes, education levels and other policy variables more directly under govern-ment control, such as the level of sanctions and the likelihood of their enforcement. This is not to deny that other – non-economic – factors also influence the illegal transactions, but to stress that economic variables have a role to play in this setting, and that such variables can be employed in a normative analysis as they are, after all, partly under the control of the policy-maker. Moreover, to state that eminently economic variables have only negligible effects on most individual agents' choices concerning illegal activities seems to be at odds with a growing body of empirical evidence.

A simple list of the main activities which can be labelled as 'illegal' makes this point clearer: fiscal evasion and elusion, administrative and political corruption, access to black and illicit markets, commercial and financial frauds, violations of antitrust and other regulatory legislation, especially in the job market, manipulation of public subsidy schemes, organised fiscal evasion, etc. etc. Accordingly, most agents – even if they are not social deviants – are often in a position to choose the proportion of their resources to allocate to illegal activities.

Moreover, it is plausible that the main factors in determining such choices are precisely the ones which characterise the typical economic choice: the costs and benefits of the different options, the degree of uncertainty surrounding costs and benefits, the long-term consequences of increasing or decreasing one's reputation and so on. To this, one should also add that in the area of the illegal activities there is a significant increase of the share of transactions which are directly or indirectly under the control of highly-structured and highly-diversified organisations. This increase signals a trend towards greater efficiency in the allocation of resources used in the production of illegal commodities and a growing need for the agents involved to adopt management schemes which minimise organisational costs in order not to disappear in the course of competition.

Building on these considerations, the Department of Economics of Bologna University, together with the Centro Interuniversitario di Studi Teorici per la Politica Economica and the Centre for Economic Policy Research, organised a conference on the activities of criminal organisations in order to contribute to a wider diffusion of the more fruitful applications of economic analysis to this area, both in their theoretical aspects and in their implications for deterrence policy.

2   Alternative views on the nature of organised crime

The term 'organised crime' has been used with various meanings by scholars and prosecutors in different countries. Some authors use it to define a set of relations among illegal organisations, while others use it to indicate a group of illegal activities performed by a given set of agents. For instance, the definition used by the Task Force on Organized Crime of the 1967 President's Commission at the beginning of its report is as follows: 'The core of organized crime activity is the supplying of illegal goods and services – gambling, loan-sharking, narcotics, and other forms of vice – to countless numbers of citizen customers.'[2] This definition clearly establishes a direct link between the core activities of organised crime and the management of illegal markets. While ordinary crime is typically appropriative and aimed at an unlawful redistribution of resources, organised crime arises in order to perform activities for which there is a spontaneous demand. Although it is not denied that the criminal organisation can use violence in order to achieve economic results in its legal activities, this is typically not so when it is involved in its activities in illegal markets. Indeed, according to this view, the criminal organisation looks very much like a (highly structured) *firm* whose business is that of producing illegal goods and services for the consumers.

Schelling (1971) argues that the above definition of organised crime cannot be accepted because it does not give a central role to those activities involving the threat and/or practice of violence against other legal and illegal business. According to Schelling, the difference between ordinary criminal activities – which may be highly organised – and 'organised crime' is that only the latter seek to govern and control the whole economic structure of the underworld. Schelling's argument is built in two distinct logical steps. First, it is argued that the very notion of organised crime brings in itself an idea of 'exclusivity, or to use a more focused term, [of] monopoly'. Indeed, according to Schelling, the very core of the business of the criminal organisation is to acquire a rule-making role in a given area (be it geographical or economic) so as to levy taxes and impose regulations over legitimate and/or illicit businesses. This allows it to reap most of the rents from the illegal transactions without running the full cost and risk involved in the direct management of the businesses. Second, the rule-making role necessarily requires the organised use of violence, either through threats or actions, not only to extort from the illegal firms but also to impose a monopoly of violence over a given area. According to Schelling therefore, the core activities of the criminal organisation are closely linked with illegal markets not because of its direct control over production and distribution in those markets but, quite on the contrary, because the active firms in the illegal markets are less able to protect themselves from harassment because they cannot seek protection from the law-enforcement agencies and cannot hide as they need to advertise their operations to attract demand. In this respect Schelling's idea of the criminal organisation is much closer to that of a *government* establishing its own rules in the areas over which it extends its power.

More recently, Reuter (1983) provides and motivates a third definition of organised crime which implicitly rejects both the above approaches: '[O]rganized crime consists of organizations that have durability, hierarchy, and involvement in a multiplicity of criminal activities.'[3] This definition is rather general as it neither mentions any specific legal or illegal activity or market nor alludes to the existence of a close correlation between organised crime on the one hand and illegal markets or a trend towards monopolisation of the underworld on the other. However, the definition is also precise enough to exclude from 'organised crime' those illegal firms dealing with only one illegal activity or not having a stable and hierarchical structure. Reuter rejects the President's Commission approach because it includes within 'organised crime' only activities in the illegal markets. Such a definition is clearly too restrictive as there is clear evidence of the involvement of criminal organisations which operate in legal activities, ranging from the production of crucial inputs in given industries to the organisation of large-scale frauds to governmental subsidy schemes, and to the allocation of public procurement.[4] For similar reasons – lack of empirical evidence – Reuter objects to the definition of organised crime given by Schelling. Indeed most of Reuter (1983) is dedicated to the confutation of the thesis that there is a central control of the illegal markets due to the monopoly of violence and corruption established by organised crime over the firms active in those markets.

Observing the evidence put together in the last ten years by different investigative agencies and independent scholars, both Schelling's and Reuter's definitions seem to stress crucial elements for an understanding of the peculiar features of organised crime, while the President's Commission's definition has increasingly lost analytical relevance.[5] Indeed the growing empirical evidence on the national and international activities of criminal organisations has made it clear that they are active in so many different markets that one can hardly use a unitary interpretative scheme. On one hand, there are several illegal markets (or legal markets where criminal organisations operate) where there are no significant barriers to entry (e.g. numbers, loan-sharking, prostitution, smuggling, counterfeiting, etc.), for which it seems rather implausible to infer the existence of some sort of centralised control. These markets seem to be competitive and the elements which could constitute monopolistic rents are usually swept away by the forces of competition and by the conflicts between rival organisations.

On the other hand, there are markets (again either legal or illegal) where criminal organisations tend to integrate themselves vertically so as to reach some degree of central coordination (e.g. money laundering, large-scale distribution of narcotics – especially in international markets – and supply of violence for extortionary purposes). Although in these markets there is undoubtedly room for competitive activities – whose intensity may follow cyclical patterns – there are efforts on the part of the most powerful criminal organisations to reach some coordination between themselves. Such coordination is usually sought through the establishment of cartels – mostly on a territorial basis – and through the strengthening of vertical relationships between organisations specialising in the provision of different inputs needed to provide a given illegal service (e.g. violence, corruption, financial expertise). As is well known, this idea of centralised control over large parts of organised criminal activity has been recently advocated by the Italian prosecutors who started the so-called 'maxi-trial' against the heads of the Sicilian mafia.[6] The prosecutors' thesis is based on evidence concerning the existence of a committee of local heads of mafia families which acted as a centralised decision-maker for their more important economic activities. The advantages arising from centralisation were said to come from different sources: (a) economies of scale in some basic services needed to perform illegal activities; (b) exploitation of monopolistic prices in some markets less open to external competition; (c) internalisation of negative externalities due to oversupply of violence; (d) avoidance of resource dissipation through competitive lobbying and corruption; (e) better management of a portfolio of risky activities; and (f) easier access to national and international financial markets.

However, the proceedings of the maxi-trial and further empirical evidence suggest that there are strong forces which push the criminal organisations away from a high degree of central coordination. Among these forces the most relevant seem to be the following: (a) the risks involved in illegal transactions decrease more than proportionally with their size since it is impossible to make contracts binding; (b) the property rights over the commodities are not well defined and can be subjected to seizure by the enforcement agencies so that large investments in any given activity are discouraged; (c) the participants in illegal activities run a risk of detection which is growing with the number of people involved because some members of the organisation may cooperate with the investigative agencies; and (d) there are inherent problems in keeping the financial markets efficient as they are thin markets.

To establish which of the two theses better describes the supply of illegal activities is not only a theoretical problem. Indeed, the most appropriate deterrence policy clearly depends on how the illegal markets are structured in terms of barriers to entry, the number of active firms, their coordination in terms of pricing and marketing strategies, and their attitudes towards the use of violence. If the illegal supply is highly centralised, an increase in deterrence against the illegal transactions may increase entry costs in that market and therefore increase rents for the incumbent firms. On the other hand, if the illegal markets under observation are mainly competitive, a lowering of the barriers to entry may increase the overall output which has a negative effect as the output is an illegal commodity.

Accordingly, both approaches to the definition of organised crime – as a central decision-maker in the underworld and as a non-coordinated group of firms mainly dealing with illegal markets – have received some support from the existing evidence. In the present collection of essays both these views of the criminal organisation are adopted. This is because we – and most of the authors of the conference papers – think that both aspects are relevant to a fuller understanding of the role and activities of organised crime. Moreover, which feature of organised crime is more relevant depends not only on the specific historical and institutional settings but also on the purpose of the analysis. For instance, if one is interested in the internal structure of a criminal organisation, it is perhaps more appropriate to investigate it as a firm where agents at different levels maximise their objective functions. The analogy with a firm holds even more tightly if one is interested in the analysis of the investment decisions of the criminal organisations or their competitive behaviour with respect to rivals in the output market. On the other hand, the analogy with a governmental structure is much more useful when the analysis focuses on racketeering activities or the management of military conflicts against other organisations.

Irrespective of the analogy chosen to describe organised crime, its investment decisions strictly depend on the role played by the legal government as law-enforcer and law-maker. In this respect, the legal government's definition of the illegal markets, and also its choice of regulation in the legal markets and of fiscal legislation, can be regarded as the most important factors in determining the areas in which the criminal organisations choose to allocate their resources. Moreover, the strength of the legal government as a law-enforcer is a crucial variable for understanding the extent of the criminal organisations' extortionary activities. For these reasons we focus in this introduction on the relationships between the activities of the criminal organisations and the features of the legal government as both law-maker and law-enforcer. In doing so we also deal with some of the policy implications of the conference papers which have not yet been fully investigated, and which constitute an interesting agenda for future research.

There is a further aspect of the relationships between organised crime and governmental bodies which is not usually investigated by the economists supporting one or the other approach to the analysis of the organised crime but is central to the analysis of many sociologists working in the field.[7] This aspect involves the collusive relations between criminal organisations on one hand and politicians and bureaucrats on the other. Here, one could consider very different activities ranging from the organisation of groups of voters in exchange for a share of the public contracts to the bribery of police officers. These collusive agreements between public decision-makers and criminal organisations have been very little analysed although, by analogy with the positive theory of regulation, one would think that they are not so rare.

In the next section we deal with the origin of criminal organisations as institutions for seeking rents in competition or collusion with the legal government. Such a theory builds on the idea that institutions – including criminal organisations – arise in order to perform either appropriative or productive activities depending on which of the two involves higher returns from the use of scarce resources. Although this approach is not completely new (Hirshleifer, 1988, and Baumol, 1990), it has been fruitfully applied in different papers in this volume and has further potential for future research targeted at the role of the criminal organisations as competitors to the legal government is levying taxes and providing public goods and services. Such a line of research is particularly relevant as it allows one to understand better the analogies and differences between the coercive activities of both the legal government and the criminal organisations. In Section 4, we turn to the analysis of the productive activities of the organised crime sector, that is of those activities for which there is a voluntary demand. In this setting the contributions to this volume investigate the specific features of criminal organisations as firms in terms of both internal structure and competitive strategies in the output markets. However, here we also deal with the interesting situations in which the criminal organisations collude with parts of the public administration in order to extract rents. In Section 5, we discuss the policy implications which can be drawn from the contributions dealing with the above aspects of the criminal organisations' activities and finally, in Section 6 we discuss an agenda for further research with particular reference to the definition of better deterrence policies against organised crime.

3   Theories of the state and criminal organisations

> If entrepreneurship is the imaginative pursuit of position with limited concern about the means used to achieve the purpose, then we can expect changes in the structure of rewards to modify the nature of the entrepreneur's activities, sometimes drastically. The rules of the game can then be a critical influence helping to determine whether entrepreneurship will be allocated predominantly to activities that are productive or unproductive and even destructive. (Baumol, p. 897)

Most contributions to this volume focus on the conflictual relations that arise between criminal organisations and governmental agencies because both need to perform their functions to obtain a monopoly or near monopoly in coercion over a given territory. In order to understand the features of the criminal organisations as governmental institutions one needs to analyse the circumstances in which the legal government's agencies acquire an undisputed monopoly over coercion or, alternatively, the criminal organisations succeed in establishing control over an area – be it geographically or functionally defined.

 In this respect the theory of the origin of economic institutions under anarchy has many relevant implications for an economic theory of the origin of organised crime.[8] Indeed, in the communities in which, for different reasons, no group of agents has an established comparative advantage in appropriative activities, agents in several groups continue to invest their resources in such activities. Further, the ongoing allocation of resources in appropriative activities decreases the incentives to establish a stable definition of efficient property rights and hence the relative advantage of investing in productive activities. Even in the case in which a group of agents reaches the monopoly over coercion (becoming effectively the collective decision-maker) without giving rise to open conflict, there are some areas of the economy in which the group prefers not to impose direct regulation over the activities under its control. A first reason for this lack of direct regulation is to be found in the excessive monitoring costs needed to enforce it. Such a case occurs, for instance, in competitive markets where the high number of agents involved and the logic of competition do not allow for the collection of large rents from regulation net of its costs.

Another situation in which the collective decision-maker prefers not to extract potential rents – more interesting for the analysis of criminal organisations – is that of the markets which the collective decision-maker itself defines as illegal. In such circumstances the agents who have control over the monopoly of coercion abstain from direct regulation, leaving other organisations to compete for the rights to impose their rules. In the next section we will show how the economic approach, which views the criminal organisations as groups of agents competing for the monopoly over coercion, can provide a coherent interpretative scheme for the analysis of the activities of organised crime as well as its origin.

The approach proposed independently by Hirshleifer (1988) and Baumol (1990), and based on the idea of rent-seeking, suggests that the entrepreneurs allocate their resources between appropriative and productive activities depending on the relative returns of the two activities. This choice is made both when there is regular enforcement of the property rights over resources and when such enforcement is not realised (the case of anarchy), and indeed such property rights are defined in the working of the model as the result of a rent-seeking conflict between the different agents.[9] Under anarchy one of the main preliminary conditions for the intentional exchanges to take place is lacking, so that the voluntary features of the economic actions, which characterise market exchanges, fall in second place after the coercive features.[10] In such a case, where a strong governmental authority is lacking, the investment of resources in appropriative activities allows each individual agent to participate in the distributive conflict which none can escape – even if only for self-defence – because no agent can credibly commit himself to respect the initial resources of the other agents.

In their essay in this volume, Skaperdas and Syropulos, following the Hirshleifer and Baumol approach, show that if agents are equally productive in both their appropriative and their productive activities, the level of investment in the latter depends mainly on the characteristics of the conflict technology, and more precisely increases with its efficiency, because in such a case even small differences in the investment can bring about large differences in the final distribution of resources. Analogously, the amount of resources allocated to appropriative activities increases with their productivity in such activities because this increases the resources which can be obtained at the end of the conflict. On the contrary, if agents' productivities in different activities differ (under anarchy), those who have a comparative advantage in the productive activities are likely to receive smaller shares of the overall resource endowment. Moreover, the greater is the comparative advantage of a group of agents in appropriative activities, the smaller is the overall investment in such activities, because the agents who suffer from the comparative disadvantage know from the start that their investment in those activities have a minimal effect on the distributive share they will obtain, but it will reduce the overall endowment of resources to be distributed at the end of the conflict.

Hence, the agents who contribute more to the growth of the available resources – as they have a comparative advantage in productive activities – end up with smaller shares of the overall resources than the agents who have a comparative advantage in appropriative activities. Further, if there is an exit option out of anarchy, there is migration by those agents who have a comparative advantage in productive activities, giving rise to a progressive decrease in their proportion of the total and a fall in the overall productive capacity of the community. If one assumes that the interaction between asymmetric agents is repeated over an indefinite number of periods, the situation is rather more depressing concerning the effects of the redistributive conflict, but it also shows some counter-weighing effects. As for the negative aspects, every agent is aware that the supremacy obtained in the first interaction tends to consolidate the comparative advantages in the appropriative activities and, in view of the pay-offs which can be obtained in the following repetitions, they are induced to increase their investment in appropriative activities. In the following interactions, however, once the pre-eminence of some agents becomes established, there are less and less incentives for agents in any group to dissipate their resources in an actual conflict because the latter would have a predetermined outcome. As a consequence, the appropriation of other agents' resources – even if it is still based on the possibility of an actual recourse to force – takes place through the imposition of generally accepted redistributive rules.[11]

These results only appear to contrast with the predictions based on the possibility of sustaining cooperative agreements in strategic situations repeated over an indefinite number of periods. Indeed, they only tell us that the sustainability over time of such agreements is possible, but not that it is more likely than their break-down. Further, such results are typically obtained under the assumption that the incentives for the agents to choose a given strategy do not change over time, while in the case of conflict under anarchy the agents' incentives to invest in appropriative activities are decreasing over time. For this reason, agents have particularly strong incentives to choose conflictual strategies in the first repetitions, making it impossible to consolidate cooperative agreements in the following rounds of the social interaction.

The competition among different communities – by analogy with what happens among firms – not only induces the disappearance of those communities which are unable to avoid the dissipation of their resources in the redistributive conflict but also enforces the definition of property rights over economic resources, which tends to maximise the overall efficiency of the community. This protects the resources of those agents who do not belong to the group having a comparative advantage in the appropriative activities and thus maintains their incentive to invest in productive activities. Further, following the specialisation of resources into different productive activities, agents in a growing number of groups acquire greater weight in the management of the monopoly over coercion because, when the complementarity between different groups increases, more groups can credibly threaten to reduce the overall efficiency of the community through the adoption of different exit options.[12] Accordingly, in the development of the social interaction, the groups holding a comparative advantage in the appropriative activities lose weight in the management of the monopoly over coercion, and their ability to violate the other agents' property rights reduces, which helps to preserve the resources available for appropriation.[13] Given the complementarity existing between different groups, none of them can acquire full control of the monopoly over coercion and one expects a continuing conflict to obtain the greater weight in the definition of the redistributive rules.[14]

4   The activities of organised crime

When either the legal government or the criminal organisations have established a monopoly over coercion, there are many analogies between criminal and governmental institutions in their management of the economic transactions under their control. In this section we show how organised crime plays its role as a substitute for the government employing the typical tools which characterise public intervention in the economy, from levying taxes to restricting entry in different markets, from regulating the quality of goods and services to the coercive provision of public goods.

On the basis of the allocative theory of resources between productive and appropriative activities, we have seen that organised crime can be defined as a set of organisations competing (and/or colluding) with the government and among themselves to obtain the monopoly over coercion in a given territory. However, the nature of such organisations is rather complex and, as we have seen in Section 2, it can be better understood if one focuses on its analogies and differences with the two institutions which have a central place in modern economic systems: the firm and the government.

4.1   The criminal organisation as a firm

This research perspective is explored in the works of Polo and of Gambetta and Reuter, and is also taken up with a normative perspective by Fiorentini and Celentani *et al.* The common starting-point of these works is the observation that control over the territory – be it geographic or functional – is a necessary condition for criminal organisations to carry out their activities. As has been shown in the analysis of anarchy, different organisations invest a considerable part of their resources in military technology and/or in corruption to acquire the monopoly over coercion. But, even when an organisation holds such a monopoly in an area, and the conflict with other organisations becomes latent, there remains an incentive to invest in appropriative activities to dissuade further attempts to contest such control.

In this respect, investment in military technology for criminal organisations is analogous to investment in research and development or in advertising for legal firms. In fact, the investment in each of these activities is not aimed at the production of goods and services, but instead at increasing their profitability by deterring the entry of rival firms. In the case of the criminal organisations, the investment in violence and corruption is intended to increase the profitability of the illegal commodities sold or imposed through a strengthening of the incumbency position. There are, however, rather severe limits in expanding the size of criminal organisations holding control over coercion in given areas. Indeed, the criminal organisations need to monitor strictly the activities of their members to be able to punish credibly their opportunistic behaviour, since they cannot rely on external judicial intervention. These monitoring costs increase more than proportionally with the number of their members, and therefore represent a rather stringent limit to the efficient operating scale of such organisations. Moreover, criminal organisations are also liable to disruption from the cooperation of some of their members with the deterrence agency, and again this risk increases more than proportionally with the numbers of their members. These two effects help to explain the observed trend towards several small local monopolies both in a geographical and in a functional sense.[15]

Even if a significant part of organised criminal activities cannot take place but inside local monopolies, there are illegal goods and services that can be produced and marketed efficiently only above a relatively large scale of operations (money laundering, manipulation of large-scale public interventions). In these cases criminal organisations often enter directly into the production and marketing stages to prevent some illegal firms under their control from acquiring sufficient financial means to contest their monopoly over coercion. Moreover, to prevent the competition for larger market shares from carrying over to an open conflict with the criminal organisation managing the nearest local monopoly, each criminal organisation tries to define collusive agreements for the collective management of the supply of such goods and services. However, the problem of monitoring the terms of such agreements, in which each transaction requires the smallest possible diffusion of information, usually makes the agreements themselves unstable. If such problems arise, while legal firms involved in cartels can start a price war in order to punish the firms that violate the collusive agreements to get a greater market share, criminal organisations have no alternative but to start an open military conflict to achieve the same result.

A further service provided by the criminal organisation – operating as a firm – is analysed by Gambetta and Reuter and involves the creation and the enlargement of the rents which can be reaped in legal markets. As we already noticed, in legal markets there are transactions which are defined as illegal by the legitimate government. Among these transactions, which fall under antitrust legislation, the most relevant is the establishment of collusive agreements among firms operating in a legal market. In practice, the dispersion of relevant information in many different sources (shops, plants, customers) makes it almost impossible to monitor effectively the implementation of such agreements. In order to overcome these difficulties, however, the criminal organisation can offer itself as an enforcer of cartel agreements in order to ensure their stability through the punishment of opportunistic behaviour by individual firms, and through deterrence activities against those firms wishing to enter the market and thereby diminish the profit margins. In this respect, the criminal organisations operate as agents of the cartel of the legal firms when the latter cannot monitor the cartel agreement except with the help of a regulatory agency created by the government, for instance because they operate in competitive or contestable markets.[16]

A perhaps even more relevant service provided by criminal organisations in legal markets is the protection against the consequences of violating restrictive regulations or fiscal rules imposed by the government. As we will see, such protection takes place through the coordination and the centralisation of corruption activities and can constitute an important constraint on government intervention in the economy.[17]

4.2   Organised crime and government intervention in the economy

Once the monopoly over coercion has been acquired by a criminal organisation, the latter can perform inside its territory those activities which typically characterise a collective decision-maker's intervention in the economy: levying of taxes, coercive provision of public goods, and regulation of private agents through non-fiscal tools. These different activities have been investigated by several authors at the conference, and in particular by Grossman and Tanzi, and can be distinguished between those taking place in markets defined as illegal by the government where the criminal organisation completely substitutes the latter, and those taking place in legal markets where the criminal organisation competes with the collective decision-maker in providing public goods and in levying taxes.

In the illegal markets the criminal organisation can often be regarded as the equivalent of the policy-maker and therefore, once the monopoly over coercion is relatively stable, its main interest consists in maximising the rents to be extracted from its territory. By analogy with what happens in market economies, the institutional framework used to achieve this objective is not centralised control over the commercial and productive activities on the part of the collective decision-maker, but instead a system of decentralised markets. The organisation holding the monopoly over coercion is interested in giving general rules of behaviour to the individual firms, leaving to them the choice of the profit-maximising production processes and reaping the rents through the use of franchises to enter the market and through lump-sum taxes – which are often preferred due to the high costs of monitoring illegal transactions.[18]

As a counterpart to the fiscal pressure applied by the criminal organisation, the latter often provides public goods that increase the profitability of the firms active in illegal markets. In first place, the criminal organisation supplies a key service for the development of any illegal economic activity, that is the provision of a stable institutional framework and of reasonably well-defined property rights through its control over coercion and corruption. In second place, the criminal organisation provides a service of arbitration and resolution of controversies which is at least as important since agents cannot rely on an external judicial authority to control opportunistic behaviour with respect to the rules and conventions established by the criminal organisation.[19] A last public good provided by the criminal organisations to the illegal firms is the introduction of entry restrictions in order to avoid excessive competition that would dissipate profits and therefore reduce the rents available for the criminal organisation itself. In this respect, however, as noticed by Gambetta and Reuter, criminal organisations sometimes find it more profitable not to supply this service because they fear a threat to their monopoly over coercion from those firms which are given a monopolistic position in the illegal markets.

In this area, Grossman centres his analysis of the role of the mafia as a public good provider around the definition of a *kleptocratic* state. According to such a definition, the state is nothing but an agency whose objective is to maximize the total rent from the taxpayers under the constraints of re-election and mobility of the economic inputs. Building on this assumption, the competition between the mafia and the state as alternative providers of public services might have some beneficial effects for the consumers as the presence of the mafia effectively constrains the monopolistic role of the governmental authorities and therefore increases the equilibrium supply of public services. Under these circumstances, the only ones who are damaged by the competition between mafia and state are the members of the groups who benefit from the political *status quo*. Hence, from a positive point of view, Grossman foresees that strong popular support for anti-mafia policies will form only if the members of those groups are a minority of the population. More generally, however, if the appropriative activities of the mafia are very disruptive or threaten the viability of the state, so that the mafia could get a new monopoly over the provision of public services, the support for a strong deterrence policy will be widespread. Accordingly, in Grossman's model, what the consumers should fear most is the possibility that the political establishment and the mafia reach a collusive agreement in order to share the rents from the monopolistic provision of public services. While the assumptions ιcerning the kleptocratic features of the state may be regarded as ρalatable and even unrealistic for most areas of the developed countries, there is convincing evidence of popular support to criminal organisations in those settings where the groups benefited by the political establishment have been a small minority of the population.[20]

On similarly pessimistic lines as far as the role of the governmental agencies is concerned, Tanzi argues that in countries where interpersonal relations are relevant in activating economic transactions, the only way to deter corruption is to reduce significantly the scale of public intervention. This line of analysis seems to be particularly relevant when one considers the possibility of collusive agreements between organised crime – acting as a broker of votes in a given area – and the elected members of the public administration. In different instances there has been evidence of large-scale agreements where organised crime ensures political support for groups of candidates, while the latter repay the favour through a favourable management of public procurements and the provision of public services or subsidies.[21] Most scholars think that by now the greatest business of the Sicilian mafia is precisely that of appropriating the different sources of public expenditures and of organising frauds against the local, national and European Community schemes of subsidisation.[22] Having this evidence in mind, Tanzi's policy advice is to reduce all forms of public interventions which are particularly subject to manipulation in those countries where interpersonal relations in business are particularly relevant. This condition appears to be satisfied in those circumstances where the organised crime sector operates effectively as the centre of the allocative mechanism of public funds and Tanzi's advice can therefore be regarded as a relevant point of any overall deterrence policy against organised crime.

5   Problems in normative analysis

If the positive analysis of criminal organisations presents several unresolved problems, this is even more the case as far as the normative analysis is concerned. Accordingly the papers given at the conference which have a large normative component tackle their objects from different perspectives. By and large, however, one can distinguish between the papers that analyse deterrence policies against legal firms involved in illegal activities (Cowell and Gordon, Karpoff and Lott) and those dealing with deterrence policies against the criminal organisations (Celentani et al., Fiorentini).

5.1   Deterrence policies against firms involved in illegal activities

The papers of Cowell and Gordon and of Karpoff and Lott both focus on the counter-intuitive effects of punitive legislation against firms involved in illegal activities. The former deals with tax frauds while the latter is mainly concerned with commercial frauds, but their main common policy conclusion is that a sophisticated (and costly) deterrence policy in terms of monitoring and penalties against illegal activities may be inefficient from a social point of view.

Cowell and Gordon evaluate the audit strategies available to a tax-enforcement authority wishing to minimise indirect tax evasion when the taxpayers have the option of selling their output in a black market where sales are untaxed. The two alternative auditing strategies are auditing firms randomly and conditioning the auditing probabilities on reported output. In the second case, the approach taken by the enforcement agency is to adopt a simple cut-off rule which excludes from investigation those firms reporting less than a given amount of output. The main result is that when firms are able to sell all their output in an illegal market the simpler random mechanism may be a better deterrence tool than the more sophisticated alternative – contrary to most of the literature on this topic. This is because some firms might choose to become 'ghosts', therefore avoiding completely detection based on the cut-off mechanism.

Notice that Cowell and Gordon draw our attention to a crucial constraint for policy-makers irrespective of the area where they operate: private agents can always shift their transactions – at some cost – from a legal (taxed) market to an illegal (untaxed) one. Therefore, whenever a new policy is introduced, great care should be given to the design of a deterrence mechanism that reduces the incentives for the private agents to increase the scale of their illegal transactions. There is a clear analogy here between the paper of Cowell and Gordon and that of Grossman. While the latter focuses on the implications of the illegal markets constraint for a government imposing taxes in competition with a criminal organisation, the former analyses the effects of the same constraint for a tax enforcement agency choosing an efficient tax auditing strategy.

On similar lines, the contribution of Karpoff and Lott discusses the effect of two different deterrence mechanisms – court-imposed penalties and loss of reputation – on private corporations' decisions about committing commercial frauds. The authors find empirical evidence suggesting that an increase in criminal penalties against fraud over their current level in the United States may have negative effects because it would decrease the deterrence role played by the loss of capital value following the discovery of such frauds. In its turn, such a reduction in the role of loss of reputation will have negative effects because criminal penalties are only imperfect substitutes as they are difficult to monitor and administer and they do not affect the sunk investments of private corporations. The conclusions of the paper are relevant for they shed some light on a different aspect of the illegal markets constraint. To discipline illicit behaviour through sanctions is especially costly against highly structured criminal organisations that can bribe even high-level enforcers. However, if such criminal organisations enter the markets for legal consumer goods and services they are at least partly subjected to the market discipline. Hence, it should be a priority objective to devise mechanisms for the allocation of public resources which embody at least some elements of market discipline.

5.2   Deterrence policies against criminal organisations

Drawing any normative conclusion in the case of the activities of criminal organisations is particularly difficult due to their distributive effects. Indeed, everyone – economist or not – would agree that the activities of criminal organisations have an overall negative effect on economic activity because of the emphasis they bring on appropriative activities and the dissipation of resources which follows. What makes things less clear-cut is the fact that there are different groups of agents who, even if they are not themselves members of criminal organisations, still benefit from their presence and from the services they provide. In other words, together with the purely coercive activities, which usually represent a net cost for the community (even if the criminal organisations' taxation often substitutes for and does not add to that imposed by the government), there are also illegal activities in which the exchanges come about on a purely voluntary basis. For these transactions it is not at all certain that the benefits – measured in terms of income produced in voluntary transactions – are larger than their costs.

These preliminary aspects of the normative analysis of organised criminal activities are the central point of the papers of Celentani et al. and Fiorentini. Indeed, both papers tackle the problem of defining a sensible objective function for a deterrence agency. The former authors attempt a purely normative answer to this problem by modelling an agency interested in minimising the overall profits of the criminal organisations and showing that in some circumstances such an objective is analytically equivalent to the minimisation of the output traded in illegal markets. However, it is not always obvious that minimising the profits obtained selling illegal output is a sensible policy target. If this were the case, in fact, a straightforward policy, which could easily be implemented, is to legalise the illegal markets so that – due to the contestability of such markets – the criminal organisations' profits would be greatly reduced.

Fiorentini instead analyses the deterrence activity against criminal organisations, assuming that the deterrence agency reacts passively to the actions taken by such organisations. This is because the agency is under the control of elected decision-makers who are not interested in minimising violence and/or corruption. Indeed, having crime reduced to a minimum is not electorally productive because the general public may believe that this is due to exogenous reasons. On the other hand, what is electorally productive – because it is clearly visible to the general public – is to show that the enforcement agency is capable of responding successfully to active criminal organisations. Moreover, elected decision-makers seem to believe that effective deterrence activity against larger criminal organisations is more electorally productive than that against smaller groups.[23] From this positive description of the deterrence agency's behaviour it is difficult to draw policy implications. What can be said is that more efforts should be made to understand the logic of government interventions against the activities of criminal organisations when the latter compete among themselves in order to achieve a monopolistic control over illegal markets.

6   Alternative deterrence policies

The distinction between the two main roles of the criminal organisation – as a government and as a firm – is especially fruitful when applied to the analysis of policy-making. In this respect, we can distinguish between three main areas of deterrence policies against organised crime: first, the traditional deterrence strategies based on investment in investigative activities and in the judicial and penitential systems in order to increase the probability of detection of crimes related to the criminal organisations' activities; second, the deterrence strategies related to the regulatory activities of the government; third, the deterrence policies against money laundering and the investment of illegal profits in legal activities. In Section 5 we have considered the normative problems investigated by authors who were mainly involved with what we have defined as 'traditional' deterrence policies. In this section, we will discuss the other two types of deterrence policy which have not been dealt with extensively in the economic literature, but which represent one of the most interesting directions of research in this field.

6.1   Deterrence and regulatory activity

In this very wide-ranging area of deterrence one usually includes the choice between prohibiting or regulating the transactions of some goods and services, thereby creating or restricting opportunities to earn criminal rents through the production, smuggling and distribution of those commodities. Moreover, as has been made clear in Tanzi's paper, in this area one should also consider the degree of public intervention in the economy whose increase often brings with itself an increase in the volume of rent-seeking activities on the part of organised crime. Our brief agenda for further research will start with a survey of the most recent advances on the issue of prohibition and will then give room to the analysis of the relationships between corruption and public intervention.

6.1.1 Prohibition or regulation   In this area perhaps the crucial problem from an economist's point of view is that of determining the elasticity of demand for the illegal commodities. Indeed, if the demand schedule is sufficiently elastic, the increase in output which generally follows the introduction of a more liberal regulatory regime increases significantly the consumption of the commodity that was restricted for ethical or humanitarian reasons. This notwithstanding, relatively few empirical works make use of reliable and systematic data concerning the demand for illegal commodities.[24] As far as the demand for gambling and betting is concerned, there is some evidence which points to a rather elastic demand.[25] Moreover, criminal organisations seem to have had a competitive advantage over other legal competitors or even the state in matching the increased demand following decriminalisation. As far as the demand for drugs is concerned, things are made much more complex due to the different degrees of physical dependence given by different drugs. However, the existing evidence concerning the few cases of decriminalisation of soft drugs seems to indicate that their demand is relatively inelastic.

From a theoretical point of view the question concerning drugs which generate a physical dependence is more complicated because while the demand is surely very inelastic for old consumers, this might not be so for the new ones. For this reason economists have always suggested a policy of price discrimination by which the old consumers can buy drugs at a low or zero price – thereby avoiding the negative spillovers due to the appropriative activities of the addicted – while the new consumers should face a very high price.[26] However, as most drugs have relatively low storage costs, these measures of price discrimination – where implemented – have always been circumvented by the establishment of a secondary market where the addicted who can obtain the drugs at low price resell them to the new consumers.[27]

More recently Becker and Murphy (1988) propose a model in which utility-maximising consumers can determine a steady-state equilibrium in their consumption of addictive drugs over time. Becker and Murphy show that temporary changes in the price of drugs have relatively modest effects on consumption levels in the short run. This is often interpreted as a proof that the elasticity of demand for hard drugs is very low. However, in the long run the demand for drugs is more elastic – *ceteris paribus* – than for commodities which do not lead to addiction. From a policy viewpoint this result means that even for hard drugs a strong deterrence policy which keeps prices very high might have some effect in reducing overall consumption in the long run.[28]

Even more difficult to assess is the effect of a change in the regulatory regime of the drug markets on the profits of the organised crime sector. In the light of the most recent investigative evidence, which indicates increasing competitive pressures in the international markets for drugs and therefore a relative decrease in profit margins, it could well be that relaxing the regulation of those markets would have a relatively moderate effect on the profits of organised crime.[29] A policy of lower regulation would perhaps have the effect of increasing the number of firms active in the markets as well as increasing the overall supply. However, what is perhaps the major obstacle towards any attempt to decrease the level of deterrence in the drug markets is given by the international coordination problems. Indeed, it is hardly likely that a non-drug-producing country will unilaterally lift its deterrence policy against illegal drugs and thus run the risk of becoming the commercial centre of all the organisations operating in the international markets.

6.1.2 Public intervention and corruption   The topic which has been most extensively investigated in this area is that of the relations which should be established between the payments to civil servants and the value of the economic transactions over which they have a relevant discretionary power. More explicitly, Becker and Stigler (1974) propose to design the career profile and the wage schedule of the bureaucrats so as to equalise the marginal revenue from accepting bribes – proportional to the rents administered by them – with the marginal costs of losing their future salaries and their pensions. A more provocative proposal, again put forward in Becker and Stigler (1974), is the following: if there are problems in monitoring the efficiency of the deterrence agencies then could it be convenient to make use of private organisations for investigative and policing functions? Needless to say, there may be many possible shortcomings in the implementation of such a proposal in terms of opportunistic behaviour on the part of all agents involved. However, one should also take into account that overall expenditure on private security has become almost equal to public expenditure in the same area in many communities, and not only in the US. A less travelled topic in the economic analysis of corruption has to do with the application of the theory of organisation design to the structure of the police. A relevant problem in this area is that of the optimal number of police structures which should be active in a given territory. While from a technical point of view having more than one police force is likely to bring about duplication of costs with relatively few advantages in terms of specialisation, the existence of independent police authorities may help to increase the costs of bribery and allow some form of yardstick competition between the agencies.

A more specific area where a large proportion of corruption seems to arise is that of public procurements. In those regions where organised crime is more deeply established, the available empirical evidence shows that all large-scale public projects are under its control.[30] This for three main reasons. First, the criminal organisations have often reached agreements with the local politicians to exchange votes with the management of a relevant part of the economic resources under public control. Second, the criminal organisations can manipulate the public procurement mechanisms, acting behind the scenes through several firms controlled indirectly and threats to the rival ones. Third, even if the winning firms are not under the control of organised crime, they must come to terms with it when they operate in the territory because organised crime has complete control over key input markets such as the labour market and makes use of its extortionary power.

For the first two problems, economists usually suggest centralising the procurement mechanism at the national level to limit the discretionary power of local politicians and to design complete projects where no changes are possible once the projects are under way. However, the third problem cannot be addressed by introducing institutional changes alone. Indeed, only when the legal government has a firm control of the territory in which the public projects are to be realised can local and foreign firms compete for public procurements being reasonably sure that their profits will not be taken away by the criminal organisations. However, an alternative mechanism can be used – except in the case of natural monopolies – which should reduce the negative effects of organised crime's control over the input markets. If the government does not pay directly the private firms who win the public contracts, but gives them franchises to run them for a period of time, consumers can to some extent discipline the supplier by looking for substitutes. Even such a mechanism should be managed centrally and great care should be taken in setting the number of years of franchise. Its main drawback is that most local public projects have strong elements of natural monopolies and therefore cannot be disciplined effectively by consumers.

6.2 The recycling of financial flows of illegal origin

Very much has been written on this topic in order to devise mechanisms at the institutional level to monitor and deter the use of financial intermediaries in the recycling of illegal profits.[31] In our view, however, there are yet two research directions which should be explored with the aid of economic theory. The first is the credibility of the international agreements stipulated in order to increase the monitoring of transactions in financial markets. From this point of view, many economists are rather sceptical about the possibility of giving sufficient incentives to less developed countries or to fiscal havens (but not only to them; also Switzerland, Luxembourg) to implement such agreements. This is because these countries receive very large revenues from financial intermediation and have relatively few negative externalities, at least in the short run. Moreover, the list of countries competing to attract financial capital is almost endless given the great mobility of capital in financial markets, and such countries are also those in which those markets are almost completely out of the control of even the domestic monetary authorities. Due to the difficulties entailed in devising and implementing effective sanctions against the governments of the countries involved in large-scale money laundering, some economists have suggested shifting the target of the deterrence policies more closely on to the financial institutions involved in such activities.

The second is the problem behind these schemes: creating a conflict of interests between financial institutions and their clients involved in illegal transactions.[32] To achieve this objective, the most frequently proposed institutional reform is to shift part of the penalties for crimes related to money laundering from the clients to the financial institutions. A similar logic has been applied in a recent Italian law according to which the cigarette producers have been held responsible for the smuggling of cigarettes. The deterrence mechanism worked as follows: whenever the Italian police seized more than a given amount of a brand in a given period, the brand itself could not be marketed for a subsequent period. The logic behind the rule is that the producers cannot ignore the destinations and marketing channels of very large output flows. While this could become very punitive for firms, because of the multiple transactions which can take place before an easily storable commodity reaches the final consumer, the *rationale* of the regulation is interesting because it represents an implicit privatisation of the deterrence function. And indeed following the same principle of shifting the burden of deterrence from large and often paralysed intergovernmental institutions to private organisations, it could be made compulsory for financial institutions to produce an auditing certificate especially targeted at the monitoring of suspect transactions. Such certificates would be released by private auditing firms which – given the new incentives – should specialise in monitoring the recycling of illegal profits.

6.2.1 The investment of illegal profits in legal activities This is an important area of research both for the development of more efficient deterrence mechanisms and for a better understanding of the workings of complex criminal organisations. However, in order to understand the issues at stake one should keep in mind that money laundering takes place when the criminal organisations have *already* obtained illegal profits and it is therefore not obviously preferable for such profits to be invested in other illicit activities rather then recycled into legal markets. From a normative point of view it cannot be said in general which of these two options is the worse. From a positive viewpoint, however, it is up to the criminal organisations to decide which alternative to choose taking into account their relative profitabilities. The economist and the legislator are faced by a trade-off: either we restrict the area of the transactions under the control of organisations whose interests are prevalently illegal or we restrict the area of the illegal transactions properly defined. This trade-off should be regarded as the proper starting-point for any analysis of legislative measures against the use of illegal profits in the legal economy. This is because it is virtually impossible, in the presence of illegal profits, to block both investment in other illegal activities and recycling in perfectly legitimate ones.

If one accepts this premise, any deterrence policy against the investment of illegal profits in legitimate activities becomes, at least logically, a problem whose solution depends on the policies against the formation of illegal profits. However, the movement of resources between illegal and legal activities can still be regarded as an adequate starting-point for defining a deterrence policy against highly structured criminal organisations if one can show that policies specifically targeted to this area are more effective than those implemented against the realisation of illegal profits. On this point most economists are rather sceptical, above all because it is difficult to devise policy tools giving sufficient incentives to legal firms not to enter into any relations with illegal organisations.

Indeed, many legal firms find themselves in situations where they cannot refuse to accept the very low-cost financial *help* offered by the illegal organisations. Moreover, to pass legislation which shifts most of the punishment on to the legal firms accepting such help can be excessively punitive when the latter have been threatened and, in similar circumstances, it is almost impossible to distinguish the actual responsibilities of the legal firms. Indeed, even the existing evidence in the Italian case shows a great variation in the judiciary's attitude towards the legal firms involved in transactions with organised crime.[33]

However this may be, if one is willing to set some guidelines for the judiciary, one should try and learn more about criminal organisations' different incentives to allocate resources to different industries. The few existing analyses of the allocation of illegal profits in legal activities show that the industries chosen usually share the following features: technological maturity, absence of large irreversible investments, large proportion of public demand, and preferential localisation in regions where there are problems in the definition of the property rights.[34] These features confirm that the criminal organisations cannot easily increase their market share in those legal markets where the competitive struggle mainly concerns the accumulation of human and technological capital, where there are frequent changes in the demand structure. On the contrary, the real comparative advantage of criminal organisations in legal markets comes from the low opportunity cost of capital and from the monopolistic control of key inputs in given industries. These features of the legal industries in which the criminal organisations are active have even more serious implications when one takes into account the mobility of capital in the financial market. This is because the legal firms controlled by the criminal organisations can easily be sold without large capital losses – because of the relatively small irreversible investments – so that effective deterrence measures taken in a single country are likely to bring about swift movements of illegally controlled capital towards new countries.

6.2.2 Codes of self-regulation There has recently been a growing interest in the establishment of codes of self-regulation at the industry level, targeted especially against the entry of criminal organisations in the ownership structure of legal firms.[35] Even in this respect, the theory of organisational design suggests that it is difficult to devise an institutional setting in which agents with potentially very conflicting interests at the market level will cooperate to monitor and isolate the rival firms involved in transactions with organised crime. Two main manipulations of those settings are possible, First, legal firms may abuse their power to denounce their rivals to the judiciary in order to achieve competitive gains, especially if they can take advantage of the very long periods of time needed by the ordinary judiciary to complete a trial. Second, and more likely, the agreements against organised crime – which need an institutionalised exchange of information among firms in each industry – might work as operative arms of industry cartels, perhaps even with the participation of firms indirectly controlled by organised crime.

The occurrence of opportunistic behaviour is far from unrealistic as the establishment of self-regulatory codes is usually thought of as a partial substitute for the standard monitoring activity of the police agencies. Indeed, such industry-level agreements should represent one of the possible institutional applications of the aforementioned shift of the deterrence system from the centralised agencies on to the organisations active in the markets which may have contacts with organised crime and should play a monitoring role – with the enforcement of several penalties if they do not undertake this new policing role. However, the realisation of such decentralised deterrence systems – operated by the firms which may be threatened by the criminal organisations and which may have collusive interests with them to use low-cost capital and to appropriate a larger share of the consumer surplus – does not seem to overcome most of the problems typically encountered by more traditional deterrence agencies.

7   Conclusions

To summarise, the analysis of the criminal organisations' activities developed in the previous sections allows one to define a general normative proposition: the activities of organised crime depend strictly on the policy-maker's choices. This for three main reasons. First, the larger is the area of markets in which the transactions are regarded as illegal by the government, the greater are the incentives for the criminal organisations to compete to establish local monopolies over coercion. Second, the heavier is the fiscal and regulatory pressure on the legal markets, the greater are the incentives for legal firms to shift resources to the illegal markets or to undertake transactions which are out of the control of the collective decision-maker. Third, the investment in deterrence activities can have a destabilising effect on the local monopolies held by incumbent criminal organisations, thereby increasing the investments in violence and corruption on the part of all the organisations involved.

On the basis of these observations it follows that, together with the other constraints relevant for economic policy-making, a policy-maker must take into account the constraints arising from the possibility of creating illegal markets in which any regulatory activity is ineffective. Such constraints cannot be avoided completely by means of larger investments in deterrence activities. Indeed, apart from their costs and from the distortions which they impose on legal transactions in general, the greater the effectiveness of such deterrence activities, the more they create incentives to invest in corruption and manipulation of the deterrence agencies themselves.[36]

NOTES

1 There are remarkable exceptions to this trend, that is contributions which have focused on the activities of the organised criminal sector. Among these exceptions one needs to point out Schelling (1967), Buchanan (1973) and Jennings (1984).
2 Quoted in Schelling (1971), p. 71.
3 Reuter (1983), p. 175.
4 For more details on the involvement of organised crime in legal activities see Reuter (1983), Arlacchi (1988) and Savona (ed.) (1993).
5 For a survey of this empirical evidence see Catanzaro (1992) and the contribution of Anderson to this volume.
6 The contributions in Savona (ed.) (1993) provide a good introduction to the investigative activities related to this trial.
7 In the work of Savona in Camera dei Deputati (1993) one can find an economic analysis of how the organised crime sector manipulates the system of public contracts in Italy.
8 Schotter (1981) and Rowe (1989) are stimulating introductions to the economic theory of institutions.
9 Among the economists who have analysed the problems of choice in a situation of anarchy one must recall Harsanyi (1955) and Buchanan and Tullock (1962). Much later, and building over the aforesaid authors, one needs to recall the better-known contributions of Rawls (1971) and Nozick (1974).
10 The same Robinsonian definition of economic science puts the individual agents' choices in a central position making it clear that, without free choice, it is improper to talk of economic actions.
11 One should note the difference between this approach and the functionalist approach to the origin of institutions, which originates from a conflict between (groups of) agents that can threaten one another with mutual destruction in the search for the monopoly over coercion.
12 Besides secession or individual migration, 'exit options' also include political action aimed at achieving greater participation in the management of the monopoly over coercion.
13 In this sense the implementation of democratic rules signals on one hand the growing ability of groups having a comparative advantage in the productive activities to pose an economic threat and, on the other hand, a trend towards appropriative activities in the form of a redistributive rule having features of apparent generality.
14 From this viewpoint there is substantial similarity between the redistributive

activities which take the form of a military conflict between different groups and the redistributive conflict which takes place in the political market through either an electoral mechanism or a competition between pressure groups. In this respect, the economic theory of interest groups foresees that – disregarding the problems due to the logic of collective action which favour smaller groups – there is a tendency for those groups whose endowments are more heavily affected by redistributive legislation to be able to impose (to block) those interventions which are favourable (unfavourable) to them.

15 On the internal structure of the criminal organisations one should see Anderson (1979) and Arlacchi (1988). We will show in what follows that a relatively small efficient scale of operation does not mean that the economic operations of the criminal organisations have borders which coincide with the areas under their control.

16 Gambetta and Reuter (1993) show evidence of cartels with more than 200 firms.

17 The works of Cassese and Marini in Camera dei Deputati (1993) are mainly dedicated to the issue of designing a public administration which is less manipulable with respect to corruption of organised crime.

18 One should notice that the reasons for direct intervention by criminal organisations are very similar to those defined in handbooks of public economics to warrant the use of public intervention in legal productive activities.

19 See Reuter (1983) for a very accurate description of the role of New York criminal organisations in solving disputes among members of the underworld.

20 To limit oneself to developed countries, the evidence is particularly convincing for areas such as Sicily and Northern Ireland.

21 Catanzaro (1992) provides a systematic analysis of these agreements between local politicians and criminal organisations.

22 For an analysis of the frauds against the EC and related ones, see the contributions of Mori, Pansa and Pistorelli in Camera dei Deputati (1993).

23 This description of the objective function of elected decision-makers as for deterrence policies against organised crime is the fruit of several discussions with members of the Italian Anti-Mafia Parliamentary Commission during the preparatory works for a conference held under the auspices of the Italian Parliament on 'The Economics of Organized Crime', held in Rome, May 1993. The proceedings of the conference have been published in Camera dei Deputati (1993).

24 See, however, Miller (1991) for an economic analysis of some experiences of drug 'liberalisation'.

25 Reuter (1983) shows the results of an empirical investigation on the markets for illegal betting and for numbers.

26 See Moore (1973) for a pioneering analysis of price discrimination in the markets for drugs.

27 There have been many cases of controlled distribution of methadone or even of hard drugs to scheduled consumers, but there is much scepticism about their implementation mostly because they allow the establishment of parallel markets.

28 For an empirical assessment of the Becker and Murphy 'rational addiction' theory see Sickles and Taubman (1991).

29 Traver and Gaylor (1992) represents one of the most complete surveys of the available evidence on the working of the international drug markets.

30 See the work of Cassese in Camera dei Deputati (1993) on the different techniques used by the criminal organisations to control the allocation of public contracts.

31 There are many international organisations mainly constituted to deal with the problem of money laundering: ISPAC (International Scientific and Professional Advisory Council of the United Nations Crime Prevention and Criminal Justice Programme), CICAD (Inter-American Drug-Abuse Control Commission), FATF (Financial Action Task Force of the G7 Heads of State and Government) and GAFI (Group of International Action against Money Laundering) are only a few of the best-known ones.

32 See the work of Viesti in Savona (ed.) (1993) for a survey of what has been done so far in terms of the international coordination of the fight against money laundering.

33 In this respect perhaps the most radical example is the case of an Italian judge who ruled that accepting financial help from the organised crime sector cannot be regarded as a crime because there is always a presumption of threats being implemented by the criminal organisation.

34 The work of Barca in Camera dei Deputati (1993) is a good survey of the relations between legal firms and criminal organisations.

35 The Hong Kong administration has recently (1992) established a special commission independent from the political authorities to investigate the cases of corruption among the police.

36 The actual level of enforcement of the rules depends mainly on the level of wages in the deterrence agencies and on the existence of direct victims of the violations. For these reasons, one should evaluate the congruence of any deterrence measure or of refunding schemes for the victims of coercion with respect to the possibility that individual agents can manipulate such measures and schemes by corrupting their enforcers.

REFERENCES

Anderson, A. G. (1979), *The Business of Organized Crime: A Cosa Nostra Family*, Stanford CA: The Hoover Institution.

Arlacchi, P. (1988), 'Saggio sui mercati illegali', *Rassegna italiana di sociologia*, 3.

Baumol, W. J. (1990), 'Entrepreneurship: Productive, Unproductive, and Destructive', *Journal of Political Economy*, 98(5), pp. 893–921.

Becker, G. S. (1968), 'Crime and Punishment: An Economic Approach', *Journal of Political Economy*, 76(2), March/April, pp. 169–217.

Becker, G. S. and K. Murphy (1988), 'A Theory of Rational Addiction', *Journal of Political Economy*, 96, pp. 675–700.

Becker, G. S. and G. J. Stigler (1974), 'Law Enforcement, Malfeasance, and Compensation of Enforcers', *Journal of Legal Studies*, 3(1), January, pp. 21–35.

Buchanan, J. (1973), 'A Defense of Organized Crime', in S. Rottemberg (ed.), *The Economics of Crime and Punishment*, Washington DC: American Enterprise Institute for Public Policy Research, reprinted in R. Andreano and J. Sigfried (eds.) (1980), *The Economics of Crime*, Cambridge MA: Schenkmann.

Buchanan, J. and G. Tullock (1962), *The Calculus of Consent: Logical Foundations of Constitutional Democracy*, Ann Arbor: Michigan University Press.

Camera dei Deputati (1993), *Economia e criminalità*, Proceedings of the conference organised by the Anti-Mafia Parliamentary Commission, Rome.

Catanzaro, R. (1992), *Men of Respect: A Social History of the Sicilian Mafia* (translated by Raymond Rosenthal), New York: The Free Press.

Ehrenfeld, R. (1992), *Evil Money: Encounters along the Money Trail*, New York: Harper Business.

Fiorentini, G. (1993), 'Rent-seeking in Cartels run by Criminal Organizations', IIPF conference on 'The Economics of the Illegal Markets', Berlin.

Gambetta, D. (1992), *La mafia siciliana*, Torino: Einaudi.

Harsanyi, J. (1955), 'Cardinal Welfare, Individualistic Ethics and Interpersonal Comparison of Utility', *Journal of Political Economy*, 63, pp. 309–21.

Hirshleifer, J. (1988), 'The Analytics of Continuing Conflict', *Synthèse*, 76, pp. 201–33.

Hirshleifer, J. (1991), 'The Paradox of Power', *Economics and Politics*, 3, pp. 177–200.

Jennings, W. P. (1984), 'A Note on the Economics of Organized Crime', *Eastern Economic Journal*, 10(3), July–September, pp. 315–21.

Martin, J. and A. Romano (1992), *Multinational Crime*, Newbery Park: Sage.

Miller, R. (1991), *The Case for Legalizing Drugs*, New York: Praeger.

Moore, M. (1973), 'Policies to Achieve Discrimination on the Effective Price of Heroin', *American Economic Review*, 63, pp. 378–96.

Nozick, R. (1974), *Anarchy, State and Utopia*, New York: Basic Books.

Rawls, J. (1971), *A Theory of Justice*, Cambridge MA: Harvard University Press.

Reuter, P. (1983), *Disorganized Crime: The Economics of the Visible Hand*, Cambridge MA: MIT Press.

Rowe, N. (1989), *Rules and Institutions*, New York: Philip Allan.

Savona, E. (ed.) (1993), *Mafia Issues: Analysis and Proposals for Combatting the Mafia Today*, International Scientific and Professional Advisory Council of the United Nations Crime Prevention and Criminal Justice Programme, Milan.

Schelling, T. C. (1967), 'Economics and Criminal Enterprise', *The Public Interest*, 7, pp. 61–78, reprinted in R. Andreano and J. Sigfried (eds.) (1980), *The Economics of Crime*, Cambridge MA: Schenkmann, and in Schelling, T. C. (ed.) (1984), pp. 158–78.

Schelling, T. C. (1971), 'What is the Business of Organized Crime?' *Journal of Public Law*, 20, pp. 71–84, reprinted in Schelling, T. C. (ed.) (1984), pp. 179–94.

Schelling, T. C. (ed.) (1984), *Choice and Consequence*, Cambridge MA: Harvard University Press.

Schotter, A. (1981), *The Economic Theory of Social Institutions*, Cambridge: Cambridge University Press.

Sickles, R. and P. Taubman (1991), 'Who Uses Illegal Drugs?', *American Economic Review* (Papers and Proceedings), 81, pp. 248–51.

Traver, H. and M. Gaylor (1992), *Drugs, Law and the State*, Hong Kong: Hong Kong University Press.

Part I
Theories of the state and the origin of criminal organisations

2 Organised crime, mafia and governments

ANNELISE ANDERSON

1 Introduction

The mafia in Italy is an economic, social and political problem of considerable magnitude. Of this there is no doubt. Most striking is the murder of two anti-mafia crime-fighters in 1993, following the earlier murders of anti-mafia government officials, which demonstrates the willingness of the mafia to use violence and intimidation at the highest levels.

The term 'mafia' has been adopted internationally, most recently in the countries of the former Soviet Union. Russians refer, for example, to the Red Mafia. Economists prefer to talk about organised crime, but a mafia is more than a criminal gang willing to use violence and implies more than criminal activity that happens to be organised. Even a small criminal group, such as a gang that robs banks, has some organisational structure; someone drives the getaway car and someone else rides shotgun. Violence and some division of labour, or even a relatively elaborate organisational structure with positions that may be vacant and need to be filled, do not describe a mafia. The term is not applied to terrorist groups.

An organised criminal group engaged in illegal market activity – drugs, illegal liquor, gambling – is more likely to warrant the use of the term mafia. One of the critical features of such activity is that arrangements and agreements are made among participants that are not legal contracts. To go beyond personal relationships in which deals are completed at face-to-face meetings, participants need some larger structure or organisation that is able to enforce agreements and punish or redress violations thereof. Such arrangements may greatly increase the size of the deals they can undertake, the scope of their market (or the distance over which they can do business and the number of people with whom they can deal) and the use of violence or force as a necessity on the part of the participants.

33

An organisation that is able to enforce agreements and punish violators is also likely to determine whose agreements it will enforce and what kinds of agreements it will enforce. It may come to control entry into various lines of criminal activity and the behaviour (at least to some extent) of those who come under its protection. At this point we have some of the characteristics of a mafia: it is performing governmental functions – law enforcement and criminal justice – in that sphere where the legal judicial system refuses to exercise power. Alternatively, in certain respects or for particular illegal markets it may be compared to a cartel, a franchiser or a trade association, with the significant difference that it does not leave to the state the monopoly of violence.

Because many of its activities are illegal, another aspect of an organisation with the power to enforce agreements among participants is its potential power to deal with the legal criminal justice system. Its leaders may succeed in bribing individuals at any level or location in the criminal justice system – police, courts, corrective institutions – to mitigate the severity of law enforcement. Cases may be dismissed, juries bribed, sentences reduced, parole lifted. The organisation may agree in some cases to use its powers on behalf of others who are not generally under its protection.

It may also use its law enforcement connections against rival groups; the police crack a case and the mafia eliminates a competitor. T. C. Schelling (1971), perhaps the first economist to address the mafia phenomenon analytically, considers the suppression of rivals, possibly in collusion with the police, one of the basic skills of organised criminal groups, and he argues that their basic business is extortion from the criminal enterprises that actually supply illegal goods and services to the public. He defines organised crime (1967, p. 115) as 'large-scale continuing firms with the internal organisation of a large enterprise, and with a conscious effort to control the market', and he also discusses the governmental functions of these groups.

At the same time the group is likely to make considerable efforts to prevent the cooperation of its members with the police. Jennings (1984) considers the use of resources for this purpose to be the defining characteristic of organised crime, and he develops a model to predict what kinds of crime will be undertaken by organised criminal groups as a function of the value of the non-cooperation and the cost of enforcing it.

If this were all, the damage done by mafias would be limited. The subversion of the criminal justice system becomes a far more serious problem, however, when the legitimate government loses or lacks the power to protect citizens and legitimate businesses from criminal activity. Theft and fencing become more attractive when those who fence stolen goods are not prosecuted; but worse, the subversion of the criminal justice system allows the mafia to run protection rackets, that is, to extract payments from legitimate business enterprises and perhaps to control entry and conditions of operation (preferred suppliers, for example, or hiring) of these enterprises. Here the criminal organisation is using its influence in the criminal justice system of the legitimate government to perform activities comparable to the taxing and regulating powers of legitimate (mercantilist) government. The corruption of the legitimate government may extend beyond the criminal justice system to other regulatory agencies or to agencies that award contracts or grants.

At this point we have not an organised criminal gang but a full-fledged mafia with serious consequences for the economic growth of the legitimate economy. The mafia creates monopolies in local enterprises, controls entry and maximises revenue by extracting monopoly profits as protection payments; new investment may be discouraged and old investment driven out. Pino Arlacchi (1986, pp. 229–30) points out that in the 1970s and early 1980s the area of southern Italy with the highest growth rates were those with the lowest levels of both organised and conventional crime, whereas those with the greatest mafia presence were the only economically stagnant regions of Italy.[1]

Thus the essential characteristic of a mafia that differentiates it from other groups engaged in violent or criminal activity is corruption or substantial influence in at least some agencies or bureaux of the legitimate government. It is this relationship that warrants the use of the term mafia around the world. The questions of interest are why mafias develop, how damaging they are, and what can be done to eliminate them or their most undesirable consequences.

2   Why mafias develop

History suggests three origins of mafias, or three conditions that encourage their development: an abdication (possibly combined with rejection) of legitimate government power, excessive bureaucratic power and the potential of illegal markets. These conditions may interact, each providing growth opportunities to a mafia originating for another reason.[2]

2.1   Abdication of power

The origin of the Sicilian mafia dates, according to scholars, to the second half of the nineteenth century, especially the period after the unification of Italy. Sicily had a long tradition of resistance to outside domination. Catanzaro notes that both 'before and after unification, people tended to use new systems of private protection for securing their land and property' (1992, p. 6). The Sicilian case is thus an example of the rise of a mafia in a vacuum of power,[3] or of the inability or unwillingness of the state to ensure public order in a society that had turned, over hundreds of years, away from state power to private means of protecting property and ensuring order (Catanzaro, 1992, p. 20). Instead, the state implicitly let local powers control peasant unrest. Catanzaro concludes that '... in contrast to what had happened in the past, [violence] occurred within the framework of the weak authority of a state that formally held, but failed to exercise, the legitimate monopoly over violence. It therefore compelled the state to come to terms with those who exercised de facto power at a local level and to delegate to them the functions of exercising that monopoly. Indeed, in practice, the state deferred to their authority, for although it officially prohibited private violence, it nevertheless granted the power to govern on behalf of the central government to that same local ruling class that made use of it' (Catanzaro, 1992, p. 76).[4]

Owners of estates hired *gabelloti* (custodians) to run the estates in their owners' absence, and the mafia became prominent in these positions and achieved, at the same time, control over products and manufactured goods going to market as well as the peasants. Scholars of the period thus find that the mafiosi played critical roles of mediation between peasants, landowners, and the state, and between the countryside and the outside world (Chubb, 1989, p. 9).

Between 1925 and 1929 the Fascists made a concerted effort to eliminate the mafia and re-establish government control of the use of violence, but the man implementing this effort – Prefect Cesare Mori – was dismissed when he targeted the more powerful people who were supporting the Fascist regime (Catanzaro, 1992, p. 110). Thus this effort replaced mafia control of the relationship between peasants and landowners with state control, but did not eliminate the problem; so the mafia re-established itself when Fascism fell, and was given a further boost when the Allied occupation in 1943 turned to local powers for assistance in governing (Catanzaro, 1992, pp. 113–14).

The Italian government is not the only government that has turned to private violence to accomplish what it was unwilling to do for itself. The US Navy turned to the imprisoned leader of the American mafia, Lucky Luciano, to protect the New York docks from Nazi sabotage during World War II (Sterling, 1990, p. 56). They were indeed protected, and it is a reasonable assumption that the methods used were not ones the US government would have been willing to employ.

2.2 Excessive bureaucratic power

Excessive bureaucratic power is a possible contributor to the development of mafias on the territory of the former Soviet Union, where government agencies and people with power in local government during the communist regime exercise power over the distribution of resources and entry into legitimate business, sometimes with the help of gangs. The vacuum or rejection of legitimate government power may also be a factor in the rise of ethnic mafias in the autonomous regions of Russia, in a way similar to the rise of the Sicilian mafia.

In general, excessive bureaucratic power and discretion, especially when the criteria for bureaucratic decisions are unclear and difficult to monitor and evaluate, provide the potential for corruption – for bribery, shakedowns or extortion. The corruption of a bureaucratic agency may begin with the clients of the agency – the members of the regulated industry. Thus building contractors may seek to speed up the work of the agencies that give building permits. It is more likely, however, that the bureaucrats originate the activity by demanding payment. Getting a government contract may require a kick-back; tips or bribes may be necessary to secure a wide variety of government services. In the former Soviet Union bribes are often necessary to secure even medical services.

This sort of corruption is virtually world-wide and does not necessarily lead to the development of full-fledged mafias, but to sporadic corruption that can be corrected or to a standard pattern of paying government functionaries for their services. (Government positions may be a means of giving favoured people access to a share of the spoils – a bureaucratic mercantilism.) It takes on the character of a mafia when access to bureaucratic decisions is used to exclude competitors through violence or threats of violence, and thus to control entry or access to contracts. At this point the efficiency benefits sometimes attributed to bribing government officials to do faster or better what they ought to do anyway collapse; bureaucratic corruption in collusion with criminal gang violence – 'the mafia' – become means to monopolising industries, awarding inflated contracts and operating outside public safety standards. The activity may be extraordinarily persistent, defying repeated investigation and prosecution.

2.3 Illegal markets

In the United States prohibition was a major impetus for the growth of mafia organisations. Prohibition created the potential for a major illegal market in alcohol, and it is to the years of prohibition that America can trace the growth in scope and power of its mafias. Illegal market enterprises generate considerable cash – indeed, only those that do so may be attractive – that can be used for bribes and investment in other industries. It is a good deal easier for legal authorities to overlook voluntary trade among consenting adults, even if illegal, than it is to take bribes to permit crimes that involve victims. Law enforcement agencies may be able to meet their quotas for arrests relatively easily if they cooperate with those who emerge as market leaders in the illegal industry to exclude new entrants or drive out competition by enforcing the law in cooperation with the group that becomes dominant.

Illegal drug markets have been a major factor in the virulence of the Sicilian mafia in the last several decades. In the Soviet Union the communist command economy criminalised a wide range of market exchange. Substantial illegal market activity involving bribes at many levels of the ruling hierarchy (Simis, 1982, pp. 126–79) is probably the origin of the mafia phenomenon in Russia today.

3   The American and Sicilian mafias and the business firm

The Sicilian mafia was originally a group of families controlling territories. Accounts suggest that while all of these groups – often made up of a single natural family and always headed by a dominant male figure – were competitive with each other, they were not in themselves firms. (When more than one natural family made up a *cosca*, or mafia clan, the families were often related by marriage.)

Rather, members of the family entered into various illegal and legal businesses with each other and with outsiders. Some accounts suggest that the Sicilian mafia between 1860 and at least 1957 was not a membership organisation but a natural outgrowth of culture, politics and law enforcement. It (or the families that composed it) thus re-emerged after a variety of efforts to eliminate it – most notably the effort of the Fascists under Cesare Mori in the 1920s – much as a new dominant male will emerge in a pride of lions if the pride loses its current dominant male. Arlacchi (1986, pp. 44–5) concluded in 1983 that 'there does not exist – and there never has existed – any secret, hierarchical and centralized criminal organized called the *mafia* ... The *cosca mafiosa* is a simple organism, but a solid one, without formalism or bureaucracy. Within it are neither statutory ordinances, initiation rites nor courts of judgment.' Nor, according to a statement he quotes, are there membership lists. Nevertheless, Arlacchi (1986, p. 79) speaks of the difficulty of recruiting in the 1950s and 1960s, and his more recent writings, based on extensive interviews with participants, find evidence of more formal organisation. Other accounts report initiation ceremonies as early as the first decade of the twentieth century, and a major figure in the Sicilian mafia who turned state's evidence in the early 1980s, Tommaso Buscetta, reported being 'made' a member of a mafia family in 1945 in a ceremony with rituals and oaths (Sterling, 1990, p. 72).

In the United States there were fewer mafia families (about 24 rather than hundreds) and they were larger; they were definitely membership organisations; and by 1931 they had formed a commission of leaders of families. A detailed case-study of one of these families and its legal and illegal activities as of 1970 (Anderson, 1979) found that the mafia family itself was not a business firm; rather, its members entered into various businesses on their own account. The group's main illegal market activities were numbers gambling and loan-sharking. The group controlled entry into numbers gambling (and other forms of gambling) in one section of the city where it operated (both the entry of its own members and of independents), and several firms operated in the numbers gambling industry. A few leaders of the group owned a numbers lay-off operation – an insurance mechanism for the retail firms – but lay-off services were also provided by other large numbers firms. Bribery and corruption to ensure police inaction and to deal with the criminal justice system were handled centrally.

The group did not control entry into loan-sharking; members of the group had established several loan-sharking firms that loaned their own funds or, for a percentage, those of others. The owners of loan-sharking firms generally did their own collecting but could turn to the services of some men in the group who were known as strong-arm men, that is, enforcers. A loose network existed for checking out potential borrowers with other members of the group and other organised criminal groups in the city and elsewhere.

Thus the group provided certain goods and services – capital, corruption, violence (and the reputation for the effective use of violence), and the evaluation of credit risks – primarily to its own members but also to non-members if they were permitted to operate on its territory. The use of violence generally required the approval of the boss of the group, and permission was sometimes denied. Entry into some businesses (e.g. gambling) required the permission of the boss; for other activities, such as selling stolen goods, reporting the activity to one's *capo* (the group leader of about ten men at the lowest level of the organisation) was sufficient.

Four activities were forbidden: kidnapping, white slave traffic, counterfeiting and narcotics traffic. These are all federal crimes and were thus likely to be costly to the group as a whole because of vigorous law enforcement at the federal rather than the state and local level and the lesser or non-existent ability to corrupt the criminal justice process. Neither this group nor any other American mafia family killed police officers, judges or politicians. Transcripts of wire-taps on this and other organised criminal groups in the 1960s also show that a good deal of the time of the bosses and other group leaders was spent talking about problems of leadership and control of members who talked too much, engaged in activities that endangered others, took too large a cut from others' businesses, borrowed too much, didn't pay debts, and cheated one another (Anderson, 1979, pp. 33, 37).

The boss of this group had contacts with the commission created in 1931, made up of the bosses of the major families; the commission generally dealt with disputes among families. As Claire Sterling describes it, 'The Commission was designed to set policy guidelines, fix territorial boundaries, settle intramural disputes, and rule on in-house killings' (Sterling, 1990, p. 81).

In short the mafia family as a whole was not a firm; it was a governance structure within which members undertook their own legal and illegal enterprises, and some of the members who held no position in the hierarchy were more successful financially than those who did. Its governance hierarchy was thus not the same as its economic structure. It used violence and negotiations to monopolise a territory within which its members operated certain illegal enterprises (especially gambling), thus functioning as a government, albeit an incomplete government. It established and enforced some rules for members, including their access to services it provided, and settled disputes among them, as in fact do many organisations, such as stock exchanges and professional associations. It gave permission for entry into some businesses for (presumably) a fee or a share of the gross revenues, as a franchiser might.

That narcotics traffic was forbidden in this family as well as others (at a minimum, members of American mafia families were supposed to inform superiors and warn friends) is related to a relationship the American mafia leadership is believed to have negotiated with the Sicilian mafia in 1957: it invited the Sicilian mafia to take over the importation of heroin into the United States and its wholesale distribution, presumably to achieve some of the financial benefits without the risks of US law enforcement.

Initially the Sicilian mafia bought heroin processed by the Corsicans in Marseilles, but after the French cracked down the Sicilians established their own processing plants for turning morphine base into heroin, primarily in Sicily.

Although drug trafficking was not entirely new to the Sicilian mafia or the Calabrians, it brought changes in the organisational structure of the families. Lucky Luciano, who had helped establish the American mafia commission, had been deported to Italy in 1946, a reward for his contribution to the war effort, and he recommended that the Sicilians establish a commission like the American one. They did so in 1957, calling it the *cupola*. It was disbanded in 1963 but re-established in 1970 (Sterling, 1990, pp. 81, 104, 131). The members of the commission were the leaders of districts, each comprising two or three mafia families (Catanzaro, 1992, p. 199).

The families remained in control of activities in their territories, but the *cupola* made rules about activity on the territory of other groups, about relationships among groups, and about recruiting (Catanzaro, 1992, pp. 199–200). Nevertheless it still seems to be the case that neither the *cupola* nor the families were functioning as business firms, and individuals continued to go into business, legal or illegal, themselves or in various partnerships with other members. Each drug shipment was financed as an independent venture. One informant reported realising that a seized shipment was one that he 'had a piece of' – a $30,000 investment (Sterling, 1990, p. 258).

Journalist Claire Sterling (1990, pp. 203–4) describes it this way:

> The Mafia's till, a revolving fund for quick turnaround expenses in the heroin business, to which all the clans contributed, contained some twenty billion lire, around $15 million in 1981. The whole venture was organized on a corporate basis, paying dividends of 1,600 percent. Indeed, the Mafia was issuing heroin shares like a company on the stock market's big board.
>
> The work was parceled out among the clans. Some procured morphine base, and heroin occasionally, through the Turkish Mafia. Others were linked up directly to suppliers of refined heroin in Southeast Asia: pure China White from the Golden Triangle, coming to Sicily in massive shipment of two hundred, three hundred, and even five hundred kilos. Different clans ran the refineries in Italy, while still others were in charge of the transporting, distributing, marketing, and money laundering. The product was available to everyone in the consortium. Orders could be placed overseas as if from a Sears catalog; the merchandise would be shipped in bulk with special markings for individual customers.
>
> Made Men of Honor had considerable latitude. They could cross Family boundaries for the heroin business, and use outsiders – chemists, couriers, launderers – for many chores. They were able to take part in the production process or just buy some points in it. They could invest individually or in a group. They might take their quota of the product and get it to market, or wait until it was sold abroad and paid for. Those preferring this last got a higher cut, since they shared the risk of police seizures.

> A flourishing cottage industry in body carriers was spreading the
> wealth to whole villages. . . .[5]

Arlacchi (1986, p. 193) quotes a 1972 story that financiers – perhaps
professional people – were offered a profit of $2 million on an outlay of
$100,000 over six months; they risked losing the investment in its entirety
but the shares of the deal could be sold back to the originator if the
financier needed cash.

In spite of the *cupola*, which was supposedly 'directing the entire heroin
consortium' (Sterling, 1990, p. 205), a major war erupted in 1981
between two major groups of clans: those who imported the morphine
base and those who marketed the heroin in the West. The proximate
cause was cheating. The marketing clans had been routinely skimming;
on this occasion they simply kept $10 million, claiming that the
Americans had not yet paid. But the war for control of the drug traffic
was in the minds of both groups in any case, perhaps the mafia version of
a hostile take-over. The brutality of the war was also responsible for the
first major break in the code of silence of the Sicilian mafia: several major
figures turned state's evidence. In the end the control of the drug traffic
was more centralised than before.

4   Transaction cost analysis and the Sicilian mafia

One of the more recent developments in economics that may be applied
to problems of the mafia and organised crime is that of transaction costs.
As Oliver Williamson (1985, pp. xii, 17) explains it, any economic
transaction that can be analysed as a contract is a subject for transaction
cost analysis. Transaction cost analysis assumes that people are bound-
edly rational: they have goals and purposes and try to choose appropriate
means to achieve them, but they do not know everything about either
current or future states of the world, and thus cannot write contracts that
cover all contingencies that might arise. It further assumes that people go
further than pursuing their self-interest: they are opportunistic and will
take advantage, if the opportunity arises, of those with whom they deal.
Finally, the courts are not assumed to adjudicate disputes either routinely
or costlessly; contracts are assumed to be worked out primarily as they
are in the real world, by the parties involved, that is, through private
rather than court ordering.

Transaction cost analysis thus involves the costs of 'drafting, negotiating and safeguarding' agreements and the costs, later, of renego-
tiating, the bonding costs of establishing secure commitments, the costs
of setting up organisations (not necessarily the courts) to oversee

disputes, and the costs of changes in the circumstances assumed when the contract was written or the agreement reached (Williamson, 1985, p. 21). Transactions vary in their frequency, the uncertainty associated with them, and the extent to which they involve transaction-specific assets. Five types of asset specificity have been identified: site specificity, physical specificity, human asset specificity, general purpose assets dedicated to specific customers, and brand name capital (Williamson, 1989, p. 143). Transaction-specific assets pose risks or potential costs for the parties involved, especially when circumstances change or contracts come up for renewal; having made an investment in specific assets or a commitment to deal with a firm that holds essential specific assets, the parties are in a bilateral negotiation and may be able to take advantage of one another.

Effort to economise on transaction costs (as well as normal production costs) is thus considered to explain different forms of organisation – the market or the firm and various non-standard contracting practices. Economising on transaction costs rather than technology alone is thus seen as the critical factor in how economic activity is organised – the scope of the firm and the extent of vertical integration. The firm itself is seen not as a technical production function but as a governance structure that seeks to economise on the transaction costs resulting from bounded rationality, opportunism and the consequences of specific assets. When one firm invests in specialised assets to produce output to be sold to another firm, contract renegotiation problems arise and the purchaser may find it desirable to integrate backward.

Transaction cost analysis has also been applied to families and to the family as the owner of a firm. Robert A. Pollack (1985, p. 594) reasons that family governance is especially suitable to low-trust environments (where outsiders cannot be relied upon in one way or another) and to simpler technologies. Mafia organisations in Sicily, and in Calabria as well, have traditionally been based on territory and centred on the male members of a particular nuclear family – a father and sons or several brothers. This group is called a *cosca*, and it may have a variety of relationships with friends and kin; sometimes several natural families form a *cosca*, and in stable cases intermarriage (the taking of hostages, perhaps) among them is common (Catanzaro, 1992, pp. 168–9). These *cosche* have been highly competitive with each other and murder among them has been common.

In Italy two of the mafia's major businesses (in addition to protection rackets) have been construction (or the obtaining of construction contracts for specific firms and some control over how they are carried out) and heroin. The following discussion focuses primarily on the heroin traffic.

One of the major risks of doing business in illegal markets is the risk of law enforcement activity, including the seizure of contraband and possibly other assets and the loss of personal freedom through successful prosecution. Criminals are vulnerable not only to direct police observation but also to testimony against them by other criminals, victims, corruptees and other witnesses.

The most important relationship of the criminal organisation, one that can be looked at as a contract, is thus likely to be its arrangements for non-enforcement of the law and mitigation of penalties. Corruption may be easier if the crimes are viewed as consensual (e.g. gambling) by the public and the government; if the criminal activity is an ongoing activity that produces an attractive stream of cash flows; and if the criminal organisation can offer the legitimate political system some benefits, especially cash and votes, which will lead to greater tolerance of the behaviour of individual judges or other corruptees who may act favourably to members of the criminal group.[6] Corruption of the criminal justice system is made more difficult if the system has overlapping jurisdictions. Federal agencies trying to combat organised crime in the United States in the 1960s encouraged the establishment of statewide Attorney Generals' offices to deal with problems in particular districts of the state.

These observations are only suggestive of the importance of the design of the criminal justice system and public opinion in influencing the kinds of contracts criminal organisations can make for mitigating law enforcement; the criminal justice system thus influences the behaviour of the criminal organisation.

In the United States the American mafia has found it desirable to avoid criminal activity in those areas where largely incorruptible federal agencies have jurisdiction. A major contractual event in the heroin trade was the negotiation by the American mafia in 1957 to have the Sicilian mafia take over the importation and distribution of the heroin traffic, that is, to give the Sicilians the franchise for this activity. This contractual arrangement, assuming that it did indeed occur, is of considerable significance and should yield to transaction cost economics. Quite a few members of the American mafia were imprisoned as a result of narcotics convictions at the time this arrangement was made (Sterling, 1990, p. 86), and the groups were known to the police and under frequent surveillance. By contrast the Sicilians could operate in the United States with far less surveillance and far less threat of law enforcement action while paying the Americans for the privilege.

The most striking difference between the American and Sicilian mafias is that the American mafia refrains from killing police officers, judges and politicians. Sterling (pp. 323–4) lists 24 'distinguished cadavers' of men murdered in Italy between 1979 and 1988, and others have occurred since then. This is part of the implicit contract; it is not clear what actions the American mafia believes the US law enforcement community would take in the case of a violation, but the American mafia itself would possibly take action against the violator. American law enforcement officials were astounded at an informant's report that a contract (to kill) had been put out on a US undercover agent whose work had resulted in the arrest of a Sicilian mafioso. The agent's boss is supposed to have negotiated the cancellation of that contract with an American mafia boss (Sterling, 1990, p. 319).

In contrast to the situation in the United States, the political tolerance of the mafia in Sicily has been considerable – perhaps to the point where various law enforcement bureaucracies were not able to take effective action against the murder of their own members. The reasons for the difference between the United States and Italy in this regard are worth further investigation. The need may be for a credible commitment to take drastic action in the event of murder of police officers and public officials.

The claim is sometimes made that trust is important in criminal enterprises. In fact the problem of breach of contract – of disloyalty (tipping off the police for personal benefit or as a means of competition, turning state's evidence, switching loyalties to another leader, becoming an informant for the police) and cheating – is extensive. The organisational structure of criminal groups and the structure of the firms that are created to undertake criminal ventures (as well as legitimate enterprises) reflect the probability and magnitude of these costs and the effort to deter disloyalty and cheating by structures and penalties that make violations costly. These transaction costs are great enough that criminal entrepreneurs seem to find it worth while to forgo economies of scale in the production process to reduce disloyalty and cheating. Transaction costs, then, lead to far smaller firms than would exist if the heroin business were legal. Major figures in the international drug traffic are found testing samples of product in their kitchens and standing on the streets of Brooklyn waiting for deliveries (Sterling, 1990, pp. 176–7, 285). Disloyalty as a major transaction cost is of course consistent with what law enforcement officials in both the United States and Italy know: that informants and defectors are extremely effective weapons against the mafia.

The centrality of the natural family as the core of Sicilian mafia groups and the fact that so many actual ventures, legal and illegal, are undertaken by individuals or members of a natural family is a means of organising economic activity that places a high cost on disloyalty and cheating; one can abscond to Brazil with the profits only at the expense of leaving one's home and family, and if wealth and the ability to earn profits in the future are a function of family rather than individual assets, there may be no benefit in cheating one's brother. The American mafia and, perhaps to a lesser or more recent extent, the Sicilians have also attempted to extend this kinship tie by recruitment into the mafia family. This induction is buttressed not only by rituals and oaths but by a hostage situation (the Sicilian requirement that new members have murdered someone) and the threat of death if oaths – especially the oath of silence – are violated. Strong penalties indeed. Illegal market activity is carried out in an organisational setting in which severe penalties can be imposed for breach of contract.

Another major event in the economic organisation of the heroin trade was the vertical integration into processing by the Sicilian mafia after French action shut down the Corsican processing laboratories. Laboratories that convert morphine base to heroin qualify as specific capital, and vertical integration backward is consistent with transaction cost theory. There is specific human capital (chemists) involved here as well; the Sicilians hired the French chemists. Some 15 processing plants were located in Sicily and northern Italy by the 1980s, probably a greater number than production economies alone would allow. The greater number allows processing to continue even if one is shut down. These plants were apparently financed and operated by individual families (or even individuals); information was not available on whether they compete with one another for processing the morphine base brought in by the importing families, whether they buy and resell, or process for an exporter. (Wherever enterprises are competitive, the potential exists for law enforcement to subvert one group at the expense of another.)

The heroin traffic also requires ownership or some control of other sorts of legitimate enterprises that can be used for specialised purposes, such as firms that export legal goods, financial institutions and transportation. Like export ventures themselves, these businesses are closely tied to families (Catanzaro, 1992, pp. 205–8). Furthermore, the heroin trade involves specific human capital: not just any member of the family can be sent to negotiate a deal or evaluate the quality of a shipment.

As an export industry the heroin traffic differs in one major respect from legal exporting: shipments cannot be insured.[7] Each shipment is a venture in which the goods are at risk, and each is specifically financed by varying participants; thus the risk is diversified.

Finally, R. H. Coase (1988, p. 10) notes that the buying and selling of securities takes place on stock exchanges that have well-structured sets of rules for the behaviour of members; their main problems are securing the agreement of members and enforcing their rules. The arrangement works because the right to trade on the exchange is valuable and occurs in a limited area that brings members together. This is an organisation of economic activity that may bear comparison with that of organised criminal groups; the family hierarchies or the commission of leaders of major families provide a governing structure within which the activity of members takes place. This development took place earlier in the United States than in Italy, where the *cupola* became important only after 1970, a development Catanzaro attributes to the increased coordination and capital requirements of the drug traffic, for which the family-based *cosche* were too small. He describes the *cupola* as 'in fact a true and proper system of sovereignties in competition with each other [as evidenced by] the widespread practice of infiltrating one's men as spies into competing families.' For the American mafia the commission was an effort to control the costs of internal warfare and the consequences of the activities of individual members on law enforcement activity. For the Italian mafia the *cupola* may be more a device to centralise control of the heroin traffic under some families rather than others, and this objective may conflict with the organisational consequences of the kinds of transaction costs involved in this illegal market.

5 Public policy implications and further research

The purpose of this paper has been to explore the application of one relatively recent development in economic theory – the transaction cost approach – to the problems of the mafia in Sicily.

In contrast to the neoclassical view of the firm, major characteristics of the transaction cost approach are more realistic assumptions about human nature (especially opportunism) and an emphasis on the micro-economic details of the functioning of the firm that goes beyond the view of the firm as a technological production function, emphasising instead the firm as a governance structure that seeks to deal with transaction costs as well as production costs. What goes on inside the firm and inside organisations created to monitor and enforce contracts is therefore considered essential information. This economic approach is, I think, a good fit with the problems posed by the mafia in Italy.

Public policy begins with value judgements about the desirability of alternative states of the world and proceeds with determining how to use scarce resources to achieve agreed objectives. In a democratic society it is important that the policy objectives have public support. In the field of law enforcement especially it is also important to keep the objectives in mind; otherwise results may be measured by output statistics – numbers of arrests and convictions, days spent in court, and so forth – rather than what is actually achieved.

Yet the nature of mafias – that they are always involved with corruption of the legitimate government – makes it difficult to establish and carry out policy. The very people who are supposed to do so, or are supposed to support the policy, may themselves be corrupt. Nevertheless in most places there are honest and courageous crime-fighters, as Italy has amply demonstrated over the years. Italy has also used a variety of jurisdictional methods and other devices to work around the corruption within law enforcement and other agencies, as has the United States, and it has followed the United States in establishing legislation that gives law enforcement officials a better chance of making cases, such as a witness protection programme.

The law enforcement effort will be severely hampered, whatever the public policy objectives, if law enforcement and public officials (and their families) risk assassination. In the United States the consequences of killing police officers or federal agents (and presumably judges) are apparently high enough that this simply does not occur. One might interview US mafia informants (as well as lesser criminals) to determine why they have arrived at this decision and how it is enforced. One might also interview law enforcement officials about the actions they would take in the event of assassination. But a reasonable hypothesis is that police officers support each other, and making one of their members an intentional target would lead to an all-out effort against the instigator. There is no reason to believe that members of Italy's law enforcement agencies are any less strong in their loyalty to each other or that they do not know what to do. The difference is rather that the politicians have not let them proceed. One approach is for those appointed to positions of leadership of law enforcement agencies to refuse to take these jobs if they are not guaranteed the power to bring the full forces of law enforcement against those who kill crime-fighters or threaten them and their families.

It is a fundamental assumption of a public policy oriented towards achieving defined objectives that mafia organisations respond to the costs imposed on them by law enforcement. Some activities can be made more expensive than others; behaviour can be changed. This assumption seems to be borne out by the comparison of the behaviour of the American and Italian mafias.

Mafia families are governance structures and they are also relatively small organisations. The pool from which heads of families arise or are selected is not large. Nevertheless members vary considerably in personal qualities and values, from men with statesmanlike wisdom and skills to sociopathic killers. In the world's larger nation states, leaders who emerge probably have qualities appropriate to the times. But the size of mafia families and the nature of the succession process is unlikely to produce the kinds of leaders most desirable from a public policy perspective. Yet the family heads are the people who exercise the powers of governance – the control of members and the relationship with the legitimate government. Some of them will respond more readily to signals from the law enforcement community than others, and some will be more effective than others at managing their members. Law enforcement can affect the leadership by targeting the most undesirable leaders.

As for specific objectives, they should depend, as already mentioned, on value judgements about the consequences of mafia activity and the resources needed to change existing conditions. In this regard mafia control of entry into legitimate business, protection rackets (and associated violence), and the control of public contracts seem especially pernicious, as they defeat competition, reduce the profitability of legitimate business and thus investment in the region, and divert taxpayers' funds (sometimes to politicians). Protection rackets require the threat and effective use of violence, whether against persons or property. Their continued existence requires the complicity of local law enforcement officials or their inability or unwillingness (perhaps out of fear) to protect people and enterprises threatened by violence. The protected businesses may support the racketeers because they control entry, as Reuter (1992) found in a case-study of racketeering in the garbage industry in New York City.

A prerequisite for a successful campaign to eliminate protection rackets and control of entry into legitimate business is the elimination of threats to law enforcement officials. It might also be worth while to do an economic analysis of the costs to the population (in higher prices, lost jobs and so forth) of the consequences of protection rackets in order to provide a base for support of the policy. Success requires that those threatened be willing to turn to law enforcement officials for help and protection. It also requires effective protection and successful prosecution of those making the threats.

A major area of Italian mafia activity has been corruption in the public contracting and procurement process. Kick-backs and bribery on government contracts are a recurrent problem for governments around the world. It is generally dealt with by a variety of administrative and law enforcement methods: investigations, audits, procedural rules for competitive bidding, and so forth. The problem becomes less tractable when kick-backs occur at the highest levels and contract procedures are a way to reward the recipients for favours provided to the government or ruling party, such as controlling the population or delivering the vote. One approach would be to reduce or eliminate the funds available.

In public contracting as in other areas, corruption itself mitigates against effective law enforcement. The diversion of public funds in overpriced contracts, work not done and kick-backs is one cost of this corruption. But the recurrent theme is that corruption itself is the major cost of mafias, in its violation of public trust and in the resulting inability of the government to protect either citizens or its own officials from violence.

One potential objective of public policy that is sometimes put forth is that of reducing the flows of funds to the mafia and thus its ability to use its cash flows to corrupt, enter other businesses and so forth. Drug traffic (in addition to public contracts) has been a major source of funds and profits for the Sicilian mafia. It is unusually profitable, of course, precisely because it is illegal. The profitability extends to local drug trafficking, where the lifestyle of the drug dealer competes in US cities and elsewhere with legal employment opportunities. The high cost of illegal drugs also increases conventional crime. The obvious solution is legalisation, a policy challenged on the grounds that it may increase the use of drugs and thus their debilitating effects on users. Meanwhile the insights from the transaction cost approach are consistent with what law enforcement officials know and other analysts have described (e.g. Arlacchi, 1986, pp. 196–210) about the risks and vulnerabilities in this endeavour, although the ownership structure of, for example, the heroin processing laboratories in Sicily remains obscure.

In general the merit of the transaction cost approach is that it reminds us to look inside organisations and their relationships with other organisations to determine why they are organised as they are, for it is here that we find the transaction costs with which the organisation is wrestling and thus its greatest vulnerability. Some economists approach organised crime with theoretical models that ignore the empirical facts, such as the fact that the governmental structure of mafia families is not the same as the economic structure of the organisations that actually undertake criminal activity. This empirical observation highlights the importance to mafias of organising to protect against cooperation with the police and to corrupt the law enforcement and political processes. The transaction cost approach thus provides support for the view of law enforcement officials that informants are crucial to prosecution efforts, for informing and turning state's evidence are activities the governance structure is designed to prevent.

The transaction cost approach also suggests that mafia families and mafia enterprises need to deal with the problem of property rights in illegal enterprises. These property rights are limited in significant ways – they are not, for example, heritable. If the owner of a 'piece' of a heroin shipment dies before he is paid, does his widow get the return from the investment? How does the ownership and control of a protection racket change hands? And is it possible that the time of transfer is the time when vulnerability is greatest?

One of the empirical observations that can be made about mafia families in both the United States and Italy is that they are always involved in legitimate as well as illegal enterprises. In the United States (Anderson, 1979, pp. 103–15) these legitimate businesses provide diversification against the risks of illegal enterprises as well as a place to do business and a tax cover – that is, a legal source of income. The US government has often used tax evasion based on a net worth case to prosecute members of organised criminal groups. To defend against a net worth case, an individual must counter the charge that he has not reported sufficient income on his tax returns to account for overt consumption and the change in his net worth over the period of time chosen by the authorities. If the individual wants to consume and invest openly amounts earned illegally, these earnings must be converted to legal income reported on tax returns. In other words, the money must be laundered. (It should be noted that laundering money for the purpose of converting illegal income to apparently legitimate income results in the collection of taxes on illegal income.) The estates of widows can also be audited, placing at risk offshore investments or investments made covertly. As far as I know, the Italian government has not used tax evasion based on net worth analysis as a prosecution technique.

Very little information has come to my attention on the internal financial arrangements of mafia families and mafia enterprises, although more might be available in Italian-language sources. The problems of property rights in illegal enterprises and covert legal investments suggest that this area is potentially rewarding for identifying vulnerabilities and devising law enforcement strategies.

Although criminal activity is harder to observe than legal activity, there is nevertheless an enormous amount of material available in court records, journalistic accounts, and the publications of the Parliamentary Anti-Mafia Commission that is worthy of what we might call economic archaeology by those able to read the record. In recent years Italy has succeeded in developing informants who may be able to provide answers to some of the outstanding questions.

Finally, an ultimate objective of public policy towards the Italian mafia might be its assimilation into the larger society. This is what is happening to the American mafia, which aspires to legitimate rather than mafia careers for its children. It might be worth while to try to separate the historical and cultural reasons from the economic reasons (primarily the consequence of law enforcement) for the difference between the American and Italian mafias in this regard to determine whether public policy can promote such an outcome.

The description of the organisation and operations of the Sicilian mafia in this paper, based as it is on sources available in English, is incomplete and thus only suggests possibilities for further study. Nevertheless, I hope I have succeeded in demonstrating that analysing the Sicilian mafia through the lens of transaction cost economics can provide insights into its relationships with law enforcement and its vulnerabilities that may lead to more effective strategies of law enforcement.

NOTES

1   This relationship leaves open the possibility that a common factor is involved in both the mafia presence and the poor economic performance. The work of political scientist Robert Putnam (1987) suggests that the weakness of civic associational culture could be responsible for both. Putnam studied representative regions in Italy in the 1860–1920 period and in the 1970s. He found that civic participatory culture in the earlier period was a strong determinant not only of civic culture in the later period but also of economic development (e.g. the percentage of the labour force in industry); indeed it was a stronger determinant than the level of economic development in the earlier period itself.

2   No claim is being made here that the existence of one of these conditions will always produce a mafia or that one of the three is always found as a prelude to the mafia phenomenon.

3   See Skaperdas and Syropoulos, this volume, for an analysis of how gangs, which they interpret as primitive states, arise in a situation of anarchy. They note that when government makes a product or service illegal it also ceases to enforce other laws, such as contract law, in the illegal market. They also note that the inability to govern does not require geographical distance (as in Sicily) but may occur in places such as the inner cities in the United States. They emphasise that these primitive states arise not out of cooperation but out of coercion, and initial endowments of resources are important in determining the outcome.

4   A great deal has been written about the history of the Sicilian mafia. This identification of a few important features, as well as later descriptions of the organisation and functioning of the Sicilian mafia, is based on a limited number of sources in English and cannot begin to convey the richness of even those sources.

5   The sources for Sterling's summary include Commissario Antonino Cassara's report to the Sicilian judiciary entitled 'Greco + 161' (13 July 1982), which summed up information from a number of important informants, and testimony by informants reported in Stajano (1986).
6   Becker and Stigler (1974) address a number of these issues.
7   Consider an agricultural crop grown in certain regions of the Third World for ultimate use in relatively small quantities, but perhaps in a variety of forms, by a large number of individual consumers in the United States and Western Europe, and sometimes also in the country of origin. The crop is grown, perhaps as a secondary crop, by many farmers, who may perform some preliminary sorting or processing. It is collected by village merchants or itinerant traders who may further process and package it for resale and shipment to consuming countries, or sell it to exporters who may do so. An intermediate stop may occur in a country serving as an entrepôt or a processing area. Prices may vary with supply changes resulting from weather and other influences on agricultural output, including political exigencies.

In the importing countries broker-agents may serve to bring together seller and buyer; dealers then market the product to those who will process it further and sell at retail. Direct sales from the producing country to the dealers or the manufacturers who will produce the final product are more likely when quality standards are higher and more uniform; there need be less reliance on middlemen to evaluate the goods or search for the product the manufacturer wants to produce.

This is a general description of the world trade in spices – specifically pepper, cinnamon, nutmeg, cloves, allspice, chillies and paprika, ginger, turmeric, vanilla and coriander. Unlike heroin and cocaine, considerable quantities of some spices are sold to food-processing companies rather than directly to consumers. And the trend for most spices is in the direction of increasingly direct relationships between importers who do the final processing and exporters, bypassing broker-agents and often dealers as well. Governments, growers' associations or trade associations in the producing countries have attempted to rationalise the sale of various spices, provide a more consistent product, and reduce price fluctuations (Purseglove, Brown, Green and Robbins, 1981).

REFERENCES

Anderson, A. G. (1979), *The Business of Organized Crime: A Cosa Nostra Family*, Stanford CA: The Hoover Institution.

Arlacchi, P. (1983), *La mafia imprenditrice*, Bologna: Il Mulino.

Arlacchi, P. (1986), *Mafia Business: The Mafia Ethic and the Spirit of Capitalism* (translated by Martin Ryle), London: Verso.

Becker, G. S. and G. J. Stigler (1974), 'Law Enforcement, Malfeasance, and Compensation of Enforcers', *Journal of Legal Studies*, 3(1), January, pp. 21–35.

Catanzaro, R. (1992), *Men of Respect: A Social History of the Sicilian Mafia* (translated by Raymond Rosenthal), New York: The Free Press.

Chubb, J. (1989), 'The Mafia and Politics: The Italian State Under Siege',

Western Societies Program Occasional Paper No. 23, Ithaca NY: Cornell University Center for International Studies.

Coase, R. H. (1988), *The Firm, the Market, and the Law*, Chicago: University of Chicago Press.

Jennings, W. P. (1984), 'A Note on the Economics of Organized Crime', *Eastern Economic Journal*, 10(3), July–September, pp. 315–21.

Pollack, R. A. (1985), 'A Transaction Cost Approach to Families and House-holds', *Journal of Economic Literature*, 23, June, pp. 581–608.

Purseglove, J. W., E. G. Brown, C. L. Green and S. R. J. Robbins (1981), *Spices*, 2 vols, London: Longman Group Limited.

Putnam, R. D. (1987), 'Institutional Performance and Political Culture in Italy: Some Puzzles About the Power of the Past', Working Paper, Cambridge MA: Harvard University Center for European Studies.

Reuter, P. (1992), 'Collecting Garbage in New York: Conspiracy Among the Many', Washington DC: The Rand Corporation, August.

Schelling, T. C. (1967), 'Economic Analysis and Organized Crime', Appendix D of President's Commission on Law Enforcement and Criminal Justice, *Task Force Report: Organized Crime*, Washington DC: US Government Printing Office, pp. 114–26.

Schelling, T. C. (1971), 'What is the Business of Organized Crime?', *Journal of Public Law*, 20, pp. 71–84, reprinted in Schelling, T. C. (ed.) (1984), *Choice and Consequence*, Cambridge MA: Harvard University Press, pp. 179–94.

Simis, K. M. (1982), *USSR: The Corrupt Society*, New York: Simon and Schuster.

Skaperdas, S. and C. Syropoulos (1995), 'Gangs as Primitive States', Ch. 3, this volume.

Stajano, C. (ed.) (1986), *Mafia: L'atto d'accusa dei giudica di Palermo*, Roma: Editori Riunati.

Sterling, C. (1990), *Octopus: The Long Reach of the International Sicilian Mafia*, New York: W. W. Norton & Co.

Williamson, O. E. (1985), *The Economic Institutions of Capitalism: Firms, Markets, Relational Contracting*, New York: The Free Press.

Williamson, O. E. (1989), 'Transaction Cost Economics', in R. Schmalensee and R. D. Willig (eds.), *Handbook of Industrial Organization*, Amsterdam and New York: Elsevier Science Publishers, Vol. I., Ch. 3, pp. 135–82.

Discussion

MAURIZIO FRANZINI

In this stimulating essay, Annelise Anderson discusses questions of great importance for understanding the organisational structure of the mafia and the relationship between mafia and government. Here I shall examine the central theme of the essay and the scope of the approach she suggests. The main aim of 'Organised Crime, Mafia and Governments', in the author's own words, is 'to explore the application of one relatively recent development in economic theory – the transaction cost approach – to the problems of the mafia in Sicily' (p. 47).

As is by now well known, Transaction Cost Economics is one of the principal branches of research of New Institutional Economics, and is closely associated with the name of Oliver Williamson. Ms Anderson gives a concise account of the main features of Transaction Cost Economics – the aim of which is to demonstrate that transactions with different attributes are assigned to different governance structures so as to economise on transaction costs – and she suggests that this approach could be useful in analyses of the Italian and US mafias. In particular, she proposes considering the mafia to be a governance structure. In her historical interpretation, the author argues that the American mafia became a governance structure long before the Sicilian mafia. The latter is said to have achieved this status only in the second half of the 1950s, when the *cupola* was established.

Having chosen to regard the mafia as a governance structure, Ms Anderson criticises the widespread opinion that the mafia is a firm. For example, she writes: '... the mafia family as a whole was not a firm; it was a governance structure within which members undertook their own legal and illegal enterprises' (p. 40).

As a governance structure the mafia accomplishes several tasks, none of which is typical of a business firm. In the American case, the mafia 'used violence and negotiations to monopolise a territory within which its members operated certain illegal enterprises (especially gambling), thus functioning as a government, albeit an incomplete government. It established and enforced some rules for members ... and settled disputes among them. ... It gave permission for entry into some businesses for (presumably) a fee or a share of the gross revenues ...' (p. 40). As these tasks concern both the setting of rules and rule enforcement, their range is very broad.

Most of the questions discussed by the author are concerned with enforcement, although she extends the discussion beyond the enforcement of rules for mafia members to the relationship between mafia and governments. She goes on to say that '[B]ecause many of its activities are illegal, another aspect of an organisation with the power to enforce agreements among participants is its potential power to deal with the legal criminal justice system. Its leaders may succeed in bribing individuals at any level or location in the criminal justice system –

police, courts, corrective institutions – to mitigate the severity of law enforcement' (p. 34).

More specifically, Ms Anderson maintains that disloyalty is a 'major transaction cost' and that '[T]he organisational structure of criminal groups ... reflect[s] ... the effort to deter disloyalty and cheating by structures and penalties that make violations costly' (p. 45). The existence of these problems, which Ms Anderson calls 'transaction costs', may explain, among other things, why the mafia is not bigger than it is or why more illegal transactions are not internalised. The author applies the same arguments as Coase to explain optimum firm size.

Corruption and violence are undoubtedly two typical aspects of the mafia which deserve close attention. Ms Anderson is perfectly right when she stresses their importance. In particular, she implies that corruption is a truly distinguishing feature of the mafia and it may extend beyond the criminal justice system and involve other public agencies, especially those with the task of awarding contracts. She goes so far in this direction as to suggest that '[T]he essential characteristic of a mafia ... is corruption or substantial influence in at least some agencies or bureaux of the legitimate government' (p. 35).

This definition of the essential characteristics belongs to a different level of analysis and is not easily reconcilable with the conception of the mafia as a governance structure having the primary aim of solving serious enforcement problems.[1] True, it is not quite satisfactory to define the mafia exclusively in terms of a governance structure. For example, this point of view leads to the absurd conclusion that the Sicilian mafia did not exist before the 1950s, until the *cupola* was established. The word 'mafia' may have many meanings but it is not always easy to understand the reciprocal compatibility between the many definitions used by Ms Anderson.

Going back to what I regard as the main point of the essay, bribery and violence are essential functions for efficient criminal organisation and the approach of the author may be very helpful in explaining the mafia's frequent use of them. After correctly identifying the problem, Ms Anderson does not explore it in depth, leaving the curiosity that her approach has aroused, unsatisfied.

In fact, the author's main conclusion is of another type, namely that Transaction Cost Economics 'provides support for the view of law enforcement officials that informants are crucial to prosecution efforts, for informing and turning state's evidence are activities the governance structure is designed to prevent' (p. 50). This is a rather disappointing conclusion for such a sophisticated approach. After all, there is little doubt that informants are important in the struggle against crime. We could expect more than this from a New Institutional Economics approach to the problem of the mafia. In the rest of this comment I shall explain the reasons for this statement.

Ms Anderson uses a mixed approach which is partly historical and partly theoretical. The complexity of the questions under consideration makes it necessary, in my opinion, to go into the theoretical potential of New Institutional Economics in relation to an interpretation of the mafia. In particular, greater clarity is required in the definition of concepts and problems.

The first problem is to define the role we want to attribute to mafia-type governance structures. Ms Anderson does not distinguish clearly between efficiency and distribution. When she refers to the American mafia, she emphasises the coordination problems, that is, organisational efficiency. When she speaks of the Sicilian *cupola*, she seems to favour distributional aspects or the predominance of one mafia family over another (see for example at p. 47). Coherent analysis in a New Institutional Economics framework should concentrate on the problem of efficiency. Although this notion is not unambiguous when there are many more constraints than the technological one, it can be defined with some precision. In particular, it requires minimisation of appropriately defined transaction costs.

The second question regards the concept of the mafia as a governance structure rather than as a firm. The new institutional approach allows the contrast between these two concepts to be overcome. As the author mentions, the concept of firm as governance structure is typical of this approach and is based on the organisational features of the firm rather than the mere transformation of inputs into outputs. To conceive the mafia as a governance structure means focusing on its organisational features, its pattern of internal relations and the rules governing its members. The mafia has members, but this does not mean that it does not also have clients. When the mafia is defined as a firm, the services it sells to clients willing to pay, more or less spontaneously, are emphasised. Many authors regard protection as the service offered by the mafia (see Gambetta, 1993); there is nothing to prevent an organisation from selling protection and being a governance structure at the same time. This conclusion seems inevitable if we admit that the mafia has both members and clients.

By making reference to protection, it is possible to present the enforcement problems to which Ms Anderson rightly dedicates much space in a different light. Widespread opinion has it that the mafia cannot be regarded as monopolising the protection market; a similar idea crops up repeatedly in Anderson's essay. There are actually many mafia firms which sell protection services to 'final consumers' and which operate in a complex relation of conflict and cooperation. For the reasons clearly stated by the author, each of these firms needs protection in its turn: protection from violent and opportunistic behaviour of other firms and from state repression.

Hence a demand for protection arises even from firms that sell protection in turn. To the best of my knowledge, this problem is neglected in the literature, probably because it is assumed, for no convincing reason, that firms are able to protect themselves. Rather than being made as an assumption, this concept ought to emerge from an analysis of when it is advantageous to produce one's own protection and when it is better to buy it. With the new institutional approach, it comes naturally to tackle questions of this kind. What is to prevent us from regarding the mafia as an organisational structure that protects mafia firms on the basis of the advantages it offers with respect to individual protection?

Through this approach it would be possible to distinguish mafia in the strict sense from mafia in the broad sense; besides the structure that offers services of protection to firms (if it exists), the latter also includes the group of mafia firms. However, the mafia phenomenon is characterised by the existence of a centralised structure offering protection to firms or, in other words, what I have called mafia in the strict sense. Using this key, it is possible to trace more clearly the distinction between mafia and criminal firms in general.

In Anderson's essay, the reason for the diversity of the mafia does not emerge clearly. All criminal firms are vulnerable to law enforcement and collaboration of their members with the police. In the end all illegal transactions are subject to transaction costs of this type. What then, characterises the mafia? The use of bribery and violence, or successful use of both these 'instruments', would probably be Anderson's reply. I think a better reply would be: centralisation of services of protection to mafia firms, and hence, in agreement with Anderson, the existence of a governance structure for this purpose.

Following this line of reasoning, it becomes essential to tackle the problem of whether it is worth while, from the point of view of efficiency, to centralise these services. The following factors are relevant. Every mafia firm needs protection from other firms and from the government. The first need indicates an area of conflict between firms, the second, an area of possible cooperation and agreement. The institutional solution used by mafia firms also depends on the relative importance of these two needs. The means to use in either case seem, at first sight, to be quite different: violence towards rivals and bribery of the government.

The centralisation of bribery, and hence the use of a centralised structure, probably offers much greater advantages than the decentralised solution. If this is so, there is another reason for cooperation between mafia firms: not the advantages that firms expect from protection against violence from others, but their benefits from the centralised management of bribery of the government. There is no reason to suppose that the two explanations are mutually exclusive. Hence the mafia can have success if it offers good bribery services and, subordinately, protection from other firms. The author's hypothesis of centralised corruption as an explanation of the mafia phenomenon is thus confirmed by a completely different line of reasoning.

The problem I have outlined acquires significance in the light of recent Italian experience. The spread of corruption culminating in Tangentopoli (Bribe-opolis) has certainly made individual access to bribery less costly, changing the advantages between the centralised and decentralised solutions. In other words, the progressive degeneration of public morality may have created serious problems for the stability of the mafia's organisational model based on centralisation of protection services. A decrease in certain evident advantages of cooperation between mafia firms, caused by events largely independent of mafia activity, may have favoured an institutional crisis within the mafia, generating disbandment of which the criminal justice system was able to take advantage. To the many explanations of the factors determining the fortune or misfortune of the mafia, we could perhaps add that too much corruption is detrimental to organised crime.

The method of analysis that I have suggested could even permit an in-depth examination of 'institutional' problems to be solved in the presence of transactions that are extremely vulnerable to the divulgence of private information. This aspect, to which Anderson is referring when she emphasises the role of informants, is not a characteristic of illegal transactions: it is enough to mention the example of the problems arising from industrial espionage. In such cases, exclusion from the organisation is not necessarily to the detriment of the person excluded; on the contrary, it could damage the organisation if the person excluded reveals information.

With reference to the mafia, the revelation of information is to the detriment of the organisation if corruption does not ensure benevolent protection by government authorities.[2] Again, violence and bribery play a decisive role. The threat of violence, together with the threat that a member leaving the organisation may not receive the necessary protection from the law enforcement authorities because of bribery, enable the bosses of the organisation to exercise full control over their members. It may in fact be in the bosses' interests to give their members a distorted image of their capacity to influence state authorities and of their relationships with heads of government, making loyalty to the mafia organisation advisable for its members. In a more general context, it could be said that confidence in the capacity of the governance structure to influence the government plays a central role in urging mafia firms towards centralisation.

Since new institutionalism, or more generally the economic theory of organisations, tackles universal problems such as incentives, coordination and enforcement, it can help us to understand essential aspects of the mafia phenomenon. As I have tried to show, it also helps to distinguish problems of little significance from those of importance. In order to proceed in the right direction, it is necessary to go beyond the simple notion of transaction costs and utilise all available instruments, including game theory. The potential fruits of Anderson's approach are many, but before we can enjoy them, much work is needed.

NOTES

1 Another statement of the author, that corruption 'takes on the character of a mafia when access to bureaucratic decisions is used to exclude competitors through violence or threats of violence, and thus to control entry or access to contracts' (p. 37), does not help to clarify the questions being examined.
2 It is worth recalling that a criminal organisation is vulnerable to informants, even those who are not members of the organisation. An interesting discussion of the factors on which community cooperation with the police depends may be found in Akerlof and Yellen (1993).

REFERENCES

Akerlof, G. and J. Yellen (1993), 'Gang Behavior, Law Enforcement, and Community Values', in H. J. Aaron, T. E. Mann, and T. Taylor (eds.), *Values and Public Policy*, Washington DC: The Brookings Institution.
Gambetta, D. (1993), *The Sicilian Mafia: The Business of Private Protection*, Cambridge MA: Harvard University Press.

3   Gangs as primitive states

STERGIOS SKAPERDAS and
CONSTANTINOS SYROPOULOS

1   Introduction

The term 'organised crime' consists of two words that to a certain extent
contradict each other. On the one hand, a 'crime' is by definition an illegal
act that usually, but by no means always, goes against society's norms and
mores. Criminal acts and the persons committing them are relegated to the
margins of the polity and the state and they are considered an aberration,
an exception to the rule, something random. On the other hand, the
adjective 'organised' means 'having a formal organization to coordinate
and carry out activities'.[1] An organisation usually implies the presence of
written and unwritten rules and norms of conduct together with sanctions
against possible offenders. That is, even illegal organisations have a
semblance of a legal framework and a culture. The contradiction in the
term 'organised crime' lies, then, in the fact that criminal organisations
cannot be considered aberrations and random individual phenomena, but
rather they can represent a challenge to the existing legal framework and
possibly to the state and the political system itself.

But the relationship between state authorities and gangs[2] or other
elements of organised crime is seldom completely antagonistic. Often the
relationship is symbiotic, a 'live-and-let-live' arrangement. For the
police, the justice system, the politicians all have to come to terms with
the fact that the state does not have complete control and frequently in
the duopoly of violence that exists in the gang's territory the gang has the
largest market share. Hence, despite the occasional mobilisations of the
state and the official proclamations, tacit arrangements of division of turf
and self-restraint on the part of both gangs and state authorities
represents the more normal state of affairs.[3] Of course, there are also
cases of bribery and material participation of state authorities in gang
activities, but there is no need to invoke these to say that the relationship
is symbiotic.

The implicit or explicit delineation of boundaries between the gang and the state and, occasionally, the melding of the two means that there is space within which the gang has a near-monopoly in violence. This space could be a large rural district in western Sicily at the turn of the century, the territory of a powerful, well-organised New York gang, or just the club-house and its immediate surroundings of a small East Los Angeles gang. Since monopoly in violence is arguably the most important characteristic of the concept of the state, we believe it could be useful to think of organisations like gangs as states.

In Sicily the mafia used to regulate most important aspects of economic activity, and created and enforced its own version of justice.[4] Most US urban gangs examined by Jankowski (1991) have a hierarchical structure with a president, vice-president, war-lord and treasurer. Moreover, within their territories these gangs perform similar functions to those of the Sicilian rural mafia. Gangs also develop organisational cultures and ideologies that contribute to their cohesion and expansion. These are characteristics shared with ordinary states and researchers on organised crime and gangs have explicitly recognised the similarities. Thus, Bequai (1979) states that '[organised crime] is in essence a de facto government with its own private army and system of laws' (p. xi), while Jankowski shows 'how gangs behave as private governments' (p. 89).

Gangs, as we generically use the term here for long-lived organisations with primarily illegal economic activity, should be distinguished from short-lived groups of ordinary bandits and brigands. Although there have been historical examples of long-lived bands of brigands (they could even be called armies), which had symbiotic relationships with state authorities that allowed some permanence in membership, geographical location and economic activity, in most rural societies that was the exception.[5] A gang should also be distinguished from an urban 'crew', a group of individuals who get together to accomplish a specific task requiring team action which disbands after the task is accomplished. A long life and the tacit recognition of economic or geographic borders on the part of state authorities and others are characteristics absent from these ephemeral teams, but present in our concept of the gang.

Whereas the near-monopoly in violence, long-life, organisation, and *de facto* boundaries provide gangs with key attributes of the state, the absence of a permanent bureaucracy differentiates them from empires and modern states. Rather, gangs are more akin to tribal, feudal and other small states with little, if any, codification of their norms and sanctions and with minimal differentiation of leadership and other governing duties; this is the sense we try to convey with the term 'primitive state' in our title.

Our knowledge of the emergence of states[6] and, more generally, the emergence of institutions, is rather limited. The view we advance in this paper is that primitive states and gangs emerge out of anarchy primarily through coercion. We first examine a formal model of anarchy. We find that those who have the comparative advantage in the use of force and are thus less productive in useful activities tend to prevail. Moreover, in addition to the resources wasted on violence, the redistribution of income discourages productive innovation and thus may constrain economic growth. We then discuss the evolution of gangs (and primitive states), emphasising the effect of coercion in their establishment and the role of ideology in keeping them in power. Although the discussion is partly based on insights gained from the model, we freely venture beyond the model, offering ideas that could be formalised and developed more fully in the future.

2   Origins in anarchy

Our starting-point is anarchy, a condition without enforceable property rights or behavioural norms to prevent the use of coercion. We first briefly review the reasons that the territories in which gangs emerge can be considered anarchic and then examine a formal model. A main feature of the model is that agents allocate their resources between productive and appropriative, or more generally, unproductive activities, with the former generating useful output and the latter influencing its distribution. Two questions we explore are: (i) Which agent is more likely to prevail in anarchy and eventually impose its own rule? (ii) What are the main determinants of welfare and the degree of inefficiency?

2.1   The absence of control by the state

Gangs emerge out of situations in which there is a power vacuum that the state is unable to fill. Jankowski (1991) describes one particular environment as follows.

> Low income areas in American cities ... are organized around an intense competition for, and conflict over, the scarce resources that exist in these areas. They comprise an alternative social order. In this Hobbesian world, the gang emerges as one organizational response – but not the only one – seeking to improve the competitive advantage of its members in obtaining an increase in material resources. (Jankowski, 1991, p. 22)

There are several related reasons why it is difficult for the state to enforce its rule in areas in which gangs emerge. Some mafia-type groups developed in isolated mountainous regions or islands of the Mediterranean (Albania, Calabria, Corsica, Montenegro) where central authority was, for all practical purposes, absent. Indicative of this absence of authority is the administration of private justice in these regions through the vendetta, *besa*,[7] and other norms, as well as through the equivalent of the mafiosi.

Isolation, by reducing both access and the transmission of information, also weakens the responsiveness of the (usually distant) centralised authority to local concerns. In turn, this reinforces any pre-existing distrust and further undermines the ability of the state to enforce its rule.[8] Although this type of isolation, which can be characterised as political and social isolation, can be induced by geography, it can also arise independently of it. Thus, the state's ineffectiveness in enforcing its rule in poor urban areas is bred primarily by economic distance which in turn induces social and political distance from the centres of power.

Laws prohibiting the production and distribution of certain commodities (drugs, alcohol, prostitution, gambling) also imply that the state effectively abrogates the enforcement of its other laws in the affected illegal market; private parties can no longer use the ordinary channels for the adjudication of disputes and the enforcement of contracts. In a sense with prohibition the state voluntarily, although sometimes unwittingly, creates conditions that facilitate the emergence of anarchy in the affected area of economic activity.

2.2   A model of anarchy

We now turn to the model of anarchy. It is a variation of the model in Skaperdas and Syropoulos (1992), which is itself an extension of models examined by Hirshleifer (1988, 1991) and Skaperdas (1992a). There are two agents, labelled 1 and 2. Introducing a greater number of agents does not change the essential results as long as alliances do not form.[9] The agents can be either individuals or groups who have solved the collective action problem (for example, these groups could be clans) and behave as if they were individuals. Each agent has an endowment R_i of an inalienable resource which can be converted into 'guns', G_i, or a consumption good B_i ('bread' or 'butter') in the following manner ($i = 1, 2$):

$$R_i = \beta_i B_i + \gamma_i G_i \tag{1}$$

The positive parameters β_i and γ_i are coefficients measuring the technical efficiency with which each agent's resource can be transformed into the consumption good and guns, respectively. A lower value for either parameter indicates greater efficiency in production.

The consumption goods could be identical but, in general, we allow them to be different from each other. We can identify B_1 as 'bread' and B_2 as 'butter' with agent 1 being a peasant cultivating grains and agent 2 being an animal herder. The agents have identical preferences over bread and butter. In particular, they both have a linearly homogeneous utility function $U(B_1, B_2)$.[10]

Once the agents have converted their respective resources into guns and the consumption goods, the latter can be subject to capture by either party or be peacefully exchanged. Specifically, the two agents may either use their guns in conflict whose outcome is uncertain or trade their consumption goods under the threat of conflict. For a given choice of guns (G_1, G_2), the winning probability of agent 1 in case of conflict is denoted by $p(G_1, G_2)$, with the winning probability of agent 2 represented by $1 - p(G_1, G_2)$. This function $p(\cdot, \cdot)$ is symmetric so that when the agents have equal quantities of guns, they also have equal probabilities of winning. In addition, each agent's winning probability is increasing in her own quantity of guns and decreasing in that of her opponent. These properties are formally written as follows.

$$p \equiv p(G_1, G_2) \in (0, 1); \; p(G_1, G_2) = 1 - p(G_2, G_1)$$
$$\forall \; (G_1, G_2);$$
$$p_1 \equiv \partial p / \partial G_1 > 0 \text{ and } p_2 \equiv \partial p / \partial G_2 < 0 \tag{2}$$

Assuming the winner receives the entire production of the two consumption goods and letting $U(0, 0) = 0$, the expected pay-offs of the two agents in the event of conflict can be written as follows:

$$\pi^1 = p(G_1, G_2) \cdot U(B_1, B_2) \tag{3a}$$

$$\pi^2 = [1 - p(G_1, G_2)] \cdot U(B_1, B_2) \tag{3b}$$

The linear homogeneity of $U(B_1, B_2)$ implies that $pU(B_1, B_2) = U(pB_1, pB_2)$ for any p. Consequently, the expected pay-offs in (3) can also be interpreted as deterministic pay-offs according to which each agent receives a share of each good equal to his winning probability. In other words, for any given choice of guns, bread and butter, the two agents are indifferent between engaging in conflict and trading the two consumption goods in a way that results in the allocation just described.[11]

Using (1), B_1 and B_2 can be eliminated from (3), thus making the payoffs functions of the G_i, R_i, β_i and γ_i. Of these, G_1 is agent 1's choice variable or strategy, G_2 is agent 2's strategy, while the remaining variables are exogenous parameters. We focus our attention on Nash equilibrium strategy combinations, denoted by (G_1^*, G_2^*).[12] At a Nash equilibrium in which both agents have chosen positive quantities of guns and of the consumption goods, each agent's derivative with respect to her own strategy, G_1 for 1 and G_2 for 2, vanishes. In particular, for agent 1 the following condition holds at a Nash equilibrium:

$$\partial \pi^1(G_1^*, G_2^*)/\partial G_1 = p_1^* U^* - p^* U_1^* \gamma_1 / \beta_1 = 0 \tag{4}$$

where $p^* \equiv p(G_1^*, G_2^*)$, $U^* \equiv U(B_1^*, B_2^*)$, and subscripts in functions denote partial derivatives. The first term of (4) represents the marginal benefit of a small increase in guns (and an implied small reduction in bread). It is the product of the change in the probability of winning due to a small increase in guns, p_1^*, times the total 'pie', U^*. The second term in (4) represents the marginal cost of a small increase in guns. An increase in guns reduces the consumption good produced by the agent and, therefore, this marginal cost must include terms reflecting the opportunity cost of reducing useful production. These terms are U_1^* and γ_1, and $1/\beta_1$. U^* is the marginal utility of bread, γ_1 represents the (in)efficiency of producing guns (higher values reduce efficiency), and $1/\beta_1$ represents the efficiency of producing bread. Then, the higher is the marginal utility of bread, the lower is the efficiency of producing guns, and the higher is the efficiency of producing bread, the higher is the opportunity cost of producing guns. Since the agent who has the most guns has a higher probability of winning or, equivalently, receives a higher share of total utility, we could expect the agent who is contributing more to useful production and overall welfare but is less efficient in the production of guns to be less powerful.

This intuition, emanating from an inspection of (4), can be generally confirmed.[13] For more specificity and for the presentation of some other effects, we consider the following CES form of the utility function:

$$U(B_1, B_2) = [\alpha B_1^{(\sigma-1)/\sigma} + (1-\alpha)B_2^{(\sigma-1)/\sigma}]^{\sigma/(\sigma-1)} \tag{5}$$

The parameter α measures the relative valuation of bread and butter. The higher α is, the more bread is valued relative to butter by every agent.

Table 3.1: Effects on equilibrium share of agent 1 of increases in α, β_1, γ_1 and R_1

α	$\sigma = 1$	$\sigma \in (1, \infty)$	$\sigma = \infty$
α	−	−	−
β_1	0	+	+
γ_1	−	−	−
R_1	+	+	o

The parameter σ represents the elasticity of substitution in consumption between bread and butter. The larger σ is, the more substitutable (or, the less complementary) the two consumption goods are and as σ approaches ∞, $U(B_1, B_2)$ approaches $\alpha B_1 + (1 - \alpha) B_2$, the case with perfect substitution.[14]

Table 3.1 reports the effect of changes in different variables on the equilibrium share of agent 1; the effect on the equilibrium share of agent 2 is opposite to that of agent 1.[15]

The effect on equilibrium p^* of an increase in α is the own marginal utility effect previously discussed in connection with (4). The second effect, due to changes in β_1, has also been discussed: an improvement in agent 1's efficiency of producing bread (a decrease in β_1) increases her opportunity cost of investing in guns and reduces agent 1's equilibrium share. Thus, those who contribute more to total welfare, those who in a sense have a comparative advantage in useful production, receive smaller shares of the pie.

There are several implications of this effect for anarchic environments. First, the incentives for productive innovation (decreases in the β_is) are few, if any, relative to ideal perfectly competitive economies where productive innovation is rewarded.[16]

Second, when emigration to another place which provides more rewards to useful productivity is possible, those who are more usefully productive will have a greater incentive to emigrate. In consequence, the average useful productivity in anarchic environments will tend to decline.[17] This type of emigration may accentuate existing differences in the standards of living between regions, in contrast to tendencies for real income equalisation that are normally present in standard neoclassical worlds. Therefore, the persistence of average income inequality across regions could be explained on the basis of differences in institutions governing the distribution of income: guns under anarchy in one region, neoclassical competition elsewhere. This story is consistent with the patterns of emigration from southern Italy and American inner cities, where the rule of the gun is much more prevalent than in the areas of immigration.[18]

Whereas being more usefully productive confers a relative disadvantage, being more efficient in the conversion of initial resources into guns (lower γ_i) is usually advantageous. This can be inferred from Table 3.1 where a decrease in the efficiency of producing guns (a rise in γ_i) reduces the equilibrium share of agent i. The last effect in Table 3.1 concerns changes in an agent's initial resource endowments. An increase in resources of an agent increases the equilibrium share of that agent, unless the elasticity of substitution is infinite.[19] In short, for agents to increase their power in anarchy they can try to increase their efficiency of arms production or they can increase their resource endowments through, depending on the context, conquest of new territories, recruitment of new members in the gang, and (in the past) through enslavement.

We now briefly turn to the effects of some parameters of the model on the degree of inefficiency and equilibrium utility of the agents. As an indicator of inefficiency we adopt the ratio of actual (equilibrium) total utility to potential total utility,[20] where in the latter all initial resources are converted into consumption goods and none into guns. Improvements in an agent's useful productivity (reduction in β_i) increase that agent's utility, raise the utility of her competitor, and may increase inefficiency. An increase in an agent's resource endowment (R_i) increases her utility and reduces her opponent's utility and the greater is the asymmetry in the two endowments of the agents, the lower is the degree of inefficiency. Under conditions of near symmetry, increases in resource endowments intensify conflict and reduce efficiency.[21]

Consequently, when we identify the agents in the model as collectivities, an increase in resources coming from increased membership in the collectivity can reduce the average welfare of the members. Thus, beyond a certain point the original members of the group or their leadership will not wish to recruit new members unless their own welfare is enhanced. Naturally, this will only occur if the compensation awarded to new members is lower than average.

There is an additional variable affecting the degree of inefficiency to which we would like to draw attention. From (4) it can be seen that higher p_1^* implies higher marginal benefit and lower p^* a lower opportunity cost of producing guns. Therefore, the greater the ratio p_1/p (and, equivalently, $-p_2/(1-p)$) is,[22] the greater is the incentive to produce guns and, consequently, the greater is the degree of inefficiency.

It would be reasonable to posit that more destructive weapons increase the effectiveness of conflict. Since, as argued above, improvements in the effectiveness of conflict raise inefficiency, we would expect the availability of more destructive weapons to increase inefficiency with a greater proportion of total resources converted to guns. The reported recent dramatic increase in gang warfare in American cities is surely related to the increased availability of more destructive weapons. It would be interesting to know whether gangs have been allocating greater percentages of their resources to purchases of weapons over the time that these weapons have become more destructive and more available.

Overall, those with a comparative advantage in useful production tend to receive a smaller share of the pie whereas those with a comparative advantage in gun production or a greater quantity of resources tend to receive a larger share of the pie. Interpreting the model as a steady-state model with exactly the same structure – resources, other parameters, utility functions – repeated in every period, we could then say the agents with the comparative advantage in unproductive activities and a greater number of resources become the rulers of the anarchic territory or, in another interpretation, those agents have higher rank within the organisation emerging out of anarchy. Once we admit a time dimension, however, interactions among the interested agents could become more complicated and more interesting. In the next section we examine other aspects of the likely evolution of anarchic environments whose static counterpart we have just considered.

3   Evolution

Social norms, institutions and organisations have come to be seen by economists and other social scientists as primarily cooperative or efficient arrangements; firms are viewed as minimising transaction costs, with their most important component associated with durable, relationship-specific assets (Williamson, 1989); legal institutions economise on information in enforcing efficient trading arrangements (Milgrom et al., 1990); norms of cooperation in general arise when the future is important in long-term relationships (Axelrod, 1984). We can call this a 'contractarian' view of the emergence of organisations and institutions, by the fact that the agents involved make a self-enforcing contract to cooperate.[23]

While gangs usually promote the interests of their members (in part, because they eliminate much destructive conflict among them) and can thus be considered cooperative organisations from their members' viewpoint, from society's perspective it would be difficult to view gangs as promoters of efficiency since they contribute to conflict with other gangs, the police and sometimes with their own communities. Even if we were to regard the gang's supply of goods and services as productive, as we would with the goods and services produced in a primitive state, in order to maintain its borders and enforce its rule within its borders a large proportion of the gang's material and human resources is still devoted to directly unproductive activities. Primitive states and gangs are ruled by the gun. Most organisations and institutions of concern to economists are governed by contract.[24] Thus the contractarian view of the emergence of organisations and institutions can give only a partial view of the emergence of gangs and primitive states.

In this section, we first present a brief contractarian story about gang formation; we then examine the role of overt coercion and violence; finally, we discuss the effects of ideology.

3.1   How the gang could form

Suppose the anarchic environment examined in the previous section is repeated day after day indefinitely into the future. There are no complicating linkages across time. That is, guns are not durable so they have to be produced anew during every period. Moreover, saving today's resources for use in the future is impossible. In short, this is an ordinary infinitely repeated game with the model of the previous section as its stage game (which is generally asymmetric). By the folk theorem (see e.g. Fudenberg and Tirole, 1991, Ch. 5) it is well known that, as long as the agents value the future sufficiently highly, all the allocations that Pareto-dominate the single-period (Nash) equilibrium[25] could emerge as equilibria in the infinitely repeated game.

The set of allocations Pareto-dominating the equilibrium in single-period interactions, though, is not as apparent here as it is in other models. In Figure 3.1 we depict typical utility possibilities set(s) of all the feasible utility pairs, associated with our model. The shaded area is the utility possibilities resulting from the pay-offs given in (3), that is, the pay-offs given the rules of single-period interaction. Point A is the point at which neither agent produces guns, with each agent receiving half of the consumption goods and half of the total utility. Point B represents the single-period equilibrium. According to the folk theorem then, any point to the north-east of B and within the boundary CD can be an equilibrium in the infinite repetition of our single-period model. But any point within this set would involve positive gun production by at least one of the agents and, therefore, full efficiency would not be attained.

The reason for this is that, within this utility possibilities set, the agents cannot deviate from the division of utility prescribed by (3) for any given choice between guns, bread and butter. Under indefinite interaction, however, since actions in each period can be conditioned on the past, the

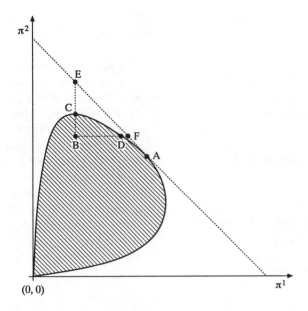

Figure 3.1 How the gang could form

agents need not be constrained to abide by (3). For example, both agents could put all of their resources into bread and butter production and still agree on an unequal division of the surplus, thus achieving any utility combination along the dotted line which represents the Pareto frontier of the fully efficient utility possibilities set. Such a division could be self-enforcing by the threat of reversion to the single-period equilibrium in *B*. By allowing for these possibilities and by appropriately redefining each agent's set of available actions, any allocation to the north-east of *B* and within the line *EF* is an equilibrium if both agents are sufficiently patient.[26]

Note that in all the fully Pareto-efficient allocations that are supportable as equilibria (points between *E* and *F*) depicted in Figure 3.1, agent 1 receives more than half of the total utility. This is because the bad single-period equilibrium allocation *B* also favours that agent who has a comparative advantage in guns or violence. Thinking of any such repeated-game equilibrium as the establishment of a gang consisting of two agents, agent 1, who receives the larger share, can be thought of as the leader and agent 2 as the follower soldier. Since the model can easily be generalised to more than two agents, we get an idea of how gangs with many members can come together and why the gang will be stratified with differential rewards across its members.

Those who get a higher share, and presumably have higher positions in the hierarchy, will tend to be those who have a comparative advantage in violence.

Although this contractarian story indicates how a gang may form and how it might sustain itself as an organisation, it has several weaknesses. First, as for all arguments based on folk theorems, it merely asserts the possibility of cooperation, not that it will be achieved and which particular form it will take. For there are many equilibria, including the single-period equilibrium, and we have no indication which one should be or would be implemented. Second, in practice, within gangs coercion and violence against their own members is ever-present but more importantly violence is continually used against non-members, mainly members of other gangs. The model, as interpreted here, does not consider non-gang members, either community residents or other gangs. Gang members as well as the ruling circle and enforcers in primitive states are small fractions of the populations over which they rule. To enforce their rule they have to exert coercion.

3.2   The importance of coercion

All power is ultimately based on the ability to use force. If a power holder's position is supported by codified law then this ultimate possibility of enforcement may gradually be forgotten in the conscious mind of the subordinate; in the case of the *mafioso* the relationship always remains much more direct. An act of force opens a man's road to power. Without having applied physical force at least once he would find it impossible to meet the other requirements necessary for the exercise of *mafioso* functions. He could not gain recognition, instill fear, or successfully control *mafioso* rivals. (Hess, 1973, p. 46)

A main threat to the leadership of primitive states and gangs is the threat of violent overthrow. As the quote above suggests, the mafioso's rise to power is inextricably linked to his willingness and ability to use force successfully. The rank and file also routinely have to face violence, either as instigators in attack or as defenders of their territory. Reflecting the importance to the gang of the fighting skills of its members, the most important initiation rite for new recruits in urban gangs is a fight against another member (Jankowski, 1991, pp. 49–50). Physical punishment, sometimes as severe as death, as an instrument of control of members and subjects alike is much more common in gangs and primitive states than it is in most modern states.

By contrast, modern states and other bureaucratic organisations rely overwhelmingly on law and contract for the discipline and motivation of their members and subjects. Although power is ultimately based on

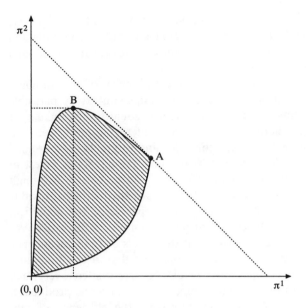

Figure 3.2   Subjugational equilibrium

force, in modern organisations 'this ultimate possibility of enforcement is forgotten in the conscious mind of the subordinate.' The contractarian view of the emergence of the state reflects this forgetfulness of the modern conscious mind.

We can gain some insight into the emergence of the state through coercion by first examining a seemingly limiting case of our model of anarchy. Figure 3.2 depicts a typical utility possibilities set for this case with the equilibrium utility pair located at point *B*. What is distinctive about this case is that, given the 'rule of the gun' prevailing in the interaction between the agents, agent 1 could not possibly receive a higher utility than that received in the depicted equilibrium; he receives his best possible pay-off. The production of guns in this equilibrium is also distinctive: agent 1 produces guns but agent 2 does not, or the more powerful party has the *monopoly of coercion*.[27] We can identify agent 1 as the despot, the ruler or the ruling class of a primitive state and agent 2 as its subjects. Alternatively, agent 1 could be the gang and agent 2 the gang's community.

Such a subjugational arrangement could arise as an equilibrium in circumstances with strong asymmetries in the following variables: (i) the relative valuations of bread and butter, with the agent producing the less valuable consumption good becoming the ruler; (ii) initial resource endowments, with greater resources providing the advantage of power; (iii) the rates of transformation between guns and butter and guns and bread, with the agent possessing the comparative advantage in gun production also having the advantage of power.

Some of the asymmetries required for the realisation of this subjugational equilibrium could be induced in a dynamic context by plausible dependences across time. One such dependence could be the linkage of every year's resource endowment for each agent to the utility received in the previous year, with greater utility leading to greater resources.[28] Another type of dependence would be to allow the agents to invest in improving the productive efficiency of guns, bread or butter. Although ordinary repeated games, including the one sketched in the previous sub-section, usually do not allow for time-dependence for analytical convenience, it would be difficult to dispute its empirical relevance. We have not derived analytical results about the effects of time dependence in the presence of asymmetries, but we conjecture that, if anything, any initial asymmetries that might exist would be accentuated over time. Given that the method of distribution employed favours the production of guns, the incentives to invest in improving the efficiency of gun production over those of bread or butter, if that were possible, would certainly be present. Since those who receive a higher share of the pie could invest more in improving their relative efficiency of gun production, there appears to be a tendency for polarisation of power and the development of ever-increasing asymmetries. A similar argument could be made about the effect of dependence of resources on previous utility. The asymmetries could eventually be arrested by the fact that not doing so would not be in the interest of the more powerful side, as it is not in the interest of agent 1 in Figure 3.2 to reduce the pay-off of agent 2 because that would imply a reduction in her own pay-off as well.

Perhaps the point we are trying to establish can be stated more simply. When force determines how many resources you receive and the amount of force you exert depends on your resources, there are compounding rewards to having an initial superiority in resources. The resultant organisation, if any, is more likely to be subjugational, authoritarian and hierarchical rather than an efficient contractual arrangement. This is not to say that organisations, once established through coercion, cannot improve efficiency later on. The rulers would always want to reduce the waste of resources associated with the use of force and protracted conflict if it could be done with minimal threat to their rule. One way to do that would be convince their subjects of their rule's legitimacy.

3.3   The role of ideology

In the long run, probably the most effective way to make other people work to further your interest is to have them believe that your interest is their interest. Another way is to have them pretend they believe your interest is their interest because of peer pressure. Material incentives, including the potential use of force, work best only in the short run when beliefs are given. That's why most firms and other organisations constantly try to inculcate organisational loyalty and pride in work for its own sake.[29] Similarly, the long-run success of gangs and primitive states depends heavily on the articulation and internalisation by members, subjects and community of a workable ideology, a logically connected system of beliefs about the world.

There are of course varying degrees to which the affected parties may subscribe to the 'official' ideology. In turn, there are layers to the ideology itself, each with a different degree of credibility and strength. Part of the core ideology of all the gangs studied by Jankowski (1991, pp. 84–5), including Irish gangs, is a picture of American society 'as structured in such a way that certain groups are discriminated against and prevented by other groups from enjoying all the benefits of society. Nearly all the gangs believed that their ethnic group had been denied access to conventional opportunities that would allow them to live more comfortable lives.' Gang members have a Social Darwinist perspective according to which illegality and predatory behaviour are the primary determinants of success not only in their own community but in the larger society as well. With this world view, the everyday activities of the gang that are considered morally reprehensible by the larger society are rationalised as legitimate by gang members.

Often participants in organised crime can see themselves as providers of public service. This was more true in rural societies, where the mafioso performed straightforward intermediary and judicial duties enjoying legitimacy from the local society, rather than in urban communities where wider legitimacy may be lacking. But even when extreme brutality was involved, the self-image of the perpetrator could be that of a 'sacrifice which he makes for the benefit of the public weal' (Hess, 1973, p. 68).

The public display of beliefs does not necessarily imply adherence to them. Part of the official organisational ideology of American gangs is that all gang members are 'brothers'; they are all 'family'. The gangs actively promote this view, with all members frequently alluding to versions of it. Yet, Jankowski (1991, pp. 86–7) found this brotherhood ideology to be largely symbolic and ultimately contradicting the intense individualism of gang members and the Social Darwinist perspective to which they subscribe. Rather, the gang, by getting its members to pay lip-service to the brotherhood ideology, hopes to alleviate the negative effects of the intense individualism of its members on organisational unity.

It appears that gangs cannot survive for long without the tacit acceptance of their communities. Acceptance can mean, though, approval in public and condemnation in private. The cost of publicly condemning those who have the monopoly in violence is usually high and, therefore, it would be difficult to observe public condemnations except in cases of uncertainty when nobody is clearly in charge. Universal expressions of support for the gang or the state can suddenly evaporate when an event makes the perceived expression of true preferences less costly.[30] Consequently, organisations established by the use of force cannot ascertain the support of their subjects or their communities with much accuracy. They can only hope that when a moment of crisis comes they will have enough loyal supporters to stay in power or that the perception of their strength will hold up sufficiently.

Organisational ideologies, almost by definition, promote the interests of the organisation but they can also encourage social fragmentation by promoting intrinsically conflictual viewpoints. The Social Darwinist perspective is not confined to American gangs. Our guess is that it would be the majority belief in most of southern Europe when pitted against a belief like 'successful are those who are most usefully productive.' Beliefs and ideologies evidently interact with institutions and together shape the economic decisions made by individuals. But, as economists, we know little about how this occurs.

4   Concluding comments

We have used the term gangs to designate long-lived organisations engaged mostly in criminal activity. We have argued that gangs can be thought of as primitive states with a near-monopoly in violence within their territories. They arise out of anarchy where those who have the comparative advantage in the use of force tend to prevail. This implies that gangs as well as primitive states, in contrast to other organisations examined by economists, emerge primarily through coercion and not through contract. The ideologies rationalising gangs to their leaders, members and communities are correspondingly different, emphasising the importance of predatory behaviour as a determinant of success.

In addition to any challenge they may encounter from state authorities, gangs have to be constantly vigilant against attacks from rivals trying to snatch away territory and its accompanying rents. Although our model of anarchy could be used to examine inter-gang warfare, it would be desirable to add the state as a third party with objectives different from those of gangs and examine in greater detail the sources of gang growth and break-down. What is the effect of increases in the efficiency of gun acquisition, a phenomenon that appears to have occurred over the past decade? Is an intensification of warfare a long-run effect of such a change, or is it a transitory phase eventually contributing to gang consolidation, with in the end fewer and more powerful gangs? What are the effects of instruments at the disposal of the state, including police protection, changes in legal codes (like the legalisation of previously prohibited activities that contribute to the gang's rents), publicity and education? These are only few of many questions that can be asked in modifications of our framework. Here we have just given an account of the origins of gangs that, we think, helps us understand their prevalence, persistence and differences from other organisations.

NOTES

* We would like to thank William Baumol, Jack Hirshleifer, Timur Kuran and the editors for very helpful comments. The financial support of the National Science Foundation under grant no. SES–9210297 is gratefully acknowledged.
1 *Webster*'s (1979).
2 Partly for brevity, we will be using the term 'gang' to signify any long-term illegal organisation. The ordinary usage of the term does not necessarily imply permanence or organisation. Here, however, a gang is meant to be a long-lived organisation, not just a group of individuals who get together for a specific purpose after the completion of which it disbands. See also our discussion on 'crews' and bands of brigands.
3 Jankowski (1991), which analyses the results of an invaluable ten-year field research project on American urban gangs, emphasises how such arrange-ments take the form of procedural rituals between police, social workers and the justice system on the one hand, and gang members on the other (see pp. 252–83). According to Jankowski, military-type police mobilisations against gangs were more common in Los Angeles than in New York and Boston, the two other cities covered in his study, but even in Los Angeles the live-and-let-live relationship between the police and gangs was the norm. The Sicilian mafia had an even closer relationship with state authorities since politicians were very closely associated with the mafia 'capos' (Hess, 1973). Such cosy relationships were interrupted during the Fascist period, but continued after World War II. Their precise nature and extent remain unknown but are becoming increasingly clear.
4 This includes the adjudication of criminal and civil disputes, but also the enforcement of cultural norms. Thus, on the last point, a young man could be forced by the mafiosi to marry the girl he has 'seduced' (Hess, 1973, p. 145).
5 Hess (1973, pp. 5–12) discusses the differences between brigands and mafiosi. Koliopoulos (1987) examines banditry in nineteenth-century Greece where in

some mountain areas the bands resembled the ideal type of gangs. Probably the most powerful organisation based almost solely on appropriative activities that was by any definition a state was that of the pirates based on the coast of western North Africa in the sixteenth century with Algiers as its effective capital. The city of Livorno in Italy was a smaller state of Christian pirates during the same period. Braudel (1973, throughout Vol. II) refers to the important economic, military and political role of pirates in the Mediterranean at that time.

6 We consider that the contractarian view of the emergence of the state out of an agreement among equal partners is not very illuminating in the understanding of the institution itself. Two complementary views to the one we develop here, based on relative coercive power and other factors, are Carneiro (1967) and Oppenheimer (1972).

7 This is an Albanian term which can be translated as 'word of honour.' A verbal promise in Albanian society, even today, represents a near perfect commitment. Those who do not fulfil their promises do not have *besa* and they can have their homes destroyed to their foundations. According to Doder (1992) this is not an infrequent sight in Albanian villages. While *besa* can solve the numerous commitment problems that have been identified by economists and other social scientists, it introduces other problems. Doder reports the difficulties one has with extracting the simplest of promises, like replacing a light bulb by a hotel employee, out of fear that it will not be fulfilled. Parenthetically, Albanian society appears very much like Schelling's (1960, p. 39) 'cross-my-heart' society, where crossing one's heart represents perfect commitment.

8 For an examination of the rather extreme social fragmentation and lack of trust in a post-war southern Italian village see Banfield (1958). Gambetta (1988) discusses this phenomenon in relation to the mafia.

9 This is an important but difficult issue in any examination of anarchic systems. Skaperdas (1992b) provides a preliminary analysis of alliance formation in the case with three agents.

10 The model is also interpretable as a production model with the two goods interpreted as production inputs and the function $U(\cdot, \cdot)$ interpreted as a production function; this is the interpretation in the papers on which our model is based.

11 Risk aversion or destructive conflict would make exchange under the threat of conflict strictly Pareto superior, but would introduce multiple exchange possibilities. Risk-seeking behaviour would make conflict strictly preferable to exchange. For a similar model with risk aversion see Skaperdas (1991).

12 Denoting by $\pi^i(G_1, G_2)$ the pay-off function of agent $i = 1, 2$, a Nash equilibrium is a strategy pair (G_1^*, G_2^*) such that $\pi^1(G_1^*, G_2^*) \geq \pi^1(G_1, G_2^*)$ for all G_1 and $\pi^2(G_1^*, G_2^*) \geq \pi^2(G_1^*, G_2)$ for all G_2. Existence of a Nash equilibrium is guaranteed if $p_{11}p < p_1^2$ (and by the symmetry property in (2), $-p_{22}(1 - p) < p_2^2$) where the subscripts 1 and 2 denote derivatives with respect to the first and second arguments of $p(\cdot, \cdot)$. This property is satisfied by all contest success functions that are concave in each agent's strategy, but they are also satisfied by others which are not 'too convex' in each agent's strategy. This property is also less stringent than those required for the existence of equilibrium in the class of rent-seeking games inaugurated by Tullock (1980) (see Perez-Castrillo and Verdier, 1992).

Uniqueness of equilibrium is guaranteed when p has the following additive representation:

$$p(G_1,\ G_2) = f(G_1)/[f(G_1) + f(G_2)]$$

where $f(\cdot)$ is a non-negative increasing function. This property is also satisfied by the functional forms used in the above-mentioned rent-seeking games. For precise statements of theorems and proofs, the reader is referred to Skaperdas and Syropoulos (1992).

13 The complete analysis for this and other results reported below is in Skaperdas and Syropoulos (1992).

14 Hirshleifer (1988, 1991) examines the latter case with $\alpha = 1/2$.

15 These effects could be reversed in some cases when $\sigma < 1$ (e.g. for β_1); there is an intuition for such reversals but an explanation here would take us too far afield. Again, see Skaperdas and Syropoulos (1992) for a complete analysis.

16 Baumol (1990) and Murphy et al. (1991) have drawn attention to the importance of the institutional framework in encouraging economically beneficial, as opposed to unproductive, entrepreneurship. Here we indicate how the distributional method prevailing in anarchy (and, we would say, in most pre-capitalist economies), in addition to directly reducing welfare by the amount of unproductive activities that are undertaken, contributes to dynamic inefficiency through the disincentives it creates for some types of productive innovation.

17 Implicitly in this statement is an n-person model instead of the 2-person model we have examined. As mentioned earlier, the basic results continue to hold in basic n-person extensions. Although the emigration of the most usefully productive agents reduces the overall average productivity, the reduction of average welfare does not necessarily follow. There is a counter-acting influence which we touch upon later. Emigration may reduce the intensity of competition by reducing the total percentage of resources converted into guns. Thus, although those who remain would be less usefully productive, they might devote a smaller percentage of their resources to warfare and, therefore, their welfare could conceivably increase.

18 Southern Italians have emigrated, among other places, to northern Italy, North America and Australia. Many middle-class residents of American inner cities have moved to the suburbs over the last thirty years. We do not wish to imply that these areas of immigration are perfect examples of neoclassical economies, but we certainly believe they approximate it a lot more than the areas of emigration do.

19 This can be understood by going back to (4) and noting that the marginal utility of an agent's own consumption good (U_1^* for agent 1) is decreasing in the resource of that agent when the elasticity of substitution is less than infinite; otherwise, this marginal utility is constant. Hence, following the earlier discussion of (4), the opportunity cost of guns is reduced whereas the marginal benefit ($p_1^* U^*$) increases, with the net effect unambiguously favouring an increase in gun production. It can be shown that the opponent also has an incentive to increase his gun production, but not so much so that his equilibrium share is increased.

80   Stergios Skaperdas and Constantinos Syropoulos

20 Since the agents in the model have identical linearly homogeneous utility
    functions, we can make interpersonal comparisons of utility and speak of
    total welfare.
21 Comparable effects are found in Garfinkel (1990) who employed a model
    different from ours. The result no longer holds, however, when the elasticity
    of substitution is infinite (see Hirshleifer, 1991).
22 This ratio is a measure of how easy it is to increase one's probability of
    winning in conflict as a result of a small change in the quantity of guns and
    for that reason we call it the *effectiveness* of conflict.
23 Such contracts are usually implicit. They are self-enforcing typically because
    of repeated interactions between agents.
24 Under some other politico-economic approaches to distribution like that of
    Aumann and Kurz (1977), the use of coercion is limited to that of the
    majority being able to tax the minority. Otherwise, distribution is determined
    in a typical neoclassical fashion where, other things being equal, the more
    productive receive higher incomes.
25 We assume uniqueness of equilibrium in single-period interactions. Footnote
    12 provides a sufficient condition.
26 One way of redefining the actions taken within each period is to suppose that,
    in addition to choosing between guns and the consumption good, each agent
    makes a proposal about the division of the surplus. If the proposals of the
    agents agree, then that proposal is implemented; if not, they revert to the
    division prescribed by (3).
27 An examination of this equilibrium in a more specific model is in Skaperdas
    (1992a). Grossman (1991) finds an intuitively similar equilibrium in a model
    with a ruler who hires soldiers to suppress potential revolts by peasants. In
    this equilibrium the ruler hires soldiers but the peasants do not spend any
    time on insurrections.
28 In Skaperdas and Syropoulos (1993) we examine a two-period model with
    such a time-dependence. We establish there that increasing the importance of
    the future may in fact harm instead of facilitating the cooperative outcomes
    based on folk-theorem arguments.
29 This is of course not a mainstream view in economics. A penetrating
    discussion of this issue and its relation to basic human psychological traits is
    in Simon (1991, pp. 34–8). For the importance of ideology in the development
    of institutions in general, we have learned from North's (1984) short
    discussion.
30 This discussion is based on Kuran's simple yet powerful model (see e.g.
    Kuran, 1987, 1989). The basic ingredients are the distinction between private
    and publicly expressed preferences and the costliness of expressing private
    preferences when they differ from the dominant position.

REFERENCES

Aumann, R. J. and M. Kurz (1977), 'Power and Taxes', *Econometrica*, 45,
    pp. 185–243.
Axelrod, R. (1984), *The Evolution of Cooperation*, New York: Basic Books.
Banfield, E. C. (1958), *The Moral Basis of a Backward Society*, Glencoe IL: The
    Free Press.

Baumol, W. J. (1990), 'Entrepreneurship: Productive, Unproductive, and Destructive', *Journal of Political Economy*, 98(5), pp. 893–921.

Bequai, A. (1979), *Organized Crime*, Lexington MA: D. C. Heath & Co.

Braudel, F. (1973), *The Mediterranean and the Mediterranean World in the Age of Philip II*, New York: Harper & Row.

Carneiro, R. L. (1970), 'A Theory of the Origin of the State', *Science*, 169, pp. 733–8.

Doder, D. (1992), 'Albania Opens the Door', *National Geographic*, 182, pp. 66–93.

Fudenberg, D. and J. Tirole (1991), *Game Theory*, Cambridge MA: MIT Press.

Gambetta, D. (1988), 'Mafia: The Price of Distrust', in D. Gambetta (ed.), *Trust. Making and Breaking Cooperative Relations*, Oxford: Basil Blackwell.

Garfinkel, M. R. (1990), 'Arming as a Strategic Investment in a Cooperative Equilibrium', *American Economic Review*, 80, pp. 50–68.

Grossman, H. I. (1991), 'A General Equilibrium Model of Insurrections', *American Economic Review*, 81, pp. 912–21.

Hess, H. (1973), *Mafia and Mafiosi: The Structure of Power*, Lexington MA: D. C. Heath & Co.

Hirshleifer, J. (1988), 'The Analytics of Continuing Conflict', *Synthèse*, 76, pp. 201–33.

Hirshleifer, J. (1991), 'The Paradox of Power', *Economics and Politics*, 3, pp. 177–200.

Jankowski, M. S. (1991), *Islands in the Streets: Gangs and American Urban Society*, Berkeley: University of California Press.

Koliopoulos, J. (1987), *Brigands with a Cause*, Oxford: Oxford University Press.

Kuran, T. (1987), 'Preference Falsification, Policy Continuity, and Collective Conservatism', *Economic Journal*, 97, pp. 642–65.

Kuran, T. (1989), 'Sparks and Prairie Fires: A Theory of Unanticipated Political Revolution', *Public Choice*, 61, pp. 41–74.

Milgrom, P. R., D. C. North and B. Weingast (1990), 'The Role of Institutions in the Revival of Trade: The Law Merchant, Private Judges, and the Champagne Fairs', *Economics and Politics*, 2, pp. 1–23.

Murphy, K. M., A. Shleifer and R. W. Vishny (1991), 'The Allocation of Talent: Impliciations for Growth', *Quarterly Journal of Economics*, 106, pp. 503–30.

North, D. C. (1984), 'Transactions Costs, Institutions, and Economic History', *Journal of Institutional and Theoretical Economics*, 140, pp. 7–17.

Oppenheimer, F. (1972), *The State*, New York: Arno Press.

Perez-Castrillo, J. and Th. Verdier (1992), 'General Analysis of Rent-Seeking Games', *Public Choice*, 62, pp. 335–50.

Schelling, T. C. (1960), *The Strategy of Conflict*, Cambridge MA: Harvard University Press.

Simon, H. A. (1991), 'Organizations and Markets', *Journal of Economic Perspectives*, 5, pp. 25–44.

Skaperdas, S. (1991), 'Conflict and Attitudes Toward Risk', *American Economic Review* (Papers and Proceedings), 81, pp. 116–20.

Skaperdas, S. (1992a), 'Cooperation, Conflict, and Power in the Absence of Property Rights', *American Economic Review*, 82, pp. 720–39.

Skaperdas, S. (1992b), 'Coalition Formation in Contests', mimeo, University of California, Irvine.

Skaperdas, S. and C. Syropoulos (1992), 'The Distribution of Income in the Presence of Directly Unproductive Activities', mimeo, University of California, Irvine.

Skaperdas, S. and C. Syropoulos (1993), 'The Shadow of the Future: Can it Harm Cooperation?', mimeo, University of California, Irvine.

Tullock, G. (1980), 'Efficient Rent Seeking', in J. M. Buchanan, R. D. Tollison and G. Tullock (eds.), *Toward a Theory of the Rent-Seeking Society*, College Station: Texas A&M University Press.

Webster's New Collegiate Dictionary (1979), Springfield MA: G. & C. Merriam.

Williamson, O. E. (1989), 'Transaction Cost Economics', in R. Schmalensee and R. D. Willig (eds.), *Handbook of Industrial Organization*, Amsterdam and New York: Elsevier Science Publishers.

Discussion

WILLIAM J. BAUMOL

The very stimulating paper by Skaperdas and Syropoulos (henceforth S&S) accomplishes many things. It extends the formal analysis of the economics of crime yet another step and shows once again how powerful and suggestive the economist's tools have become, even outside the discipline's traditional realm. The article shows, in particular, that it is useful in an analysis of one side of their operations to think of criminal organisations as quasi-governments, serving in lieu of the state in arenas into which governments fear to tread, and in other areas forcing government by the state to let itself be replaced by the gang in some of the tasks of governance. Finally, the paper stimulates the reader to venture into new directions, as these few comments will illustrate.

The basic point of the article is obviously valid, and obvious only in retrospect. The distinguishing feature of crime that is organised is, of course, the fact that it is controlled and directed by a group whose role is far more than just administrative. In particular, it determines the rules that the gang members will be expected to follow, and it adopts procedures designed to enforce those rules. Thus, the gang leadership takes on *legislative* and *judicial* tasks, in addition to its administrative activities and, by virtue of these undertakings, it becomes a government. One can easily see what other governmental roles it plays, entailing such activities as warfare, diplomacy, the provision of employment and

welfare benefits to its members, etc. In places where 'legitimate government' abdicates its role, or is simply prevented by circumstances from
performing it, organised gangs frequently spring up and fill the gap.
From the mountains of Sicily to the inner cities of the United States
something like that has occurred, and the S&S paper analyses this
phenomenon and its implications.

The authors acknowledge that their model, quite properly, builds on the
work of others. This model, which describes a mini-economy that
produces two outputs, guns and butter (or bread), is both suggestive and
illuminating. It focuses upon distribution as well as production. Gun
output is taken to provide no utility in itself, but it offers the possessors
of the preponderant share of firearms the probability that they will be
able to control the distribution process and command the bulk of butter
output for themselves.

In studying the model one is likely to feel that it does not devote enough
attention to the incentives for butter production. Why do not all the
inhabitants of the model's mini-state devote themselves exclusively to
gun production, fearing that if they fail to join the arms race in earnest
whatever butter they produce will be taken away from them by the
victorious gang? That is to say, it remains for the authors to study what
the gangs should do in their own self-interest, to provide the incentive to
others to engage in effective butter producing activity. What part should
be taken by naked coercion, and what part by incentive payments – by a
promise to share the economy's butter output with the butter producers,
with the pay-off to them possibly increasing with the total amount they
succeed in producing? Perhaps even more important, is there a defect
inherent in gangster government leading the economy to produce output
bundles that fall far short of the production frontier? It seems to me that
these are issues that S&S and others can usefully explore, and that these
efforts promise to enrich the authors' results.

The analysis stimulates other additional thoughts, some of them
considerably further afield. A little study of history, much of it
unfortunately contemporary, suggests that the authors have been
excessively modest in their hypotheses about the similarities of gangs to
governments. I suggest that there is also much to be learned from a
reversal of the comparison, this time not thinking of gangs as quasi-
governments, but rather by interpreting most governments in human
history as gangster associations.

The governments that began to emerge after the Tudors in England and
after William the Silent in the Netherlands are, after all, freaks of history.
The normal dynasty was established by effective exercise of violence, and
the rulers felt free (by divine right) to engage in wholesale murder,

torture and mutilation. The preponderance of government by homicidal maniacs is hardly fortuitous, for it is just such individuals who could reasonably be deemed 'most likely to succeed', to succeed, that is, in wresting uneasy control in a world of anarchy provided with no restrictions upon the use of force. The term 'liberty', it is true, does occur frequently before the sixteenth century but, like Magna Carta, it refers merely to the freedom of the powerful nobles to deal arbitrarily and violently with their own inferiors, without being subjected to onerous constraints by the monarch. Gangster governments ruled the earth in medieval China, in the Ottoman Empire, in pre-Columbian Mexico and Peru as much as they did in Europe, and a reign of terror was the normal state of affairs, with the head of government often no more secure against violent demise than many of his subjects. The twentieth century has, of course, had its share of government by pathological murderers organised into hierarchical organisations.

In short, I am offering two suggestions for further consideration, both apparently far fetched, but actually resting on rather moderate interpretations of the facts. The first is that governments concerned with the welfare of the governed and constrained by rule of law from arbitrary and violent measures are the rare exceptions in human history, perhaps most realistically interpreted as a curious aberration of a very recent period in rather limited portions of our planet. Second, I suggest that study of the economics of crime may offer a pay-off going well beyond its immediate subject. For this line of investigation also promises to offer profound insights into the origins and workings of governments, not as most of us know them, but like those that have ruled the bulk of humanity in the past, and continue their sway in many countries today.

Part II
The criminal organisation as a firm

4 Internal cohesion and competition among criminal organisations

MICHELE POLO

1 Introduction

Economic research on illegal activities has probably a limited importance in the literature if compared with the relevance of this phenomenon in many modern societies. This discrepancy is perhaps even more pronounced when we consider the economic analysis of criminal *organisations*.[1]

The aim of this paper is to study some issues related to the internal organisation of illegal groups and to the interaction between competition and rivalry among criminal organisations and their internal structure.[2] We adopt a very simple definition of an illegal organisation as one that cannot rely on the external enforcement of the judicial institutions and whose behaviour and possibilities are not constrained by the law.

In this setting the emergence of a set of individuals with stable and long-term relations and a hierarchical structure, i.e. an organisation, is far from being a simple task. The promoter of this group, the principal, has to hire agents to carry out the tasks required by an illegal activity. It is very reasonable to imagine that an agent, through his relation with the principal, acquires new resources that he can use for his own private benefit. A member of the criminal organisation, for instance, can appropriate goods or money of the family, or can use for his own sake information and know-how acquired during his illegal activity within the organisation.

To a certain extent, this behaviour is not specific to organisations that operate in illegal markets, and can be found even if a third party can enforce the contracts. Agency theory usually assumes, however, that the external enforcement offered by the judicial system can reduce the scope of agents' opportunistic behaviour; this latter becomes a relevant problem only when asymmetric information reduces the principal's ability to write down first-best contracts.

When we deal with an illegal organisation, in contrast, agents' opportunism can arise in every possible conceivable aspect of the internal relations, and must be restricted entirely through the structure of the incentive schemes. On the other hand, the organisation, being illegal, can use as incentive devices a very large set of instruments, including those prohibited by the law. The widest opportunism and the hardest punishment seem therefore to characterise an illegal organisation.

From this discussion it can be understood that our analysis refers to internal rather than to market relations, and it is therefore not specific to a particular kind of illegal market. It applies to all those activities which are performed within an organisation and which are illegal. More specifically, it includes the supply of enforcement services to *other* organisations or individuals, which Schelling (1971) identifies as the distinctive feature of organised crime,[3] as well as selling illegal commodities and services, as long as the organisation provides, at least in part, private enforcement of the internal agreements.

Our problem has some points in common with two issues already studied in the literature. The first is the analysis of conflict situations, in which individuals have to decide how to divide their initial endowments between productive and military activities in the absence of property rights.[4] This literature stresses the conflicting nature of productive and coercive activities: these represent alternative ways of allocating the individual's initial resources and of implementing final consumption. In our approach, on the other hand, if an illegal organisation aims at producing any kind of commodity or service, it has to provide coercive services to ensure the members' discipline. Hence, in our setting, productive and coercive activities are complements more than substitutes.

The second piece of literature which could be relevant for our analysis is that on incomplete contracts, which shares with our setting the impossibility of external enforcement and the need for self-enforcing agreements,[5] but does not allow the use of unlawful incentives as part of the private agreements. In illegal contracts, conversely, the inability of a third party to observe the contingencies is irrelevant, while the private enforcement of the agreements and the use of violence play a crucial role.

Modelling the military technology is a preliminary step in our analysis; we assume that the probability of successfully punishing a cheating agent is increasing in the dimension of the family and decreasing in the distance between the family's seat and the agent's location; hence, there exists a dimension of agents' heterogeneity, which we interpret *prima facie* as spatial distance, that influences the effectiveness of private enforcement.

In this setting we compare the internal contracts and the dimension of the organisation when a single principal acts as a monopsonist and when two principals compete for the services of the agents. In both cases we observe limits in the expansion of the organisation due to enforcement constraints and not to productive or technological reasons.

The paper is organised as follows. In Section 2 we discuss the features of the military technology and the probability of success. In Section 3 the internal long-term contracts and the dimension of the organisation are studied with reference to the monopsony case. Section 4 addresses the same issues in a market where two principals compete for the services of the agents.

2   The military technology and the probability of success

A precise formalisation of the enforcement technology is a primary goal in modelling economic relations in an illegal market. The economic literature on conflict offers some suggestions in describing the military capacity of an organisation.[6] We shall try a first step in this direction by focusing on some features of the military technology that seem salient: what we obtain is in some sense a reduced form, or a 'black box', which links the military output to certain variables.

First of all we assume military capacity to be an increasing function of the number of members of the organisation: all the relevant functions – monitoring, intelligence and violence – require labour as a fundamental input. Moreover, we consider the case of decreasing marginal returns to labour: this assumption can be justified by referring to the loss of control when the organisation becomes increasingly large, and to the limited supply of people with a strong ability in the enforcement activity.

The second key feature is related to the spatial dimension in which the military activity takes place: when an organisation is trying to hit a target, all the preliminary steps and the final violent action increase in complexity with the distance of the target. Information collecting and monitoring are in fact increasingly difficult when an organisation operates far from its seat. Hence, the military capacity is assumed to be decreasing in the distance between the target and the organisation's seat, with an increasing decline in effectiveness.

It must be stressed that the physical distance is to be intended as a proxy for the obstacles information comes up against when circulating: hence, for instance, distance has a different impact when the enforcement activity takes place in the country rather than in an urban environment, with more pronounced decreasing returns in the latter case.

Although we discussed the case of spatial distance, in more general terms we could rephrase the argument above by saying that there exists a dimension of agents' heterogeneity which implies decreasing returns in the enforcement activity. This feature is strictly related to the fact that information transmission and diffusion follow more easily specific ways and networks: hence there could be agents in particular sub-sets, such as ethnic groups, which are 'closer' one to each other not just in a spatial sense but because the social relations are more intense within that group.

Thirdly, we think that military technology is stochastic in nature, since many unforeseen contingencies usually influence the effective outcome of a contest.

According to this discussion, the military capacity of an organisation i with n_i members and located, in a linear space, at point x_i when operating at a point x_a is described by:[7]

$$K_i(x_a; n_i, x_i) = k + \ln(n_i) - (x_a - x_i)^2 + \epsilon_i \tag{1}$$

where ϵ_i is a random variable with $E(\epsilon_i) = 0$.

It is interesting to note that by setting $n_i = 1$, (1) can also be used to describe the military capacity of single individuals. Although our analysis is primarily related to studying organisations, this feature of our formalisation will prove to be very useful when discussing the individual deviations and the resulting punishment episodes.

Given the stochastic nature of the military technology, when families i and j clash in a particular place x_a, we can predict the outcome only in terms of a probability of success. Family i will win if:

$$K_i(x_a; n_i, x_i) > K_j(x_a; n_j, x_j) \tag{2}$$

Substituting in (2) the definition of military capacity, the outcome of the clash is in favour of i if:

$$\ln(n_i) - (x_a - x_i)^2 - \ln(n_j) + (x_a - x_j)^2 > \epsilon_j - \epsilon_i \tag{3}$$

The probability of success depends therefore on the cumulated density function of the difference in the idiosyncratic terms $\epsilon_j - \epsilon_i$, which we assume to be logistic:[8]

$$F(\epsilon_j - \epsilon_i) = \frac{e^{\epsilon_j - \epsilon_i}}{1 + e^{\epsilon_j - \epsilon_i}} \tag{4}$$

The probability that family i defeats j in a clash at point x_a is therefore:

$$\pi_i(x_a; n_i, n_j, x_i, x_j) = \frac{n_i/n_j}{e^{(2x_a - x_i - x_j)(x_j - x_i)} + n_i/n_j} \tag{5}$$

Some remarks are useful for later analysis. If the clash occurs at the rival's seat, i.e. $x_j = x_a$, as will be the case in the next section, the success function is symmetric around x_i, which represents the mode of the probability distribution. When instead we consider two families located at $x_i \le x_j$, the probability of success is decreasing in x_a, which will correspond to an agent's location. Finally, the closer the two families, the flatter this function: if $x_i = x_j$, i.e. if the two families are located at the same point, the probability of i's success is $n_i(n_i + n_j)$ at any point in the space; when the distance between the two families increases, the range of values of π_i on a certain interval increases as well. In other words, an organisation has a pronounced relative military advantage, in expected terms, on a certain region only if it is sufficiently far from the rival. This feature of the probability of success will play a central role when analysing the competition between two rival organisations.

3   Internal contracts and the dimension of the organisation: the monopsony case

We begin our analysis from the relatively simple case in which a principal constitutes a criminal organisation offering contracts to a number of agents and without facing the competition of rival families. The structure of the internal contracts and the economic dimension of the organisation are in this case mostly determined by the enforcement technology, i.e. by the principal's ability to punish the opportunistic behaviour of the agents.

The design of the optimal internal contracts of an illegal organisation will be our first task. It is rather obvious that their structure will differ according to the information available to the principal: we shall consider a very simple situation, in which the principal has *ex post* perfect information on the agent's actions, and can therefore verify exactly whether the contract has been respected or not. This very simple class of problems allows us to identify clearly the difficulties that arise in an illegal market as compared to those associated with legal transactions.

Moreover, we concentrate our attention on long-term relationships: this is very familiar when studying an organisation and seems particularly relevant when dealing with illegal ones. Joining a criminal group implies an irreversible investment for the agent, who can be prosecuted for that choice.[9]

More specifically, we consider long-term stationary relations, in which a set of tasks must be performed in the same way in each period. An illegal organisation i located at x_i has to carry out a (stationary) set of activities M. An internal contract therefore assigns to an agent a located at x_a a specific task: $m_i \in M$, which has to be executed in each period. If the agent accepts, he chooses in each period an action s_a consistent with the task m_i, receiving a wage $w_i^C \in [0, \bar{w}(m_i)]$, or any other action, which is interpreted as a deviation from the contract and involves a punishment $p_i^D \in [0, \bar{p}]$ thereafter. The principal perfectly observes the agent's action with a lag of one period. Finally, we shall study contracts of infinite duration in order to capture the idea that a criminal organisation does not usually allow its members to leave in the future.[10]

Our discussion implies that the principal is able to monitor his members perfectly (*ex post*),[11] while he is unable to punish them perfectly in case of deviation. In this way we want to capture the intuitive idea that the principal can design the internal structure and rules in order to force his members to help information gathering, but once a member abandons the family, he actively tries to limit the ability of the principal to punish him.

A cheating agent will be punished by the principal with probability less than 1, corresponding to the expression $\pi_i(x_a; n_i, 1, x_i, x_a)$ described in (5): the agent is favoured because he can ward off the attack of the organisation in his own location, i.e. $x_j = x_a$, but suffers a drawback since he has to fight alone, i.e. $n_j = 1$.

Although the contract is specified before the agent is enrolled, it is contingent on the agent's behaviour. In other words, it is designed in order to use the information that is generated during the economic relation.[12]

Having described the structure of the internal contracts, we can examine the design of the optimal ones. The principal has to choose a contract in order to maximise his discounted intertemporal utility subject to a participation constraint and an incentive compatibility constraint of the agent.

The contract guarantees to the agent a discounted intertemporal utility:

$$V_a^C = \sum_{t=0}^{\infty} \delta^t U_a(m_i, w_i^C, 0) \tag{6}$$

where $\delta = 1/(1+r)$ is the discount factor.

Defining the agent's *ex ante* outside option as $\bar{u}$, the participation constraint (*PC*) is:

$$V_a^C \geq \bar{V}_a = \frac{\bar{u}}{1-\delta} \tag{7}$$

It is important to stress that if the economic relation took place in a legal market with external enforcement, the information structure considered here would require only the participation constraint to hold: the first-best contract would specify a wage ensuring the agent the outside utility level and no internal punishment in case of deviation, while a cheating agent would be detected and punished directly by the legal enforcement institutions.

If the principal cannot rely on the latter, the desired behaviour of the agent can be induced only through the contract, and the incentive compatibility constraint becomes relevant.

If the agent cheats, the principal recognises his deviation with a one-period lag and therefore at the beginning of the deviation continues to pay the money transfer:[13] the utility of the agent in the first period of deviation when the optimal action $\hat{s}$ is chosen is:

$$U_a^D = U_a(\hat{s}_a, w_i^C, 0) \tag{8}$$

Once detected, the cheating agent expects a punishment p_i^D, which the principal successfully implements with probability π_i, and chooses an optimal action $\tilde{s}$. There exists obviously a wide multiplicity of punishment schemes, which differ both in intensity, i.e. the single-period reduction in utility, and in the time-path, i.e. the number of periods they last. Each particular punishment implies a different expression and a different value of the agent's discounted intertemporal utility. In terms of our analysis, what is needed is simply an ordering of the punishment schemes in terms of utility. It seems interesting and realistic, however, to specify in a little more detail the punishment schemes, restricting attention to those rules that determine a permanent reduction, at different levels, of the agent's utility from there on once the cheating agent has been caught for the first time. An obvious interpretation of these rules is in terms of violent punishments that harm the agent permanently, with the strongest punishment corresponding to the agent's assassination. Permanent punishment schemes, if successful, leave the agent with a discounted intertemporal utility:

$$\tilde{V}_a^P = \sum_{t=0}^{\infty} \delta^t U_a(\tilde{s}_a, 0, p_i^D) \tag{9}$$

If the principal does not succeed in punishing the cheating member at time t, the single-period agent's utility is $U_a(\tilde{s}_a, 0, 0)$. We can therefore compute the present value of the utility from deviation, which is given by the utility in the first period, when the deviation has not yet been detected, and a second term which is the weighted sum of the single-period utility if the agent escapes the punishment and of the present value of the permanent punishment if this latter is successfully implemented:

$$V_a^D(\pi_i) = U_a^D + \delta \frac{\pi_i \tilde{V}_a^P + (1 - \pi_i) U_a(\tilde{s}_a, 0, 0)}{1 - (1 - \pi_i)\delta} \tag{10}$$

It is immediately noticeable that, for a given contract's parameters, $\partial V_a^D(\pi_i)/\partial \pi_i < 0$, i.e. the utility from deviation decreases with the principal's ability to punish the cheating agent.

The incentive compatibility constraint (ICC) requires the intertemporal utility of the contract to be no lower than that obtained by deviating from the contract:

$$V_a^C \geq V_a^D(\pi_i) \tag{11}$$

The analysis of the optimal contract requires to specify a little more the preference structure of the players. We assume the utility function of the principal and of the agent, $U_i(s_a, w_i, p_i)$ and $U_a(s_a, w_i, p_i)$ to be continuous and quasi-concave in s_a, w_i and p_i with the following properties:

(i): $\frac{\partial U_i}{\partial w_i} < 0$

(ii): $\frac{\partial U_a}{\partial w_i} > 0$

(iii): $\frac{\partial U_i}{\partial p_i} = 0$

(iv): $\frac{\partial U_a}{\partial p_i} < 0$

(v): $m_i \neq \tilde{s}_a$

(vi): $U_a(s_a, w_i, \bar{p}) = 0, \; \forall s_a \in S, \; \forall w_i \in W_i$

(vii): $\forall m_i \in M, \exists \bar{w}(m_i): U_i(m_i, \bar{w}(m_i), 0) = 0$

Some comments on these assumptions are needed. From (iii), the principal has no disutility (cost) from punishing: we argue that the organisation has a permanent military structure, with a negligible marginal cost of operating. (v) aims to capture the latent opportunism of the agent, who in general prefers to execute an action different from the task assigned to him. In (vi) the utility associated with the strongest punishment $\bar{p}$ is normalised to 0 *for any action and money transfer*: the maximum penalty can therefore be interpreted as the agent's murder. Finally, (vii) states that the principal's utility is bounded, implying a finite money transfer to the agent for any task assigned to him.[14]

We are now in a position to analyse the optimal internal contract for the agent.

Proposition 1 *For a given task m_i and a given dimension of the organisation n_i, a long-term contract which satisfies the participation and the incentive compatibility constraints is characterised by $\hat{p}_i^D - \bar{p}$ and*

$$\hat{w}_i^C : \frac{U_a(m_i, \hat{w}_i^C, 0)}{1-\delta} = max\left\{\frac{\bar{u}}{1-\delta}; \ U_a^D + \delta\frac{(1-\pi_i)U_a(\tilde{s}_a, 0, 0)}{1-(1-\pi_i)\delta}\right\} \quad (12)$$

$\hat{w}_i^C$ *is non-increasing in the probability of success π_i or, equivalently, non-decreasing in the distance $d_i^a \equiv |x_a - x_i|$ between the principal and the agent. Define $\underline{w}$: $U_a(m_i, \underline{w}, 0) = \bar{u}$ as the reservation wage of the agent. The principal will offer contracts which prescribe $\hat{w}_i^C(m_i, d_i^a) \in [\underline{w}, \bar{w}]$.*

Proof: See Appendix.

Proposition 1 describes the optimal contract: the principal avoids the agent's deviation through a mix of stick, the punishment, and carrot, the wage. Since the latter is costly to him, while the former is not, he always threatens the maximum penalty in order to satisfy the incentive compatibility constraint with the lowest wage.[15] The expected punishment also depends, however, on the probability of been caught, and therefore becomes less severe for more distant agents. The latter can be induced to a fair behaviour only through a higher wage. In Figure 4.1 the wage schedule is shown as a function of the distance between the principal and the agent.

It is important to stress that the above result does not necessarily imply that more distant agents receive higher wages. Proposition 1 simply states that, *for a given task and a given number of members*, closer agents can be paid less. However, by offering new contracts the principal is able to enlarge his organisation, managing a more powerful army. In other words, we observe two conflicting effects: when offering new contracts, the probability of military success decreases as long as the principal has to refer to more distant agents, but increases with the dimension of the family. Whether the organisation is able to expand indefinitely or not depends on which of the two effects prevails.

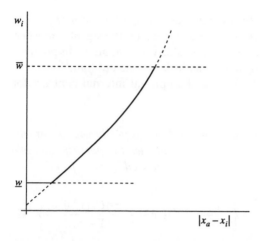

Figure 4.1   The contract wage as a function of the distance between principal and agent

The dimension of the family and the distance at which a military clash occurs have been kept independent in the description of the military capacity. However, our discussion suggests that a link exists between the two, due to the fact that the expansion of a family leads to the enrolment of more and more distant agents. We introduce some assumptions that allow this intuition to be addressed in the simplest way.

We assume that the principal and the agents are located along a linear space of unit length, i.e. x_i, $x_a \in [0, 1]$. The principal is assigned randomly to a particular location x_i while the agents, characterised by the same preference structure, are uniformly distributed on the unit interval. This assumption can be interpreted by saying that the supply of individuals with strong leadership ability in criminal affairs is scarce and determined, in some sense, by nature,[16] while the supply of agents is abundant and uniformly distributed in a social environment.

Moreover, we shall suppose that only one kind of task, m, can be profitably delegated to the agents.

Proposition 2   *When principal i acts as a monopsonist in the supply of long-term contracts, he recruits a share of members equal to* $min\{1, \bar{d}_i^a + min[\bar{d}_i^a, min(x_i, 1 - x_i)]\}$ *where* $\bar{d}_i^a$ *is implicitly defined by:*

$$U_i(m, \hat{w}_i^C(m, \bar{d}_i^a), 0) = 0 \tag{13}$$

Proof: See Appendix.

Proposition 2 shows that the military technology of the family involves a probability of success which is decreasing in distance, even if we take into account the increase in the number of members. Hence the contract wage is increasing as well: this implies that the marginal cost of the organisation will be upward sloping, due to decreasing returns in enforcement and not in production. It is worth noting that, since the contract wage is increasing in the *ex post* outside utility, if the task m implies a high value of this latter, the principal can find it not profitable to recruit all the potential agents, even if he acts as a monopsonist. The criminal organisation suffers a drawback in its expansion due to the difficulty of ensuring sufficient cohesion of its members.

This seems consistent with some empirical evidence on the drug market: narcotics offer a very high *ex post* outside utility to a cheating agent; moreover, the market has a strong spatial dispersion, in particular in the retail traffic. Transactions in the drug market seem therefore very profitable but difficult to perform within an organisation. Empirical evidence suggests that organised crime enters only in the wholesale trade, and often only in specific phases of it, while the retail trade is dominated by small groups or individuals which deal with the big families through market relations and spot payments.

Our result seems consistent with a second stylised fact pertaining to the Sicilian mafia. Although organised crime has had a very strong power in influencing the social relations and the institutions at least in the southern regions of Italy, the families usually had a limited number of members.[17]

4   Internal organisation and competition among rival families

In the previous section we studied the optimal long-term contract and the maximum dimension of an organisation which acts as a monopsonist with respect to the potential members.

Our next step is to extend the analysis to the case in which two principals compete in the same market. Competition can take place at different levels and on different grounds. Some of them can also be observed in legal environments, such as competition in the product market, through price or non-price strategies, or in the labour market, where the agents can be hired. However, it is the practice of violence that constitutes the third and fundamental dimension of rivalry among organisations, and that interacts with the more common competitive strategies also seen in product and labour markets.

It is commonly recognised that the relations among criminal organisations tend to alternate between phases of war and peace: in these latter some sort of collusive agreement is reached among the families. To analyse properly the emergence of collusion, however, we need as a first step to identify the features of the competitive phases, which describe the market behaviour if the collusive agreement is broken. This is the main reason why we concentrate our attention on a situation of strong rivalry among organisations, in which competition takes place mainly through active and prolonged military activity.

In such a situation, a member of a family is constantly under the threat of a military attack from the rival organisation. Hence, a violent punishment is no longer a consequence of opportunistic behaviour but is expected also by agents who respect the assignment of the contract: the participation constraint is therefore modified, and tends to be more stringent. Moreover, a cheating agent could receive protection from the rival family, reducing the ability of the original organisation to punish him: consequently, the incentive compatibility constraint becomes more severe for the principal.

A second important point pertains to the fact that the repeated interaction between the two families and among the principals and their agents might no longer be stationary. If the number of members of the organisations changes over time as a consequence of repeated clashes, the probability of military success changes as well and the problem is no longer stationary. Although it is possible to analyse the evolution in the dimension of the organisations during the competitive phase,[18] it is much more problematic to deal in the same setting also with the design of the optimal contracts, since we are no longer in a repeated game stationary structure. Since our main interest is in the internal relations, we prefer to maintain the stationary structure of the problem by assuming that if a member of a family is killed at time t, he is replaced in period $t + 1$ by a new agent (a 'brother') located at the same point x_a. The family's dimension and its probability of success therefore remain stationary during the competitive phase.

A double contract wage and a punishment rule for the rival agents are the two modifications of the contract structure when two organisations compete. A long-term contract is now described by the following elements. At time 0, the two principals i and j, located respectively at x_i and x_j, offer simultaneously a long-term contract to an agent a located at x_a. The contract, which is described for principal i, states a punishment $p_i^j \in [0, \bar{p}]$ if the agent joins the rival organisation, a task $m_i \in M$ to be executed in each period, a punishment $p_i^D \in [0, \bar{p}]$ if the member deviates from the task assigned m_i, and a pair of money transfers $(w_i^{C1}, w_i^{C2}) \in [0, \bar{w}(m_i)]^2$: the first ($C1$) is paid to an agent who initially joins family i until a deviation is observed, while the second ($C2$) is paid to a member of the rival organisation if he abandons his original group to enrol in family i. If the agent accepts one of the contracts, in each period t he chooses an action $s_a \in S_a$, which is observed by the principal with a one-period lag.

Finally, we maintain the simplifying assumptions of a linear space with uniformly distributed agents and that of a single task m that can profitably be delegated.

Agent a's discounted intertemporal utility according to contract i when the rival family threatens him with a (permanent) punishment p_j^i is:

$$V_a^{C_i}(\pi_i) = \frac{\pi_i U_a(m, w_i^{C1}, 0) + (1 - \pi_i)\tilde{V}_a^{P_j}}{1 - \pi_i \delta} \qquad (14)$$

where:

$$\tilde{V}_a^{P_j} = \sum_{t=0}^{\infty} \delta^t U_a(m, w_i^{C1}, p_j^i) \qquad (15)$$

$V_a^{C_i}(\pi_i)$ therefore enters in the modified expression of the participation constraint, which now, *ceteris paribus*, requires a higher wage to the agent in order to compensate him for the risk of the rival family's punishment.

The opportunities for deviation are now richer for the agent: he can still choose to deviate contrasting the original family's attack alone, as analysed in the previous section. The corresponding intertemporal discounted utility, $V_a^{D_a}(\pi_i)$, can be constructed as in (10). However, a cheating agent now has a new, and often more convenient strategy, i.e. abandoning the original family and joining the rival organisation. In this latter case the agent will receive the wage w_j^{C2} after defection and will be protected by his new family from punishment by his previous one. The present value of this strategy is:

$$V_a^{D_j}(\pi_i) = U_a(\hat{s}_a, w_i^{C1}, 0) + \delta \frac{\pi_i \tilde{V}_a^{P_i} + (1 - \pi_i)U_a(m, w_j^{C2}, 0)}{1 - (1 - \pi_i)\delta} \qquad (16)$$

where $\tilde{V}_a^{P_i}$ describes the intertemporal utility when the deviating agent is successfully punished by his original group, and is constructed similarly to (15). $V_a^{D_j}(\pi_i)$ allows us to define the incentive compatibility constraint for the agent.

With two competing families the game structure is more complex: the interaction between a principal and his agent maintains the features of a repeated game of infinite horizon; the two principals design the contracts simultaneously, however, at the beginning of the game, and are therefore competing in a Nash fashion. The participation and incentive compatibility constraints of each contract guarantee that the closed loop strategies implicit in the contracts are sub-game perfect; on the other hand, the initial choice of the contracts require a Nash equilibrium in the game between the two principals. Finally, it is worth noting that the participation and the incentive compatibility constraints depend on p_j^i and w_j^{C2}, i.e. on two elements of the rival family's strategy.

The equilibrium analysis will be in two steps. First of all we study the wage and punishment levels that ensure the constraints will hold *for a given contract of the rival family*. Secondly, we analyse the equilibrium in the game between the two principals in designing the contracts.

If the agent does not join either family, the game is over. If the agent chooses family i, w_i^{C1} and p_i^D must minimise the utility from deviation. Hence $p_i^D = \bar{p}$ is optimal and allows to set w_i^{C1} at the lowest level consistent with the incentive compatibility constraints, given the rival family wage w_j^{C2}.

Finally, if the agent initially chooses the other organisation, it is still profitable for principal i to attract him into his family. The incentive compatibility constraint works now in the opposite direction and determines w_i^{C2} as a function of w_j^{C1}. Finally, setting $p_i^j = \bar{p}$ reduces the utility of the rival contract and makes it less costly to compete for rival agents' defection.

In summary, the best reply contract defines wages w_i^{C1} and w_i^{C2} such that, given the corresponding payments in the other contract, the agent receives a slightly higher utility from family i, while the punishments p_i^j and p_i^D are set at the highest level.

We can now study the competition between the two principals. It must be stressed that, although an agent will initially choose the contract which offers him the higher utility, a principal finds it convenient to hire only those agents who do not deviate thereafter. The next proposition establishes that the conditions of no deviation are more stringent than those which induce an initial enrolment; the possibility of a future betrayal therefore limits the principal's incentive to hire new agents.

Proposition 3   *Define $\hat{\pi}_i$ as the probability of success such that $V_a^{C_i}(\hat{\pi}_i)$ $= V_a^{D_j}(\hat{\pi}_i)$ when $w_i^{C1} = w_j^{C2} = \bar{w}$. An agent a located at x_a such that $\pi_i(x_a; n_i, n_j, x_i, x_j) \geq \hat{\pi}_i$ chooses family i and successively does not deviate. The following conditions hold in equilibrium:*

(i): $\hat{\pi}_i \gg 1/2;$

(ii): $\partial \hat{w}_i^{C1}(\pi_i)/\partial \pi_i \leq 0;$

(iii): $w_i^{C2} = \bar{w}.$

Proof: See Appendix.

Proposition 3 has shown that while a slight military advantage is sufficient to attract an agent initially, the incentive compatibility constraint requires a much stronger advantage if the principal wants to discourage future defections. Consequently, the criminal organisation will not hire all the potential members that it could initially induce to enrol in the family.

The intuition of this result is as follows: when two organisations compete for the initial enrolment of a member, they offer a contract wage that ensures the agent a flow of utility which is increasing in the probability of success. A slight military advantage therefore makes the more powerful organisation's contract more attractive as an initial choice. When the two families compete for the loyalty or the defection of an enrolled agent, they still offer a flow of utility through the contract wage which is increasing in the military capacity. But now the agent, by deviating, is able to gain an extra premium before joining the rival family, and therefore the original organisation has to ensure him a higher stream of utility than the rival in order to counterbalance this initial gain from deviation. The family finds it convenient to offer such a rewarding contract to the agent only if it is able to ensure that utility level through a sufficiently high military advantage and not predominantly through a money transfer. Figure 4.2 shows how the potential members are allocated between the two organisations.

When discussing the features of the function π_i which describes family i's probability of military success, we have pointed out that the function is very flat if the principals are located close to each other: in this case they have very similar military capacities with respect to all agents and no strong advantage arises. From the previous analysis we suspect that in this case the emergence of criminal *organisations* becomes problematic. The following proposition establishes precisely this result.

Proposition 4 *Define the distance between the two principals as* $D = |x_i - x_j|$. *There exists a minimum distance* $\underline{D}$ *under which no principal finds it convenient to offer contracts to any agent a located in* [0, 1]. *For* $D > \underline{D}$ *the sub-sets of agents which join the two families are unconnected.*

Proof: See Appendix

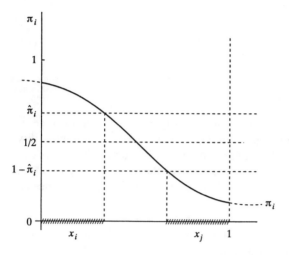

Figure 4.2   The enrolment of members with two competing families with principals sufficiently far apart

Figure 4.3 shows the case in which the two principals are located too close to induce a sufficient military advantage: in this case no organisation can be constituted. This result is not due to the fact that a long and devastating war of the two families determines *in the end* the survival of a single organisation, but derives from the too intense possibilities of opportunism that prevent the *initial* recruitment of members.

The basic analytical ingredient for this result is the influence of the distance between principals, D, on the shape of the success function. Although a complete analysis seems difficult, we can notice that if the military advantage depends on the *difference* between military capacities, from equation (1) $\partial(K_i - K_j)/\partial x_a = -2(x_j - x_i)$. Hence, if the two families are located in the same place, the probability of success is invariant in the point where clashes occur for any probability distribution $F(\epsilon_j - \epsilon_i)$. If the families are very close to each other, the range of values of $K_i - K_j$ will be small, and with continuous probability functions $F(\cdot)$ the probability of success will be almost invariant in the clash's location. Hence, there will be a non-empty sub-set of potential affiliates on which no family has a sufficient military advantage.

Our conclusion seems in line with a very stable character of the Sicilian mafia: the history of this phenomenon from the second half of the nineteenth century to our days offers examples of criminal dynasties which last several generations as well as cases in which a family is displaced by new emerging organisations. But even if the ways in which

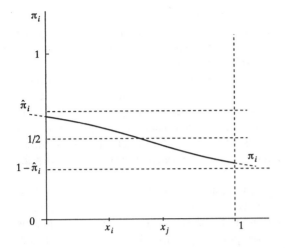

Figure 4.3   The enrolment of members with two competing families with principals too close

the leadership is handed down or interrupted vary, we observe a very stable territorial structure of the Sicilian mafia, characterised by local monopolies. Each area, which can be a village in the country or a district in Palermo, is dominated by *only one* family which controls the territory and the illegal activities in it.

5   Conclusions

In this paper we have developed a model of the organisation of a criminal group, investigating the relationships between internal contracts and (external) competition among families. Our initial conjecture was that the apparent discipline of the criminal groups should be interpreted as the successful *result* of the incentive schemes adopted, rather than as the proof that opportunistic behaviour is a minor problem in these groups.

There are several directions for further research within this approach that relate to both the internal structure and the relations among families. On the first issue, it is interesting to consider a more complex internal structure with three hierarchical levels: this corresponds more closely to the internal organisation of Sicilian mafia families, governed by a boss (*rappresentante*), managed by few military chiefs (*capidecina*), each of whom controls directly a small group of members (*soldati*).

Our analysis of the very tough competition that takes place among families is also a first step in analysing an alternative way of regulating the external relations, i.e. the emergence of collusive agreements. The latter, which typically characterise the phases of *pax mafiosa*, can only be properly understood if we can describe what happens if collusion breaks down. Moreover, there are two specific issues that seem interesting on this point. We observe agreements among families, or groups of families, of a similar power, which we could think of as horizontal collusion. But a second source of coordination is that between a big and powerful family and a constellation of minor groups: this kind of vertical agreement seems a major way of extending the control of a group over a larger territory without suffering the increasing inability to monitor very distant members.

Our approach has interesting policy implications and suggests new directions in the design of repressive interventions: the central idea is that of weakening both the internal cohesion and the external relations among families. On this latter point, the paper by Celentani, Marrelli and Martina in this volume is very close to our view of the problem. The purpose of undermining the members' loyalty is undoubtly one of the main objectives of the recent Italian law which applies strong penalty reductions to those, called *pentiti*, who abandon a family and actively cooperate in the investigations. According to our model, offering an agreement to a member which pays him a salary and strongly protects him and his relatives from retaliation means assigning a very high external utility to the member's knowledge of criminal facts. The sharp success of this law – today we have in Italy several hundred *pentiti* from all the main criminal organisations – offers indirect evidence to support our conjecture on the potential instability of criminal groups.

Appendix

Proof of Proposition 1:

First of all, if the participation constraint is met, the agent will join the organisation. Moreover, given properties (i)–(iv) of the utility functions, whichever of the participation and incentive compatibility constraints is the more stringent will be binding. From (iii)–(iv), the punishment is set at the maximum level in order to reduce the money transfer $\hat{w}_i^C$. If the participation constraint is binding, $\bar{p}$ is still weakly optimal given (iii).

For a given task, the *ex post* outside option $U_a(\tilde{s}_a, 0, 0)$ is given, and the incentive compatibility constraint, given the hardest punishment $\bar{p}$, depends on the money transfer w_i^C and on the probability of success $\pi_i(x_a; n_i, 1, x_i, x_a)$ when principal i wants to punish agent a, which is decreasing in their distance d_i^a. When the agent is very close to the principal, it may be that the participation constraint is binding, and the agent is paid the reservation wage $\underline{w}$. For more distant agents, the incentive compatibility constraint becomes binding and requires a higher wage in order to compensate the lower ability to punish a cheating agent. From (vii), finally, the principal does not offer contracts that require a wage higher than $\bar{w}$.

Proof of Proposition 2:

Since the principal offers an individual contract to each agent, he can perfectly discriminate the wage, and will offer a new contract until a non-negative surplus is obtained, i.e. $w_i^C \leq \bar{w}(m)$. From Proposition 1 we know that the wage is decreasing in the probability of success π_i. The military capacity is characterised by decreasing marginal returns in the number of members and increasing marginal losses from distance. Given agents' uniform distribution $dn_i/dx_a = 1$, i.e. the number of members increases linearly in distance. Hence, after a certain distance, the enrolment of new members does not compensate, in terms of military capacity, the increase in distance, and π_i decreases. The contract wage $\hat{w}_i^C$ therefore increases up to the maximum payment $\bar{w}_i^C$ which corresponds to a maximum distance $\bar{d}_i^\pi$. The contractual relations therefore extend up to this distance. The family could recruit all the agents or a fraction of them, corresponding to a share $2\bar{d}_i^\pi$ or a lower one, if one of the boundaries of the linear space is reached. The expression in the statement summarises the different cases.

Proof of Proposition 3

The two principals compete for the initial choice and the successive defection of the agents. Consider first the initial affiliation. Agent a chooses family i if:

$$\frac{\pi_i U_a(m, w_i^{C1}, 0)}{1 - \delta\pi_i} \geq \frac{(1 - \pi_i) U_a(m, w_j^{C1}, 0)}{1 - \delta(1 - \pi_i)} \tag{17}$$

Since both terms are increasing in the contract wage, competition for the initial choice requires each principal to set a payment higher than the rival's one. The crucial point is that the expected marginal utility of the wage depends on the probability of success π_i, since the stream of payments is received only if the agent is not punished by the rival organisation. Hence, when $w_i^{C1} = w_j^{C1}$, the marginal utility of the wage is greater for principal i if $\pi_i > 1/2$ and vice versa. The Bertrand type competition in wages therefore implies that for those agents for which $\pi_i > 1/2$, principal i is able to attract the potential members with a wage offer lower than the rival one. We conclude that all the agents for which $\pi > 1/2$ can be induced to join family i through the offer of a sufficiently high wage.

We now need to verify whether the principal is able to ensure that all those agents who can initially be recruited can also be induced not to deviate successively. The relevant incentive compatibility constraint is $V_a^{Ci}(\pi_i) \geq V_a^{Dj}(\pi_i)$, or:

$$\frac{\pi_i U_a(m, w_i^{C1}, 0)}{1 - \delta\pi_i} \geq U_a(\hat{s}_a, w_i^{C1}, 0) + \delta\frac{(1 - \pi_i)U_a(m, w_j^{C2}, 0)}{1 - (1 - \pi_i)\delta} \tag{18}$$

Consider the choice of w_i^{C1} and w_j^{C2}. For a given wage of the rival family, each principal is able to make the constraint work in his favour: increasing w_i^{C1}, principal i can determine $V_a^{C_i}(\pi_i) \geq V_a^{D_j}(\pi_i)$, while an appropriate increase in w_j^{C2} reverses the sign of the inequality. We observe again a Bertrand type competition in wages for the loyalty or the defection of the agent. Also in this case the marginal utility of the wage is increasing in the probability of success. Suppose that family i has offered the higher wage $\bar{w}$ while the rival organisation's wage w_j^{C2}, which solves the incentive compatibility constraint as an equality, is lower than $\bar{w}$. The rival principal is able to induce the agent's defection through a further rise in the wage, while family i cannot profitably respond to that offer. Hence organisation i will not offer a contract to that agent since it is not able to induce his loyalty thereafter. We conclude that it is profitable to hire only those agents for which the family has a sufficient advantage in the probability of success to overcome the single-period utility from deviation and the successive contract utility offered by the rival organisation.

Define now $\hat{\pi}_i$ so that $V_a^{C_i}(\hat{\pi}_i) = V_a^{D_j}(\hat{\pi}_i)$ when $w_i^{C1} = w_j^{C2} = \bar{w}$. For $\pi_i \geq \hat{\pi}_i$, the incentive compatibility constraint is satisfied for lower and lower wages w_i^{C1} while $w_j^{C2} = \bar{w}$, as stated in (ii) and (iii).

Finally, setting $w_i^{C1} = w_j^{C2} = \bar{w}$, the condition $V_a^{C_i}(\pi_i) \geq V_a^{D_i}(\pi_i)$ evaluated at $\pi_i = 1/2$ becomes:

$$U_a(m, \bar{w}, 0)\frac{1 - \delta}{2 - \delta} \geq U_a(\hat{s}_a, \bar{w}, 0) \tag{19}$$

which is never satisfied. Hence $\hat{\pi}_i \gg 1/2$ as claimed in (i).

Proof of Proposition 4:

The result directly derives from the fact that when $D = 0$, $\pi_i = n_i/(n_i + n_j)$ for $x_a \in [0, 1]$ and the domain of the function on the same support widens as D increases. Therefore there will be a minimum distance $\underline{D}$ such that $\max_{x_a} \pi_i = \hat{\pi}_i$. For $D > \underline{D}$ there are two sub-sets of agents for which the incentive compatibility constraint can hold, i.e. $\pi_i > \hat{\pi}_i$ and $\pi_i < 1 - \hat{\pi}_i$. With π_i decreasing in x_a, these two sub-sets will be at the opposite sides of the linear segment.

NOTES

* I thank Massimo Bordignon, Francesco Corielli, Diego Gambetta, Michele Grillo, Pierangelo Mori, Fausto Panunzi, Lorenzo Sacconi, Piero Tedeschi and the editors for useful discussions and comments. Financial support from MURST 40% and from Università Bocconi, Milano, is acknowledged. Usual disclaimers apply.
  1 See Schelling (1971) for an attempt to define the distinctive features of organised crime.

2 See also the papers by Anderson and by Skaperdas and Syropoulos in this volume.
3 See Gambetta (1992) for an interesting analysis of the Sicilian mafia according to this interpretation
4 See the seminal contributions by Schelling (1960) and Tullock (1974) and, more recently, Garfinkel (1990), Grossman (1991), Hirshleifer (1991) and Skaperdas (1992). The investment in military activity can be interpreted in a broader sense, in order to include in this modelling many examples related to rent-seeking behaviour, such as electoral competition, industrial relations, non-price competition, legal conflicts etc.
5 See, for general discussion, Hart and Holmstrom (1987). In the incompleteness story, the court cannot intervene and guarantee the execution of the contract because, for instance, the relevant contingencies are not verifiable, i.e. observable by a third party.
6 See in particular Hirshleifer (1987) and the literature on mathematical analysis of military activity quoted there.
7 This specification is similar to Hirshleifer (1987), p. 93.
8 The literature on conflict and rent seeking uses two classes of success functions, which depend on the *ratio* of the *difference* in the individual investments. Quoting Hirshleifer (1989), p. 104, 'in a military context we might expect the ratio form of the Contest Success Function to be applicable when clashes take place under close to idealized conditions such as: an undifferentiated battlefield, full information, and unflagging weapons effectiveness. In contrast, the difference form tends to apply where there are sanctuaries and refuges, where information is imperfect and where the victorious player is subject to fatigue and distraction.' The logistic is then the more familiar specification of the difference case.
9 Empirical evidence and sociological studies offer many examples and descriptions of the rites and procedures for the enrolment of a new member: the once-and-for-all nature of this choice is explicitly remarked and stressed through a rich and evocative symbolic language. See, for example, Gambetta (1992), Appendix.
10 The repeated game literature has stressed that the infinite horizon case is equivalent to one in which the players assign a stationary probability of continuing the game for another period. This is a more realistic interpretation of our assumption of an infinite horizon contract. See also Rubinstein (1992) on the use of infinite vs. finite horizon games to model repeated interaction situations.
11 We exclude therefore the case in which the agent succeeds in hiding his deviation while remaining within the organisation.
12 We implicitly assume that the principal is able to commit to such contingent behaviour. Although we do not model this problem explicitly, we could justify this assumption by referring to the reputational problem that the principal faces: since he has *ex post* very strong control of his agents, he would not be able to recruit new members if known as a greedy and unfair boss.
13 This fact is not essential to our results. The real incentive to deviate is in fact the utility that the agent can obtain through an opportunistic action and not the payment that he receives.
14 We do not impose restrictions on the maximum utility of the agent who has abandoned the organisation, $U_a(\tilde{s}_a, 0, 0)$. In principle, we would expect this *ex*

post outside option to be either greater or lower than the *ex ante* one $\bar{u}$. On the one hand, having worked within the organisation, the agent could have acquired resources or know-how that make him better off after the deviation. In this case, the benefits from cheating are not limited to the single-period gains from the action $\hat{s}_a$ but continue, contingent on not being punished, through a sequence of actions $\tilde{s}_a$ by which the agent exploits his previous experience in the family. In this case, we would expect $U_a(\tilde{s}_a, 0, 0) > \bar{u}$, which emphasises the agent's incentive to deviate *ex post*. But there is an alternative story, which on the contrary tends to soften the incentive compatibility constraint. In areas where the diffusion and acceptance of the criminal organisation is widespread, as it was for instance until a few years ago in some regions of southern Italy, a cheating agent suffers a strong ostracism in his social environment independently of being effectively punished by the organisation. In this case the *ex post* outside option could be lower than the *ex ante* one.

15 In our model, therefore, punishment does not fit the crime: this is in line with the results of the discounted repeated games literature, whose framework is adopted in the paper. In more general terms, however, the punishment schemes adopted have a poor marginal deterrence power, as stressed by Stigler (1970) and recently further analysed in Malik (1990). The interesting point is that in the Sicilian mafia murder has always been the most frequent punishment, even for minor deviations.

16 There is a rich sociological and anthropological literature on the distinctive features of a criminal boss in the southern regions of Italy. See on this point Arlacchi (1983) and Catanzaro (1989).

17 Magistrate Falcone observes that, even if the biggest families reached in some phases 200 or 300 members, the average dimension is around 50 affiliates. See Falcone (1991), p. 100.

18 The literature on generalised urn models offers important results that could be used to study the stochastic processes that describe the dimension of the two families during the war. Since the probability of success is related to the number of members while the number of survivals depends on success in the sequence of clashes, our problem is in fact similar to that of the extraction of white and black balls from an urn; extraction with or without replacement corresponds to the cases in which a family is able or unable to recruit a new member when a soldier is killed in a clash. See Johnson and Kotz (1977).

REFERENCES

Arlacchi, P. (1983), *La mafia imprenditrice*, Bologna: Il Mulino.
Catanzaro, R. (1989), *Il delitto come impresa. Storia sociale della mafia*, Padova: Liviana.
Falcone, G. and M. Padovani (1991), *Cose di Cosa Nostra*, Milano: Rizzoli.
Gambetta, D. (1992), *La mafia siciliana*, Torino: Einaudi.
Garfinkel, M. R. (1990), 'Arming as a Strategic Investment in a Cooperative Equilibrium', *American Economic Review*, 80, pp. 50–68.
Grossman, H. I. (1991), 'A General Equilibrium Model of Insurrections', *American Economic Review*, 81, pp. 912–21.

Hart, O. and B. Holmstrom (1987), 'The Theory of Contracts', in T. Bewley (ed.), *Advances in Economic Theory, Fifth World Congress*, Cambridge: Cambridge University Press.

Hirshleifer, J. (1987), 'Conflict and Settlement', in J. Eatwell, M. Milgate and P. Newman (eds.), *The New Palgrave. Game Theory*, London: Macmillan.

Hirshleifer, J. (1989), 'Conflict and Rent-seeking Success Functions: Ratio vs. Difference Models of Relative Success', *Public Choice*, 63, pp. 101–12.

Hirshleifer, J. (1991), 'The Paradox of Power', *Economics and Politics*, 3, pp. 177–200.

Johnson, N. and S. Kotz (1977), *Urn Models and their Applications*, New York: Wiley.

Malik, A. (1990), 'Avoidance, Screening and Optimum Enforcement', *Rand Journal of Economics*, 21, pp. 341–53.

Rubinstein, A. (1992), 'Comments on the Interpretation of Repeated Games Theory', in J-J. Laffont (ed.), *Advances in Economic Theory, Sixth World Congress*, Cambridge: Cambridge University Press.

Schelling, T. C. (1960), *The Strategy of Conflict*, Cambridge MA: Harvard University Press.

Schelling, T. C. (1971), 'What is the Business of Organized Crime?', *Journal of Public Law*, 20, pp. 71–84, reprinted in Schelling, T. C. (ed.) (1984), *Choice and Consequence*, Cambridge MA: Harvard University Press, pp. 179–94.

Skaperdas, S. (1992), 'Cooperation, Conflict and Power in the Absence of Property Rights', *American Economic Review*, 82, pp. 720–39.

Stigler, G. J. (1970), 'The Optimum Enforcement of Law', *Journal of Political Economy*, 78, pp. 526–36.

Tullock, G. (1974), *The Social Dilemma: The Economics of War and Revolution*, Blacksburg, Virginia: University Publications.

Discussion

PIER LUIGI SACCO

Polo's paper offers us an explanation of criminal organisations' hiring decisions and of the consequent pattern of 'colonisation' of a population of potential affiliates who are uniformly distributed along a bounded one-dimensional continuum. The perspective he adopts is that of (optimal) contract theory. Illegal organisations are *characterised* as institutions based on contractual relationships that cannot be enforced by an external, *super partes*, legal authority. On the other hand, the set of feasible actions available to an illegal organisation is not limited by legal restraints. It can (and typically does) include the use of brute force, not excluding lethal violence, as a viable alternative to legal enforcement: rather than sueing affiliates that violate contractual obligations in court, the illegal organisation threatens to punish them to an extent that depends on the available deterrence power (as determined by the organisation's 'military' technology).

As to potential affiliates, they are assumed to be opportunistically motivated: as soon as there is a clash between their own and the organisation's interests, they are assumed to pursue the former at the expense of the latter unless this option is made unattractive by the organisation's imperfect but costless deterrence power, which is assumed to be stochastic and decreasing (on average) with the affiliate's distance from the organisation's seat.

Within this framework, Polo proves that, when there is only one organisation on the stage and contracts have infinite duration, it is optimal for it to threaten the hardest possible punishment against defectors (it is costless anyway) while offering wages for a given task that are increasing with the affiliate's distance (in order to compensate for the decrease in deterrence power). Since, for obvious reasons, the organisation's deterrence power depends on the number of affiliates, a non-trivial trade-off comes about between hiring more distant affiliates whose reliability is more costly to enforce and more precarious and increasing the (overall) organisation's deterrence power through the recruitment of additional affiliates. It is in principle possible that the decision to hire one more affiliate is not beneficial at the margin in spite of the gain in deterrence power, in that the optimal contract could become too costly for the principal. Therefore, the organisation could find it optimal not to hire all potential affiliates but only relatively close ones.

When two organisations coexist, each organisation's hiring pool is no longer made up of non-affiliates only; affiliates of the other organisation are also eligible, provided that they can be made safe enough from the rival's (lethal) punishment. In fact, organisations must protect every affiliate from attack whether recruited from the rival's work force or not. In this more general framework, Polo does not investigate the dynamics of the interaction between the two organisations, but offers us a characterisation of the stationary equilibrium pattern of 'colonisation'. He shows that, at the stationary equilibrium, all affiliates who have been hired by each organisation are loyal ones; on the other hand, the competition between the two organisations has the effect of increasing the optimal cost of hiring. As a consequence, organisations will be led to hire a smaller work force than in the monopsony case; indeed, if the seats of the two organisations are 'too close' to each other, neither of them will find it optimal to hire any affiliates at all. Therefore, one concludes that criminal organisations can exist only if they are not spatially clustered; moreover, when they do exist, they are typically separated by strips of 'no-man's land' in which neither organisation hires any affiliate.

It is well known that the Sicilian territory has long been 'administratively' divided by the mafia into a number of local districts, each of which is controlled by an unique 'family' acting as a local monopolist. Does this evidence make any case for Polo's proposed explanation of the spatial activity pattern of illegal organisations? In our opinion, the answer is: yes and no. On the one hand, Polo's model does indeed show that the interaction between organisations will bring about local monopolies; on the other hand, these monopolies do not seem in reality to be circumscribed by strips of 'no-man's land' in the sense defined above. The 'enforcement problem' that plagues illegal organisations' hiring decisions in Polo's model seems to have much less bite in reality, where, typically, a family's territory ends where the rival's begins.

If this is the case, one is led to wonder whether it is sensible to assume that the hiring decisions of illegal organisations can be characterised in terms of (optimal) *complete* contracts. In fact, being an affiliate of a criminal organisation entails much more than being paid to perform a well-specified task, even if, of course, affiliates can, and often will, be chosen on the basis of idiosyncratic abilities (think e.g. of professional killers). Once enrolled, the affiliate has to perform a number of different tasks, some of which are prompted by contingencies that were not foreseen, or even foreseeable, at the moment the hiring decision was made. As a consequence, if the hiring decision is made on the basis of a contract, this will typically be *incomplete*. In fact, the internal structure of illegal organisations cannot be properly understood if one abstracts from the peculiarities of a principal–agent relationship taking place in social contexts marked by a long-standing tradition of acquaintance with criminal power.

The most distinctive feature of such a relationship is its *ritual* character. When entering the organisation, affiliates establish a relationship not only with their principal, but also with all other affiliates, to which they are bound by a series of hierarchical or peer duties (according to their relative positions in the organisation), as specified by an 'ethical code' to which the affiliate explicitly commits when joining the organisation (see e.g. Gambetta, 1992). This code also acts as a governance structure in that the settlement of the *ex post* bargaining problem arising when the affiliate is called on to perform a task that was not explicitly contracted in advance falls within its scope. The success and even the survival of the organisation critically rely on the fact that each affiliate internalises the code to a reasonable degree; if this were not the case, the level of internal conflict arising as a consequence of contractual incompleteness, and the 'litigation costs' thereof, would easily become unbearable, leading to the organisation's break-down.

An important consequence of the existence of an ethical code as a tool for the management of contractual incompleteness is a narrowing of the scope of individual opportunism. The internalisation of the ethical code is favoured by ritualised interactions between members of the organisation that often take the form of gift exchanges: as pointed out by Akerlof (1982), gift exchange rituals are relatively common not only in primitive societies but also in modern organisations as a rather powerful means of increasing internal cohesion and managing efficiently the potential conflicts that may arise as a consequence of contractual incompleteness. Gift exchange rituals may be effective in reducing individual opportunism *as long as they are part of a stable social convention*, i.e. a customary, expected and self-enforcing state of things according to the classical definition of Lewis (1969). In this case, reciprocity is stable enough to overcome opportunism in terms of expected benefits. As the social convention supporting gift exchange loses strength and reciprocity becomes less reliable, however, individual opportunism bursts out.

It is important to stress that, in modern organisations, gift exchange rituals are not mainly concerned with material donations, but rather with mutual acknowledgement of entitlements to rights and benefits, etc. In the case of illegal organisations, gift exchange also includes mutual protection from attacks by rival organisations, mutual covering from police inquiries, and so on. It is therefore clear that a break-down of reciprocity is very likely to undermine the illegal organisation's survival chances; a vital illegal organisation cannot dispense with a stable ethical code.

The slow-but-steady erosion of a convention of the above sort explains in fact the gradual loss of strength experienced by the mafia in recent years after the Corleonese families came to the head of the organisation's high council, the *cupola*. As extensively and dramatically argued by Tommaso Buscetta in his recent trial confrontation with Totò Riina, the alleged mafia chief and main strategist, the deep cause of the organisation's current dismay lies precisely in the systematic violation of the ethical code by the Corleonese, regarding both the norms ruling the relationships between affiliates and those ruling the relationship between the organisation and the 'external world'.

As to the former, Riina's career has been built on his ability to betray and slaughter all potential opponents within the organisation, including his previous protectors; as a consequence of this, the organisation's cohesion has been substantially weakened by the break-down of mutual reliability and many former affiliates have quit, agreeing to collaborate with justice as the sole means of protecting themselves from the chief's sudden, fatal death sentences. As to the latter, Riina has broken one of the 'iron laws' of the mafian code of ethics, namely the prohibition on wounding or killing women or children; as a consequence, the mafia has lost much of the connivance or even the support of local populations that have for a long time regarded it as an 'anti-state', often more reliable and effective than the official one in providing protection, work opportunities, etc. As argued by Granovetter (1985), an organisation's ability to keep opportunism at a manageable level does not rely primarily on its ability to enforce contractual obligations through (military, legal, etc.) deterrence but rather in the nature and quality of the network of social relationships in which it is embedded. The mafian code of ethics has been successfully internalised for a long time by affiliates because it embodied several norms of behaviour that were widely shared not only by the organisation's members but by the Sicilian population as a whole; as this correspondence has broken down, the organisation's hold on the population and on its own members has critically diminished and stability of the underlying social convention has become an issue.

As long as the ethical code is an important motivational factor both for the principal and for affiliates, the high cost associated with the optimal contract for affiliates whose location is distant from the organisation's seat plays a less important role in explaining the organisation's spatial pattern of activity than in Polo's model. In particular, one can expect that this cost is in reality substantially less than the one implied by the theoretical model, since affiliates will not normally consider the possibilities of acting opportunistically or of leaving the organisation unless the social convention on which the ethical code is based is losing strength. Therefore, in reality we do not observe strips of 'no-man's land' that no criminal organisation will find it worth while to occupy. On the contrary, the relatively cheap enforceability of the (incomplete) contractual relationship provides an incentive to expand the borders of the organisation's area of influence as far as possible to capture the advantages in terms of deterrence power pertaining to a larger organisational size.

This does not mean of course that one should predict that the organisation's size is growing indefinitely in the absence of rival firms; a potentially critical factor that could limit the organisation's growth is the increasing difficulty of having the code of ethics internalised by affiliates in a large group where 'face-to-face' interactions that are at the basis of the gift exchange ritual are more and more often substituted by anonymous interactions between individuals that seldom meet and hardly know each other (see Olson, 1971; Glance and Huberman, 1993). However, this sort of consideration does not imply that distance plays against organisational growth, but rather that the organisation will accommodate growth by developing a more complex hierarchy made of sub-groups (local circles, secondary organisation seats) that are small enough to restore the personal character of interactions between affiliates. The currently available knowledge about the mafia's internal organisation actually confirms this prediction. (Each family's territory seems to be divided into local units called *mandamenti*, each of which is centred on a secondary seat.)

According to the point of view just discussed, the onus of the explanation of the spatial pattern of activity of criminal organisations clearly moves from the structure of individual incentives of affiliates to the emergence of stable social conventions of the sort discussed above, i.e. from a static choice framework to a dynamic interaction framework: one has to explain how a given social convention emerges and takes over at the expense of other, rival ones. It is important to remark that the mafian code of ethics acts as a governance structure not only with respect to relationships that are internal to a given organisation, but also with respect to (illegal) inter-organisational relationships, and that the actual content of this code changes (more or less slowly) with the nature of the relationships it is supposed to rule. In other words, the mafian code of ethics can be regarded as the result of a social, evolutionary process of selection of individual behaviours and organisational practices. (For a theoretical illustration of this approach, see e.g. Bicchieri, 1990; Vega-Redondo, 1993.)

The need to adopt an evolutionary perspective also emerges from the analytical limitations of Polo's model, which must confine attention to stationary equilibria because of the difficulties brought about by organisations of changing size (viz. deterrence power) within a standard repeated games framework with complete contracting.

The next challenge seems therefore to be the following: building a model of the internal structure of illegal organisations in which contracts are incomplete and players are embedded in a wider network of (more or less) internalised social norms that co-evolve with individual behaviours giving rise in some cases to stable conventions (of which codes of ethics or, more generally, 'corporate cultures' are an important part; see e.g. Miller, 1992).

In conclusion, Polo's model is an important stepping-stone in the analysis of the internal structure of illegal organisations in that it constructs a clear and consistent analytical framework to deal with a quite interesting and difficult problem. It is not, neither does it aspire to be, the ultimate answer to the issue: it is a useful yardstick against which to evaluate avenues for future research like the evolutionary one we are advocating here.

REFERENCES

Akerlof, G. A. (1982), 'Labor Contracts as Partial Gift Exchange', *Quarterly Journal of Economics*, 84, pp. 543–69.

Bicchieri, C. (1990), 'Norms of Cooperation', *Ethics* 100(3), July, pp. 838–68.

Gambetta, D. (1992), *La mafia siciliana*, Torino: Einaudi.

Glance, N. S. and B. Huberman (1993), 'Organizational Fluidity and Sustainable Cooperation', mimeo, Palo Alto: Xerox Corporation.

Granovetter, M. (1985), 'Economic Action and Social Structure: The Problem of Embeddedness', *American Journal of Sociology*, 91(3), November, pp. 481–510.

Lewis, D. (1969), *Convention. A Philosophical Study*, Cambridge MA: Harvard University Press.

Miller, G. J. (1992), *Managerial Dilemmas. The Political Economy of Hierarchy*, Cambridge: Cambridge University Press.

Olson, M. (1971), *The Logic of Collective Action*, Cambridge MA: Harvard University Press.

Vega-Redondo, F. (1993), 'Competition and Culture in an Evolutionary Process of Equilibrium Selection: A Simple Example', *Games and Economic Behavior*, 5(4), October, pp. 618–31.

5 Conspiracy among the many: the mafia in legitimate industries

DIEGO GAMBETTA and PETER REUTER

1 Introduction

This paper considers the modes by which the mafia exercises its influence on a number of legitimate industries in both Sicily and the United States. In particular, it discusses the kinds of service the mafia provides, the economic consequences of its influence, the conditions that induce the entry of the mafia in specific industries, and the conditions and policies that make it disappear. We share the view that mafia protection in legitimate industries, although occasionally rapacious and unreliable, is frequently neither bogus nor limited to intimidating new entrants. Under some (perhaps most) circumstances, the primary beneficiaries are the owners of the firms being coerced.

This view is based both on theoretical arguments and empirical evidence. The paper relies on a series of case-studies which were autonomously developed by the authors and presented elsewhere (Reuter, 1987, 1993; Gambetta, 1993). The most important type of protection supplied by racketeers to legitimate industries, which is found in most industries we studied, is the enforcement of a variety of allocation agreements among independently owned firms, with racketeer income as payment for the service. This runs counter to two widespread conceptions of the involvement of the mafia in legitimate industries. One sees the racketeers' role as mere intimidation: the mafioso approach to 'regulated' competition would amount to thugs resorting to muscular persuasion at the expense of an innocent competitor on behalf of either a single monopolist or the mafia's own enterprise. The other sees racketeers as extortionists imposing their presence upon harmless dealers who would rather do without. Let us consider them in turn.

When the mafia looks after the interests of a monopolist, it is clearly useless as a cartel enforcer and protection is limited to the intimidation of new entrants. This, however, is seldom the case: although protectors have an interest in not expanding the number of protected firms indefinitely, they are subject to an opposite drive to increase it. First, the larger the number of firms the higher is the mafia's autonomy from and bargaining power over any single one of them (Gambetta, 1993, pp. 22–3, 85). Second, supporting a small number of firms is risky because it provides disappointed competitors with an incentive to seek protection from police or rival racketeers (Reuter, 1987, p. 6). Third, larger collusive agreements hold competition in check more effectively both because the cartel acts as a discouraging signal of determination and stability, thus reducing the need to threaten potential competitors, and because the option to exit the cartel becomes less attractive for the participants (Fiorentini, 1994).

Although in particular circumstances collusion is self-enforcing (Friedman, 1983, pp. 65, 132*ff*), whenever cartels rely on agreements, defection is a potential hazard and a genuine demand for protection may develop. Each partner must feel confident that all other partners will comply with the pact; otherwise the cartel collapses and competition creeps back in. Furthermore, even though anti-competitive outcomes can emerge without cooperation among firms – a large firm may independently decide to exclude new entrants even if rival firms share the advantages but not the cost – whenever restrictive practices require the contribution of all firms, an enforcing agency may be necessary to deter members from free-riding. There is therefore no theoretical reason to expect that the role of the mafia will be one of extortion rather than authentic protection. (Whether the price of protection is 'extortionate' is a separate question to which we return later in Section 8.)

Our argument is that the mafia solves a problem of potential cartels. It may be invited in by entrepreneurs themselves looking to organise some agreement or may initiate the activity itself; we have examples of both. Its comparative advantage is likely to be in organising cartel agreements for large number industries, as well as making cartels more stable; success, however, requires a number of other conditions, that we spell out in the course of the paper. Moreover, the mafia has a unique asset in this capacity, namely its reputation for effective execution of threats of violence; this creates a reputational barrier to entry.

We do not, however, claim that large number cartel organising is the exclusive role of the mafia in legitimate industries. The garment trucking and waterfront industries in the United States (Reuter, 1987, Ch. 3) provide instances of other kinds of predation. However, cartel organisation is an important and distinctive activity of the mafia,[1] and not just in legitimate industries. Although illicit markets do not concern us here, there are signs that the mafia can act as cartel organiser, for instance, in bookmaking in the United States and in tobacco smuggling and purse snatching in southern Italy (Reuter, 1983, pp. 42–4; Gambetta, 1993, 227–35).

2   The form of cartel agreements

The central problem for cartels is to design agreements which can be maintained over time. Three aspects of agreements, which are relevant to human cooperation generally, are also relevant for establishing cartels: the rules to be followed by members, the means of detecting rule violators, and the sanctions to be imposed against violators. Weakness in any of the three is likely to lead to defections and breakdown of the cartel (Stigler, 1964).

2.1   The rule

At least three dimensions of the rule itself affect cartel members' willingness to enter and remain in association. First, the rule must produce results that, over time, are perceived as equitable, so as to lower risk of defection and complaint. Second, the agreement must be compatible with continued entrepreneurial autonomy. Loss of autonomy – as might arise if the cartel decided that production facilities must be centralised to maximise joint profits – transforms the bargaining positions of members and those who lose production facilities become dependent on others' willingness to honour the original commitment. This may increase the demand on trust to breaking-point. Third, because of illegality, there is likely to be a strong inclination to avoid rules which require 'side-payments' among members that could provide valuable evidence for a prosecutor. More generally, illegal agreements are likely to minimise the number of transactions necessary for their effective execution.

2.2   Detection

The second important issue is the speed and cost of detecting violation. The longer it takes to detect it, the greater the return to violation and the lower the expected lifetime of the cartel (Stigler, 1964). Similarly, the profitability of the cartel will be lowered by high costs of monitoring. More generally, the higher the cost of policing agreements the lower the likelihood that cooperation will emerge.

2.3   Sanctions

The final consideration is the nature of available sanctions. Members will doubt a cartel's potential stability if violations of its rules cannot be punished without ending the cartel. A classic difficulty of price-fixing agreements is that efforts to punish price cutters lead to price reductions for all customers. The possibility of selective and cheap sanctions will increase stability.[2]

A limited number of rules can sustain collusive agreements. These are price fixing, output quotas and market sharing. Market sharing seems generally easier to enforce than, and logically prior to, the other two alternatives. In the New York carting industry,[3] for instance, in which individual customers are allocated on the basis of who served them first, cartel members have complete price autonomy. Being fixed in location, customers have little choice if other carters accept the basic rule. By contrast, if price fixing is practised – assuming that the product is homogeneous – firms usually need further allocative measures. Price fixing creates an incentive to resort to covert inducements, such as advertising, gifts, special offers, guarantees, sponsorship etc. in order to attain higher market shares. Thus, unless firms also have market-sharing rules, price fixing is likely to be unstable, even ignoring potential entry.

3   A comparison of the Sicilian and New York mafias

The differences between the mafia in Sicily and New York are several. For example, in Sicily there is a clear geographic division; individual families have specific areas in which they have sole operating authority. Members of other families can operate there only with permission. Within New York the nature of the division is harder to determine. It is certainly not territorial, perhaps reflecting the lack of effective small-area local government that would permit the use of corrupt government authority to establish monopolistic criminal enterprises. Above all, in a highly diversified and complex urban situation such as that of New York, a monopoly of protection on all transactions is hardly conceivable, even in a relatively small area. By contrast, in a village or district of Sicily, with few inhabitants, any one mafia family can still take care of its clients in most of their businesses; but as the number of exchanges multiplies it becomes increasingly laborious to supply territorially-based protection and protection itself tends to become functionally specialised. Historic roles certainly have an influence in determining where (functionally) a family operates in New York. The Lucchese and Gambino families are the only ones of the five New York families that have a presence in the carting industry, just as it is the Genovese that are most active on the docks in Manhattan. That seems to have been the case for over 40 years in the case of carting and nearly 70 years for the docks.

The capacity of the mafia to play a role in cartel organisation is probably affected by this general organisational characteristic. Sicilian industry agreements may have territorial limits because the families cannot operate outside those areas. Indeed, it appears that some sharing agreements are cumbersome to execute because of the territorial division of the mafia families; the queuing for contract bids, discussed below, is an instance where arrangements have to be worked out among different families. Also, in New York there is much more of an explicit market in property rights. Carters buy and sell customers at prices that seem to represent the capitalised value of the customer allocation agreement; it is unclear whether mafiosi levy a tax on these sales. In Sicily there is no evidence of markets in such rights. Another difference is one of scale of individual families. The mafia of Sicily are approximately 3,000, in a total of nearly 100 families. In contrast there are an estimated 5,000 mafia in New York, but grouped into only five families. Entry is more restricted in New York and the rewards of membership correspondingly greater. Few seem to enter American mafia families before their late thirties, while in Sicily members enter in their twenties.

A further important difference for our purposes is the role of the labour union. In the United States it has been the central instrument by which the mafia has acquired power in particular industries. The union provides an ideal means to dress up extortion or the suppression of competition as the expression of concern for the rights of individual workers. Interestingly, the union is critical for the initiation of a customer allocation agreement but appears not to be so central for its continuation; expectation and reputation may suffice at that point. In Sicily, on the other hand, the union is not a major institution. The mafia has much more direct ties to the political system and, as argued at length in Gambetta (1993), serves to provide quasi-governmental services that the elected government fails to deliver.

One final difference is worth mentioning. Illegal markets have traditionally been a more important source of income to the New York mafia than to the Sicilian mafia. In markets for horse-betting, certain kinds of lottery, loan-sharking and (in earlier eras) prostitution and bootlegging, the mafia has served both as a provider of the goods themselves and as guarantors of contracts and dispute settlers. In recent decades, it is the latter role that has been most significant (Reuter, 1983). There are thus parallels between the mafia's current roles in legal and illegal markets. For the Sicilian mafia, although the role of protection has been salient for a long time, markets in illegal commodities have until recently played a less important role. The growth of the heroin market since 1970 has changed that, but the Sicilian mafia in this case has played a direct role in the provision of credit and part of the service too (Gambetta, 1993, pp. 234–44).

4   Instances of mafia cartels

With only a modest number of case-studies available, even including those that have appeared in historical studies, we make modest claims as to the generality of the following summary of the prevalence of different kinds of mafia cartel rules.

We know of few settings in which the mafia has enforced *price-fixing* agreements over long periods of time. In the wholesale fruit and vegetable market in Palermo, for example, the dramatic increase in numbers of authorised market middlemen, known as *commissionari*, made it impossible to continue to fix prices. Until 1955, only twelve *commissionari* were operating and price fixing and quota control were feasible because easy to police. A 'man of respect', himself a *commissionario*, acted as guarantor of these arrangements and controlled the largest share of the transactions. Now that the *commissionari* are 77,[4] they say that it would no longer be profitable to pay someone who, like 'Don Peppe' in bygone days, enforced collusion. There are simply too many *commissionari* and, given the large number of customers that use the market every day, someone somewhere would always breach the deal. In Section 7 we provide an analysis of why the numbers grew so substantially and broke the cartel.

Output *quotas* are another important alternative. The little available evidence suggests that quota agreements require extensive and intrusive inspection for their maintenance, and these are not attractive for an illegal market. The only known case of regulating output quotas involving the mafia dates back to the nineteenth century. Franchetti, an early and insightful scholar of the phenomenon, reports the existence of two 'societies' based near Palermo: one of millers – la società Mulini – which we would call a cartel, and the other – la società della Posa – a union of cart-drivers and apprentice-millers. Both these societies are said by Franchetti to have been under the protection of 'powerful mafiosi'. Members paid a fee to the society and agreed not to compete. They kept the price of flour high by regulating output, taking turns to restrict production and receiving appropriate compensation. (Note that current EU agricultural policies are not too dissimilar.) The *capo*-mafia ensured that everybody paid their dues, that the miller whose turn it was to under-produce did not free-ride on his fellows by producing more than he was supposed to; and that the others did not free-ride on him, by failing either to pay the agreed compensation or to restrict production when their turn came (Franchetti, [1876] 1974, pp. 6–7 and 96).

The remaining collusive rule, namely *market-sharing*, can follow any one of three cases: locations, customers or queues. Which of them is adopted depends on the general conditions of the market – physical and technological constraints, size of units of demand and supply, frequency of transactions – and on which proves more suitable to monitor defectors. In what follows we assume for simplicity of exposition that agents sharing the market are sellers, but the same arguments apply to buyers. For instance, in the wholesale fish market in Palermo, middlemen share suppliers, i.e. fishermen.

4.1   Location or territory

A gets the north side, B the south side; A runs on route X and B on route Y. Trading within territorial boundaries is found in a variety of industries, such as bus companies, airlines, telephone line suppliers, estate agents and many more. When firms are few, and monitoring each other presents no great problem, firms can easily agree with no need of 'muscle'. The three top Italian producers of lead and amianthus pipes, for instance, are said to share territories – north, south and centre – when it comes to large orders. These firms do not seem to need any special agency to enforce their understanding. When it comes to small contracts, which are too arduous to police, they simply prefer to compete.

But other sectors – as diverse as construction, transport and street-hawkers – have been territorially controlled by mafiosi in Sicily. Enforcing the territorial allocation when markets are both visible and immobile (or at least well defined as bus routes are) is relatively simple. Territoriality has a logical basis that makes it the dominant alternative. In Naples and Palermo mafia enforcement has also helped prevent conflict among unofficial parking attendants, whereas in a similar market in Rome, that for cleaning windscreens at traffic lights, the mafia has not been available. In 1989 this business was lucrative: each man (mostly Polish immigrants) made between 100,000 and 300,000 lire per day ($80–250) and, according to the carabinieri, this led to violent fights over the allocation of the most profitable road junctions. The cleaners were unable to cooperate and thus attracted the attention of the authorities (*la Repubblica*, 2 July 1989).

4.2   Customers

Not all markets are efficiently allocated by territory. For instance, dealers may congregate in one location, as in wholesale markets, or agents may be highly mobile and unpredictable, as, for example, taxi drivers and, as noted by Schelling, burglars, who are both mobile and, as a matter of trade, invisible (Gambetta, 1993, pp. 220–35). Furthermore, geographical divisions are not always satisfactory because profits may be so unevenly and unpredictably distributed (e.g. because of differences in regional patterns of development) that some cartel members perceive the continuation of the agreement as inequitable. An alternative solution consists in sharing customers: cartel members, in other words agree not to accept or seek business from customers who are currently served by another member of the cartel. Where feasible, customer allocation dominates the other rules. Violations are easily detected within a short period of time and almost automatically because if a cartel member provides service to the customer of another member, that member will be aware of the loss of business of that customer. Moreover, selective sanctions can be applied by aggressive solicitation of the violator's customers.

The rule is also equitable and simple to apply. It gives to each participant what he thinks of as his already, namely his existing customers. It does not require other forms of cooperation which leave paper trails for investigators. Members can charge different prices and provide different qualities of products, though there may be limits on the variation depending on the ease of comparison by customers. This type of sharing is particularly attractive if customers are 'fixed in location and the service or good is delivered to [them]' (Reuter, 1987, p. 7) for policing is simpler. More generally, it is successful if the conditions permit an easy way to identify customers and keep track of their movements. When customers are big, for instance, they are easily shared between suppliers: A works for the electric company, B for the water company and so on.

This applies to the wholesale fruit and vegetable market too in Palermo. In fact, although most daily transactions now take place competitively, there is an exception which still provides mafiosi with an opportunity to exert their influence. A group of 6–7 *commissionari* – those said to be of 'greater respect' – collude over the contracts taken out by institutions, such as schools, hospitals, barracks and old people's homes. Each *commissionario* supplies specific institutions and the problem of competition is eliminated radically: by common agreement only one *commissionario* shows up at each tender. Relative to private customers, public institutions are fewer, take out longer-term contracts, buy fixed quantities, are generally slack about quality, careless about price and corruptible. In short, they are easy to share. The small number of participants as well as the availability of sanctions – they share the same crowded market area and could easily make life difficult for each other – are such that this agreement could in principle do without outside assistance, although some evidence suggests that this is not the case (Gambetta, 1993, pp. 206–14).

Under customer allocation agreements, customers effectively become part of the supplier's assets; they are internalised and are in some instances traded like any other form of property. Carters in the New York metropolitan area (Long Island, New York City and New Jersey) buy and sell customers both individually and in groups. The prices of those customers, roughly 40 times their monthly gross billings in the early 1980s, provide the basis for estimating the capitalised value of the allocation agreement (Reuter, 1987, pp. 48–51).

4.3   Queues

Sharing customers, however, can prove arduous. There may simply be too many of them around, or they may be too occasional or too mobile. In short, they can be difficult to identify: how could, say, restaurants share tourists or petrol stations share motorway drivers? Until the mid-1950s, when *commissionari* were very few at the fruit and vegetable market in Palermo, some ordinary customer sharing went on. Since both customers and sources of supply have increased, however, these arrangements have been abandoned. One strategy for dealing with these problematic markets involves taking turns. Provided customers can be funnelled through particular locations, queueing can help. The obvious case is that of taxis who line up at stations and airports.

Sharing customers is also meaningless if there is only one buyer, or, more generally, if there are fewer buyers than sellers. If there is just one buyer, queueing can work if purchases are repeated: sellers can then enter a (metaphorical) line and share the market on this basis. One common method of collusion found among building contractors in Sicily runs as follows: firms A1, A2, A3, ... agree that, say, A2 should obtain the contract; the others bid artificially high prices so that A2's offer is certain to be the lowest. There are certain prerequisites for a deal of this kind to work: first, only firms in the cartel can participate while free riders must be excluded. Next, A2 must be confident that none of the other firms will submit a competitive bid at the last minute. In turn, A1, A3 ... require guarantees that A2 will return the favour on a future occasion and entrepreneurs therefore keep careful records of who obtained which contract. Where a contract is publicly bid on a repeat basis, the cartel may instead allocate a contract to one firm, with others designated to provide 'courtesy' bids as camouflage for the arrangement. That behaviour has been observed among the carters in both New Jersey and Long Island. These rights can be permanent enough for the contracts to be sold from one carter to another.

5   Conditions of emergence

The ideal strategy from the entrepreneurs' point of view is to collude without paying protection money to the mafia, but this works only so long as everybody follows the rules and everybody believes it. Sometimes, racketeers can be called in simply *ex post facto* to provide a one-time service: once, in the late 1970s, according to a Sicilian building contractor, two firms suddenly defected and went after a forbidden contract so that 'the man of respect was called in and persuaded them to withdraw'. But, generally, not much is known about the conditions that foster the *continued* presence of the mafia in legitimate industries. In the United States the phenomenon of racketeer-influenced industries, despite a substantial journalistic interest, has attracted little scholarly attention. As for Sicily, research on this topic is virtually non-existent.

There seems to be just one known case, the waterfront industry in New York, in which the presence of racketeers qualifies as 'pure extortion'; and, even so, employers take advantage of their presence to control union members (Reuter, 1987, p. vii; Bell, 1960). But existing studies – e.g. Landesco (1929), Block (1982), Reuter *et al.* (1982), Reuter (1987) and Gambetta (1993) – found evidence that competitors seeking a collusive solution to market problems provide racketeers with the opportunity to acquire a role in their industry. Racketeers can enter 'by invitation' rather than on their own initiative. Recent evidence from Sicily illustrates this case. Baldassare di Maggio, a mafioso who turned state witness in 1992, said that Angelo Siino, a building contractor, 'came to me and said that if (...) we, that is Cosa Nostra, were capable of coordinating the bids we could get much bigger profits (...). In that first stage, Cosa Nostra's problem was that of making [Siino] credible in the eyes of other contractors' (*Panorama*, 11 April 1993). In order for collusion to succeed, the organisational force of the cartel must be credible: every participant must respect the agreement and in turn confidently expect that his moment to bid will come and that others will respect it. Cosa Nostra supplies these guarantees. A surveyor involved in the same enquiry said that the mafia intervenes as 'an organization which takes care of the way in which the various jobs are equitably distributed among the interested firms' (*la Repubblica*, 28 October 1992). In the interrogation which originally started this enquiry in 1990, the former Mayor of Baucina, near Palermo, summing up the role of the mafia, said that the local mafiosi 'oversaw the fair distribution of contracts among firms participating in bids' (*la Repubblica*, 14 April 1990).

There is a parallel with New York: federal prosecutors in the case United States vs. Salerno in 1985 proved that 'the Cosa Nostra families established a club of concrete contractors who decided which contractor would submit the lowest bid on each project; other cartel members prepared their complementary bids accordingly. The "lowest bid" was far higher than the price that fair competition would have produced' (New York Organized Crime Task Force [OCTF], 1988, p. 11, fn. 17).

In general, racketeers offer the prospect that the conspiracy · ill work, simply because they provide credible enforcement. Large number cartels appear generally to have short lives because there is always an incentive for a member to leave the agreement and take advantage of the restrictions imposed on the remaining members (Scherer, 1970, Ch. 6). Potential conspirators are aware of this and may be reluctant to enter into an arrangement that is probably short lived as well as illegal. By promising to take illegal but effective actions against defectors, racketeers provide potential members with credible assurance that it is likely to be of lasting benefit.

But the racketeer involvement has another benefit, once it becomes known. It reduces the willingness of customers to protest the high prices charged under the agreement or to solicit competing bids from other dealers, tempting violation. Note that the customers in the commercial sector of the carting industry in New York include major corporations competent at understanding and exercising their rights. The unspoken threat, perhaps occasionally articulated in a vague way, that aggressive action may be punished by mafia interventions, smooths customer relations for the cartel members. Given the small share of total costs associated with garbage collection, and the fact that rivals are also believed to be extorted, risky resistance is unlikely to be an attractive option. The New Jersey State Commission of Investigation (1989) noted that one carter told a reporter that a story about racketeer involvement in the industry would only help his business.

Finally, racketeers provide a reputational barrier to entry. Entrants must be concerned that they will be the target of retaliation by racketeers. Their trucks and stores may be destroyed and their customers threatened or actually subject to violence. This was certainly the case when the Brooklyn District Attorney's Office started a carting firm in 1972, as part of an undercover investigation of the industry.

Collusion alone, however, is not in itself a sufficient cause. There is no evidence of mafia control among large corporations – steel, automobiles, chemicals, rubber (Bell, 1960, p. 176; Reuter, 1987, p. 7). Entrepreneurs of this calibre can probably count on political collusion and, more generally, grander means than the mafia (e.g. Friedman, 1988). Nor does it develop in hi-tech industries. For markets to be vulnerable to the mafia, collusion must be both highly desirable and difficult to bring about. The former condition depends on inelastic demand and little product differentiation, whereas the latter is due to impediments such as numerous firms and low barriers to entry (Reuter, 1987, p. 6).

Even when all the right conditions obtain, however, a triggering event often seems necessary to attract racketeers. Slumps in the economy, for instance, can provide the activating force: in the United States during the Depression, an extraordinarily deep and rapid decline in demand intensified the incentive for collusive action and related services. The need for cash becomes an important factor: Lucky Luciano, a leading mafioso during the Depression claimed:

> [W]e gave the companies that worked with us the money to help them buyin' goods and all the stuff they needed to operate with. Then, if one of our manufacturers got into us for dough that he could not pay back, and the guy had what looked like a good business, then we would become his partner (...) we actually kept a whole bunch of garment manufacturers alive, and we helped all them unions, the Ladies' Garment Workers and the Amalgamated, organize the place. (Gosch and Hammer, 1975, pp. 77–8)

Racketeers' intervention can also be sparked off by the sudden greed of one of the cartel participants. Funeral homes in Naples, for instance, shared hospitals for many years without outside intervention: firm A was responsible for the deceased in hospital X, B for those in hospital Y and so on. They managed to keep the number of firms surprisingly low: while in Turin there are 50 firms for 1 million residents and in Rome 70 for 2.8 million, in Naples a population of 1.2 million is supplied by only 13 firms. The cartel achieved these impressive results with the assistance of corrupt local politicians and administrators who rejected new applicants. But collusive arrangements remain exposed to the risk of foundering and hence to the temptation to call in the mafiosi. At the end of the 1970s one firm tried to increase its share by enlisting the protection of an aggressive gang, La Nuova Camorra Organizzata. The other funeral homes attempted first to repel the move 'politically', then called in rival racketeers, who did not limit themselves to providing a one-time service but decided to continue levying a protection fee even after the triggering event had been sorted out. A similar case is found in the New Jersey

Table 5.1   Conditions favouring the emergence of mafia-controlled cartels

Product differentiation	Low
Barriers to entry	Low
Technology	Low
Labour	Unskilled
Demand	Inelastic
Number of firms	Large
Size of firms	Small
Unionisation	Present

garbage collection industry; there, however, the aggressive carter was not backed by outside racketeers and the other carters successfully opposed his attempts to expand by 'political' means alone.

According to one Sicilian contractor, mafioso intervention is much favoured by submissive expectations and can therefore be avoided; he himself had coordinated queues, ostensibly without being a mafioso. By yielding too quickly to the mafia – he claimed – one loses the respect which may otherwise be sufficient to control collusion: 'a lot of entrepreneurs end up in the arms of the mafia simply because they believe it is inevitable'. In New York the OCTF also found, in its investigation of the building industry, that 'sometimes contractors claim not to know exactly why they pay; experience tells them that payoffs are necessary to assure that "things run smoothly"' (1988, p. 17). The stronger the rumour that mafia services are indispensable in a certain market or area, the higher seems the likelihood that they will be requested or accepted without question.[5] In addition, institutions looking for builders may themselves feel lost without an outsider to choose for them for no-one wants to take responsibility for the allocation: in at least one case the contracting agent in Sicily actively sought the intervention of an external fixer when the latter was slow in coming forward autonomously.

6   Consequences

Although it is difficult to establish *ex post facto* whether a given collusive arrangement could have emerged without the involvement of the mafiosi, the availability of mafia services generally makes collusion more likely, more elaborate and more enduring. Thus, not only do collusive arrangements sustain the mafia, but the availability of mafia protection also provides an incentive to seek collusive solutions.

Agreements supervised by mafiosi can embrace larger numbers of both dealers and customers: in the New York carting industry, for instance, in which racketeers played a continuing role in the operation of the allocation agreement, primarily through the constant need to mediate disputes, the cartel involved the allocation of over 100,000 customers to as many as 300 carters (Reuter, 1987, p. 11). The greater the number of firms the harder it becomes to ensure that they all keep their word. An Italian building contractor spoke of a 'queue' of as many as 160 firms. It took a great deal of patience and manoeuvering before he eventually succeeded, as he put it, in 'buying' a contract: 'it is obvious that to safeguard agreements of this size one needs the threat of violence'. This threat was not supplied by an entrepreneur belonging to the cartel; at most 'he owns a few caterpillars'. Without such a threat, as the OCTF in New York also found, 'bid-rigging conspiracies may founder because the conspirators are unable to police their cartels effectively' (1988, p. 38).

Irrespective of the method adopted, the general consequences of restrictive practices, as Reuter argued, are threefold: less efficient production, higher prices, and smaller firms.

> Less efficient production is engendered by the reduced incentive for lowering production costs; a firm cannot obtain an increase in market share by lowering costs, since all existing customers are allocated. ... The agreement also permits inefficient firms to stay in the market and prevents efficient firms from growing. The higher prices result directly from the imposition of restraints of trade. ... In each dimension, the effect is likely to be greater for a racket-run cartel than for other cartels. (Reuter, 1988, p. 7)

The first victims of collusion are consumers who end up purchasing lower-quality goods for higher prices. Potential competitors come next: successful collusion makes it almost impossible for outsiders even to contemplate entering an industry, and overt intimidation becomes redundant. This is why the enforcement of internal agreements is much more important than the brutal discouragement of rivals, even though the lack of entrepreneurial energy in the south of Italy makes the function less important there. Finally, since racketeers increase the confidence of participating entrepreneurs that the cartel will endure, incentives for efficient production are even more sharply reduced than they would be in a conventional cartel, where certainty about future success is always limited and the probability of imminent competition never vanishes.

The depressing effect on quality caused by mafia involvement can go further, especially in Sicily where inter-mafia conflicts have been more common than in the United States. The operation of the mafia is based on its reputation for effective contingent violence but that does not mean that actual violence is unknown. Both in New York and Sicily an occasional killing or act of violence has been required to discipline a cartel member. Though these acts are situation specific, they also serve to enhance the reputation of the mafia and augment the reputational barrier. However, when such acts of violence become 'too' frequent because of internecine wars – in Sicily during the 1980s several entrepreneurs died in the crossfire (Gambetta, 1993, pp. 191–4) – the barrier becomes so strong that those very few who venture to take up entrepreneurial activities must be selected from risk-prone individuals who both have little chance of an alternative (and less dangerous) career and are already tightly connected with a mafia family. Even discounting for the lack of incentives for efficient production enjoyed by mafia-protected cartels, this group is most unlikely to contain characters versed in proper entrepreneurial tasks.

7 Conditions of disappearance

Again we note that our set of case-studies is too small and diverse for the development of general propositions. The examples are interesting in themselves, however, as pointing to the variety of circumstances that can lead to the demise of mafia control. The fruit and vegetable market in Palermo is now largely competitive. Agents appear more concerned with quality than with establishing or violating collusive deals. The threat of violence seems as remote as in any normal business environment. Local authorities can take none of the credit for the market's evolution: 'The contacts which our group had with the present Mayor and the assessore all'Annona', concluded the Anti-Mafia Parliamentary Commission in 1969, 'gave us the impression, increasingly so, of lack of both interest and information, often coupled with open irritation towards those trying to unsettle a status quo which was not altogether disliked'.[6]

For years local authorities tolerated unfair dealing: for instance, an area of the market designated for use by producers selling without the intervention of middlemen was invaded by the most powerful *commissionari* who then cheekily levied a 10 per cent charge from farmers wanting to share it. In 1969 the Commission asked the Mayor why an area adjacent to the market was left unused instead of being developed into further stands. The Mayor replied that it was the site of a church that could not be demolished because of its artistic value. A letter of inquiry to the Soprintendenza delle Belle Arti of Palermo went unanswered. The members of the Commission went to see for themselves: they found a small chapel of no aesthetic merit being used as a garbage dump. In the same period, beautiful buildings, such as late nineteenth-century villas by

Basile, were ruthlessly demolished in Palermo to make room for urban speculators (Chubb, 1982, Ch. 6).

It was thanks to the central authorities, the Prefects and the Anti-Mafia Commission, that the process of expansion, already to some extent 'naturally' under way, was accelerated. The present director of the market concedes that the Palermo Prefect's policy of increasing the availability of permits was crucial in alleviating the troubles of the market. Permits rose particularly during the 1970s until the last increment, in 1981, brought the number of licences to 77.

Yet, if the action of public authorities were the sole factor which brought about competition, why has the same process not occurred at the fish market? The answer lies in the diverse nature of the commodities involved. The supply of fresh fish is constrained both by limited natural resources – which are either unaffected or depleted by technological development – and by the fact that it is channelled through a limited number of clearly identified ports. Fishing firms, furthermore, are fewer and easier to control than farmers. In the fruit and vegetable trade the sources of supply are both many and widely scattered, and transport routes and delivery points outside the wholesale market can multiply unnoticed.

The rapid increase in agricultural productivity and conservation techniques after the war, as well as the improved efficiency of transport, accentuated these differences and made it virtually impossible to monopolise produce. The only example of collusion mentioned by the Commission involving *commissionari* and their emissaries concerns a case in which distribution is forced through a bottleneck: by controlling the boats linking the small island of Pantelleria to the main island, a group known as L'Associazione made sure that the local cooperative sold the zibibbo grape exclusively to them. But in general, monopolies were already being eroded in the 1960s because, according to the Parliamentary Commission, 'wealthy wholesale and retail dealers collect directly from northern Italy and introduce ever-increasing quantities of good fruit for consumption'.

A further bottleneck has also been broken. Before the rural Casse di Risparmio started to function properly, credit was in the hands of the 'man of respect'. Producers who wanted credit were obliged to sell their goods to him. As sources multiplied credit no longer had the same kind of strings attached. It is now granted sparingly to customers rather than producers and is a means of fostering competition rather than enforcing collusion. Creditors are less inclined to resort to violence against insolvent debtors lest other clients are diverted to more benign rivals.

There are also instances of the New York mafia losing its influence in industries. The trucking industry, in which the mafia notoriously had acquired influence throughout much of the nation through the instrumentality of the Teamsters Union (three of whose presidents have been convicted of corruption), now seems to be much less subject to that influence. Two factors may have been significant here; deregulation of the industry (which reduced the power of the union) and aggressive and imaginative prosecution of the Teamster leadership (which resulted in a reform leadership being installed at the beginning of the 1990s).

However, most targeted efforts to remove the mafia from specific industries in the United States have been generally unsuccessful. In response to concerns about the role of the mafia (and lack of competition) in the carting industry in New Jersey and New York City, the industry has been subject to regulation (since 1956 in New York City and since 1968 in New Jersey). A flow of cases shows that the regulation has been utterly ineffective in New York City; the evidence concerning New Jersey is less clear but anti-competitive agreements, perhaps with mafia involvement, have been alleged as late as 1988. The regulatory apparatus had indeed become one of the tools for the operation of the customer allocation agreement. The regulators allowed the sale of customers and, through inflexible price rules in New Jersey, provided the basis for contesting new entry.

8   Prices and profits

The returns to participants in these cartels are difficult to determine. The available data are best for the carting industry, where customers are treated as assets and frequently bought and sold by the participants (Reuter, 1987).

The little we know of the charges by mafia members for their services suggests that, at least where the relationship with the industry is stable, those charges are surprisingly modest, indeed well below extortionate levels. In the Long Island carting industry in the mid-1980s it appeared that the mafia took no more than $400,000 annually in tribute, though the estimated profits accruing to the carters was over $10 million. The mafia-run concrete cartel in New York City levied only 2 per cent of the contract price for its services in fixing prices. As for Sicily we have the following evidence: in 1993, Baldassare di Maggio, a *pentito* we encountered already, describing the mafia's role in organising bid-rigging in construction, reported that they kept 5 per cent; 3 per cent was for the mafioso organisation and 2 per cent was given to Siino to pay the politicians that were paid as part of the overall agreement.

The fact that customers of carters are sold at such high prices in inter-carter transactions provided evidence that the primary beneficiaries of the agreement in that industry were the carters themselves. If the mafia taxed away all the returns from the agreement, then customers would have no greater value than they would in a competitive industry; in fact they sold for a very substantial mark-up over the competitive price.

We can offer no convincing explanation for these observations. If the mafia were marketing its cartel-organising services, then these might be seen as prices intended to maximise their profits over the entire market for such services. However, the peculiar lack of mafia entrepreneurialism – no new industries have been identified as being subject to mafia control over the last decades – weakens this supposition. Nor does it seem that the mafia lacks information about the profits generated to other actors in this business. Access to accounts of member enterprises is certainly not a problem in the New York markets in which the organisation is active. Finally, we do not believe that these prices are set so as to minimise the risk of aggressive informing by other participants.

9   Conclusions

We make no claim to have identified all the relationships between the mafia and legitimate enterprises. The casino industry in Nevada, where the mafia interest was confined to tax fraud, debt collection from bettors, and some bankruptcy scams involving capital from the Central States Teamsters pension fund, represents a very different situation. On the waterfront, in New York and Florida, the mafia seems to have used its power, again through the instrumentality of a union, to extort shippers, carriers and those providing services on the docks. In neither of these industries has it acted to suppress competition on a continuing basis. Yet, we believe that the phenomenon described in this paper is one that has received too little attention. The suppression of competition is a near-universal dream of established entrepreneurs. The mafia is one of the few non-governmental institutions that can help accomplish this goal. Our impression, based on a limited set of examples, is that once the mafia has entered, its success in meeting the needs of its customers, as well as its unique reputational asset, makes the reintroduction of competition extremely difficult. The phenomenon observed here may be just a generalised form of the Stigler–Peltzman theory of state regulation (Stigler, 1971; Peltzman, 1976). The state is unable or unwilling to meet the demand of entrepreneurs for profit-enhancing and risk-reducing regulation; the mafia provides the service instead.

The phenomenon is perhaps of more analytical than policy interest, since there are signs that it is now receding, mainly because the mafia itself appears to be diminished in power in both countries. In the United States, the results of a continued federal campaign have led to the conviction and long-term imprisonment of much of the leadership. In Sicily too the mafia never had it so bad and is now under unprecedented state pressure: virtually all mafiosi who sat in the mafia 'governing body', known as La Commissione, are now in jail. Mafioso assets worth 3,500 billion lire were seized by customs police in 1992 alone. At the same time, a new crop of mafiosi turning state witnesses has been growing and their revelations are leading to further arrests and repressive actions.[7] Mafia reputation may be, initially at least, little diminished by these imprisonments, but its ability to venture into new fields is probably limited by the inexperience of, and instability in, the new leadership. Furthermore, the current dramatic political changes in Italy are likely to decrease the opportunities for political corruption and bid-rigging which used to provide the major outlet for mafia-regulated cartels of building contractors. Finally, some of the market conditions that (jointly) facilitate mafia entry as a cartel organiser – such as low technology, unskilled labour and unionisation – occur less frequently now than when it acquired its influence over industries, mostly between 1920 and 1950.

The prospects for increasing our understanding of the phenomenon are being enhanced by the very forces that are diminishing the mafia's powers. Certainly the trials of the major families in both Sicily and various American cities (including Boston, Chicago, Kansas City and New York) have provided a wealth of detailed information on the relationship between the mafia and their legitimate clients which awaits analysis.

NOTES

1 Here we prudently use the term mafia as referring to the Sicilian mafia, also known as Cosa Nostra, both in Italy and the United States. Whether other broad and enduring criminal organisations supply the same service is a matter for empirical analysis to establish.
2 A curious case of failure of cooperation due to difficulties of both policing and sanctioning is represented by radio taxis in Palermo (see Gambetta, 1993, pp. 220–5).
3 Carting is the term used to describe the collection of solid waste, whether from households or commercial establishments. It does not include the collection of hazardous waste, where different possibilities exist for collusion and fraud.
4 'Up to perhaps six firms one has oligopoly, and with fifty or more firms of roughly similar size one has competition; however, for sizes in between it may be difficult to say'. This is the rule of thumb offered by James Friedman's textbook (1983, p. 8).
5 This is analogous to the argument which holds that widespread corruption is

self-generating: the expectation suffices to produce more of the thing itself (Andvig and Moene, 1990).

6 The case of this market is illustrated in full in Gambetta, 1993, pp. 206–14.

7 For a full assessment of the mafia's prospects in Sicily see the new introduction to the second Italian edition of Gambetta's *The Sicilian Mafia*, published by Einaudi (Torino) in 1994.

REFERENCES

Andvig, J. C. and K. O. Moene (1990), 'How Corruption May Corrupt', *Journal of Economic Behavior and Organization*, 13, pp. 63–76.

Bell, D. (1960), 'The Racket-ridden Longshoremen', in *The End of Ideology*, Glencoe IL: The Free Press.

Block, A. (1982), *East Side–West Side: Organizing Crime in New York, 1930–1950*, New Brunswick NJ: Transaction Press.

Chubb, J. (1982), *Patronage, Poverty and Power in Southern Italy: A Tale of Two Cities*, Cambridge: Cambridge University Press.

Dasgupta, P. (1988), 'Trust as a Commodity', in D. Gambetta (ed.) (1988).

Fiorentini, G. (1994), 'Cartels Run by Criminal Organizations and Market Contestability', unpublished paper, Department of Economics, Università di Firenze.

Franchetti, L. [1876] (1974), 'Condizione politiche ed amministrative della Sicilia', Vol. I of L. Franchetti and S. Sonnino (eds.), *Inchiesta in Sicilia*, Firenze: Vallecchi.

Friedman, A. (1988), *Agnelli and the Network of Italian Power*, London: Mandarin Paperback.

Friedman, J. (1983), *Oligopoly Theory*, Cambridge: Cambridge University Press.

Gambetta, D. (1988), (ed.), *Trust. Making and Breaking Cooperative Relations*, Oxford: Basil Blackwell.

Gambetta, D. (1993), *The Sicilian Mafia: The Business of Private Protection*, Cambridge MA: Harvard University Press.

Gosch, M. A. and R. Hammer (1975), *The Last Testament of Lucky Luciano*, London: Macmillan.

Landesco, J. [1929] (1968), 'Illinois Crime Survey, Part III', reprinted in *Organized Crime in Chicago* (with introduction by Mark Heller), Chicago: University of Chicago Press.

New Jersey State Commission of Investigation (1989), 'Solid Waste Regulation', Trenton NJ.

New York Organized Crime Task Force (1988), *Corruption and Racketeering in the Construction Industry*, New York: ILR Press.

Peltzman, S. (1976), 'Toward a More General Theory of Economic Regulation', *Journal of Law and Economics*, 19.

Reuter, P. (1983), *Disorganized Crime: The Economics of the Visible Hand*, Cambridge MA: MIT Press.

Reuter, P. (1987), *Racketeering in Legitimate Industries: A Study in the Economics of Intimidation*, Santa Monica CA: The Rand Corporation.

Reuter, P. (1993), 'The Commercial Cartage Industry in New York', in A. Reiss and M. Tonry (eds.), *Beyond the Law: Corrupt Organizations*, Vol.

18 of *Crime and Justice: A Review of Research*, Chicago: University of Chicago Press.

Reuter, P., J. Rubinstein and S. Wynn (1982), *Racketeering in Legitimate Industries: Two Case Studies*, Washington DC; National Institute of Justice.

Scherer, F. M. (1970), *Industrial Market Structure and Economic Performance*, Chicago: Rand-McNally.

Stigler, G. J. (1964), 'A Theory of Oligopoly', *Journal of Political Economy*, 72, February.

Stigler, G. J. (1971), 'The Theory of Economic Regulation', *Bell Journal of Economics and Management Science*, 2.

Discussion

LUIGI CAMPIGLIO

Gambetta and Reuter's timely study addresses the neglected problem of the mafia's role in legitimate activities in a new and intriguing way: their idea is that 'mafia solves a problem of potential cartels', by providing a paid service to entrepreneurs asking for 'profit-enhancing and risk-reducing regulation'. In their conclusion they seem to downplay the argument proposed, arguing that in recent years the mafia has been losing power and therefore that their analysis may be of 'more analytical than policy interest'. We think instead that it is too early to be optimistic: the problems raised by Gambetta and Reuter remain important because the mafia is an overlooked danger for the process of European unification and it could prove to be a major obstacle to the well-functioning of its market.

Their analysis offers some novel insights, together with some difficulties which we now consider in more detail. Put into economic terms their model implies a market for a peculiar service, namely the 'punishment' needed for implementing a stable cartel agreement: equilibrium in the market results from a legal demand curve, made up by the firms willing to form a cartel, and the illegal supply curve, provided by the mafia.

The alternative to this framework would be to consider the mafia as an exogenous 'auctioneer', but that would simply assume what has rather to be explained, namely the mafia's economic role. The nature of this market is intrinsically multi-periodic and changing over time: before selling this service the mafia is (by definition) a monopolist facing a downward demand curve. Once, in the first period, the contract is in force and the price for the service has been paid, the various demand curves of the firms collapse in the single demand curve of the cartel, which can be considered a new, single, fictitious agent acting for the newly formed cartel. In subsequent periods the market is therefore transformed into a double monopoly relationship. Instability of cartels is a well-known fact: if the mafia is successful in implementing a stable cartel, which is the condition for it to be paid the market price of its services, then a bilateral monopoly between a monopolistic seller and a fictitious monopsonistic buyer becomes the ongoing prevailing relationship in the market.

The equilibrium of this market is robust, as one should expect when dealing with the mafia. In fact it is a well-known result that, in a sequential game, a cartel can be sustained in a stable equilibrium by a credible punishment strategy, and indeed the mafia has the capability to implement this kind of strategy, Moreover it can be shown that bilateral monopoly produces a 'double' monopolistic inefficiency, thus helping to explain the detrimental effects of the mafia on economic performance.

This framework seems to account correctly for most of Gambetta and Reuter's results: there are however problems that should be better articulated. The necessary condition which, in the first period, starts the agreement is the existence of gains from trade, namely further profits of the legal cartel that exceed the cost of its enforcement by the illegal mafia. In the case of a bilateral monopoly, the gains from trade are distributed according to the bargaining power of the two monopolists, which, in turn, is related to the distribution of information. Costs cannot be assumed to be common knowledge: the mafia will know better the costs of the cartel's firms, while the cartel, as well as each firm, will find it impossible to know the costs of the mafia. Asymmetric information will, in time, raise the share of the surplus that accrues to the mafia, unless the two monopolists can reach a credible agreement in advance, in the form of an implicit fixed-price contract.

Gambetta and Reuter produce examples of implicit contracts, like in the cartel of the concrete industry in New York City, where the mafia 'levied only 2 per cent of the contract price': however, it is not possible to assess whether 2 per cent is too little or too much unless one considers also the costs for the mafia and the profits for the concrete industry. Indeed, we will argue later, the nature of this contract seems more in the nature of a tax rather than a market price: profits for the mafia will be less volatile than the profits for the cartel because the mafia has shifted part of the market risk on to the cartel.

Moreover, this kind of contract raises again the more general point about information in a bilateral monopoly: given a structure involving asymmetric information, the two parties will usually introduce clauses that allow reciprocal auditing. When common knowledge about costs is impossible, however, because reciprocal auditing is not feasible, vertical integration of firms becomes an efficient answer to both the problems of auditing and risk sharing (Arrow, 1975). In fact one can give countless examples of this economic behaviour between legal firms: the case for vertical integration seems still stronger, as a possibility, when the mafia is present.

This possibility is worthy of exploration by the authors, because the further expansion of the mafia in the legal sectors will increasingly depend on vertical integration. The obvious example is when the mafia simply 'buys' the firm, but the most crucial case seems to be the one in which the mafia is going to have a 'minority' stake in a legal and well-functioning firm. This could easily be the case even in competitive and advanced sectors, where 'venture capitalists' fund new and innovative firms: the seeming absence of the mafia in these sectors requires an explanation which goes beyond the market and technological difficulties of forming cartels underlined by the authors.

We should consider more fully that the mafia is highly risk averse and particularly sensitive to the risk of cheating, which is usually, but not necessarily, more likely in higher-risk sectors, like high technology. Gambetta and Reuter should also better define the nature of the service exchanged, which can be thought of as the punishment or the cartel stability (allowed by the threat of punishment). The mafia provides a service which has the characteristics of a local public good: in fact cartel stability is a service that cannot be individually appropriated and for which not every firm can benefit by excluding the others. The market underlying the bilateral monopoly is indeed a market for a public good: as a consequence we have to cope with the typical problems related to the efficient provision of a public good, namely the free-rider problem and the assessment of the individual willingness to pay. The consequence is that market prices must be replaced with personalised (Lindahl) prices which correspond to the individual willingness to pay: the informational problem, already pervasive, now becomes fundamental, because we are dealing with the peculiar market structure of a bilateral monopoly for a public good. Inadequate information prevents the implementation of Lindahl prices and explains why, in the real economies, we revert to compulsory taxation for financing the provision of public goods.

We must conclude that, in Gambetta and Reuter's model, the theoretical distinction between market prices and taxes is logically blurred: their empirical examples seem to support more the intuition of taxes rather than prices. This difficulty mirrors the equally ambiguous distinction between voluntary and involuntary economic behaviour, whose explanation is much harder then expected. In a witty remark about involuntary unemployment, Patinkin (1965, p. 313) cited the Talmudic dictum that – in certain cases of private law where the formal consent of an individual is required – the court is permitted 'to coerce him until he says "I am willing" '. The remark seems especially apt when dealing with the mafia, because the distinction between voluntary and involuntary exchanges appears still more confused.

The alternative approach of the mafia as a quasi-governmental institution which levies taxes has been pursued elsewhere with more detail (Campiglio, 1993): it has the advantage of offering some new insights like that of 'comparative disadvantage'. In conclusion, Gambetta and Reuter offer a timely and provocative interpretation of the mafia: in fact there are good reasons to believe that the mafia could pose a serious danger to the process of European integration. The paper offers a rich array of insights and, hopefully, could trigger a wider debate. Economists could offer the contribution of rigorous economic arguments, exploring new lines (like that of endogenous uncertainty) and helping to design a new policy to fight effectively the economic and social tragedy of the mafia.

REFERENCES

Arrow, K. (1975), 'Vertical Integration and Communication', in *Bell Journal of Economics and Management Science*, 6, pp. 173–83.
Campiglio, L. (1993), 'Le relazioni di fiducia nello Stato e nel mercato', in S. Zamagni (ed.), *Mercati illegali e mafie*, Bologna: Il Mulino.
Patinkin, D. (1965), *Money, Interest and Prices*, second edition, Harper International.

Part III
Organised crime and state intervention in the economy

6 Rival kleptocrats: the mafia versus the state

HERSCHEL I. GROSSMAN

Until two or three hundred years ago, it was characteristic almost everywhere – and to this day, it is characteristic in the majority of countries and in countries containing the majority of the world's population – that the primary government activity was and is extraction of surpluses from the predominantly agricultural population and use of such surpluses, to benefit tiny groups of people in and near the government. Edwin Mills, *The Burden of Government* (1986), p. 134

Republicans and Democrats have forged a political class to divy up the spoils, fighting only over precisely how to pick pockets. *The Wall Street Journal*, October 24, 1990

1 Introduction

Motivated by observations such as these, recent research has developed a positive theory of what I have called 'proprietary public finance', or, more colourfully, 'kleptocracy'. [See, for example, Lane, 1958; Auster and Silver, 1979; Lal, 1988; Bardhan, 1990; Findlay, 1990; or Grossman and Noh, 1990, 1994.] This theory assumes that the objective of the state's tax and spending policy is to extract maximum rent for the group that comprises the ruling class or political establishment. Historical examples of such groups include a monarchy and its court, the professional politicians, the bureaucrats, the members of the ruling party, or the military. In stable democracies, the existing political establishment can be an explicit or implicit coalition that draws in political factions regardless of party labels. The theory of kleptocracy takes the objective of maximising political rent to be a generic property of the state and models differences in policy choices as resulting from differences in the constraints that the actions or potential actions of agents who are not members of the incumbent ruling class or political establishment impose on the state's ability to extract political rent.

143

In previous papers (Grossman and Noh, 1990, 1994), we modelled the revenue-maximising tax rate as dependent only on technology and preferences. This analysis tried to explain, within a dynamic framework that emphasised the interplay of taxation and the survival and credibility of the incumbent political establishment, why the equilibrium tax rate might differ from the revenue-maximising tax rate.

The model in the present paper is complementary. The analysis is static, but it explicitly introduces a competitor to the state in the provision of essential public services. A prime example of an essential public service that is subject to competitive provision is the enforcement of property rights. I denote the state's competitor as the mafia. Following other authors – see Anderson and Gambetta and Reuter in this volume as well as Gambetta (1988, 1993) and Zamagni (1992) for especially suggestive discussions – I take the view that in fact one main economic effect of criminal organisations derives from their role as alternative providers of public services, especially as alternative enforcers of property rights.

Within this framework, the analysis shows how the state's revenue-maximising tax rate depends not only on technology and preferences but also on the competition that the state faces from the mafia. I assume, of course, that the mafia is as greedy as the state. Nevertheless, competition between the state and the mafia can increase net total production as well as the welfare of the representative producer.

I do not assume, however, that the net economic effects of the mafia are necessarily benign. I also allow for the possibility that the mafia's activities are socially disruptive. For example, the violent methods used by the mafia to enforce property rights for its clientele can make the property rights of the state's clientele less secure. In this case, the state must allocate resources to offset these disruptive effects of the mafia's activities and to maintain the tax base. The analysis focuses on the tension between the mafia's benign competitive effect and its socially disruptive effect.

2   Production with a monopoly state

Consider a simple production economy in which the representative producer divides his resources between a non-negative fraction ℓ, devoted to legal production, on which he is subject to taxation, and a non-negative fraction $1 - \ell$, devoted to extralegal production, on which he avoids taxation. Extralegal production includes both production of illegal goods and services and unreported production of legal goods and services. Both legal production and extralegal production require the producer's own resources to be combined with public services. These productive public services are subject to congestion – that is, they are not nonrival – but they are public by virtue of being nonexcludable, at least in their use in legal production. [This assumption fits the example of the enforcement of property rights, which would involve such services as the police and the courts. It also would be possible to apply a similar analysis to public services such as licensing or cartel enforcement that increase the incomes of producers but do not enhance their productivity. Gambetta and Reuter, in this volume, describe the mafia's role as a cartel enforcer.]

The state provides the representative producer with g units of public services, $g \geq 0$. The representative producer chooses to use pg units of these state services in legal production, $0 \leq p \leq 1$, and as a result has $\gamma(1 - p)g$ units to use in extralegal production, $0 \leq \gamma < 1$.

The parameter γ measures the ability of the state to exclude state services from use in extralegal production. For example, γ could reflect the ability of the police to distinguish between legal and extralegal production and to refrain from enforcing property rights in extralegal production. In the polar case of $\gamma = 0$, state services are useless in extralegal production. For $\gamma > 0$, the larger is γ, the more useful are state services in extralegal production. As γ approaches unity, state services become as useful in extralegal production as in legal production.

Legal production and extralegal production have identical concave technologies. Specifically, the quantity of legal production is y, where:

$$y = \ell^{\alpha}(pg)^{1-\alpha}, \; 0 < \alpha < 1 \tag{1}$$

and the quantity of extralegal production is z, where:

$$z = (1 - \ell)^{\alpha}[\gamma(1 - p)g]^{1-\alpha}. \tag{2}$$

According to equations (1) and (2), private resources and public services have positive and diminishing marginal products and are complementary inputs, both of which are essential for production. Also, returns to scale in both legal production and extralegal production are constant. This assumption means that the technology does not determine optimal relative sizes for legal production and extralegal production. [In contrast, some authors – see, for example, Lane (1958) and Lal (1988, pp. 294 ff.) – assume that there are economies of scale in the provision of public services. This assumption would preclude the coexistence of the mafia and the state.]

The tax rate on legal production is t, $0 \leq t \leq 1$. The utility of the representative producer, denoted by u, increases with his net income, which is the sum of his legal production net of taxes and his extralegal production. Specifically,

$$u = (1 - t)y + z \qquad (3)$$

[This set-up assumes that extralegal production enhances utility just as much as legal production.]

The representative producer's problem is to choose ℓ and p to maximise u, subject to the production technology given by equations (1) and (2), taking t and g as given. The solution to this problem is:

$$\ell = p = \begin{cases} 1 \text{ for } t \leq 1 - \eta \\ 0 \text{ for } t > 1 - \eta \end{cases} \qquad (4)$$

where $\eta \equiv \gamma^{1-\alpha}$. Equation (4) says that, if and only if the tax rate is not higher than $1 - \eta$, the representative producer allocates all of his own resources to legal production and also uses all of his state services in legal production. Otherwise, the representative producer would allocate all of his resources to extralegal production and would use all of his state services in extralegal production. Accordingly, for the state to be viable, the tax rate cannot exceed $1 - \eta$.

3   Welfare maximisation with a monopoly state

Suppose, for the moment, that the objective of the state were to maximise the welfare of the representative producer. In this event, the state's problem would be to choose g and t to maximise u, as given by equation (3), subject to the production technology, given by equations (1) and (2), subject to the behaviour of the representative producer, given by equation (4), and subject to the state's budget constraint, $ty \geq g$. The solution to this problem satisfies the following first-order conditions: either $\frac{\partial u}{\partial g} = 0$ with $g \leq (1 - \eta)y$ or $\frac{\partial u}{\partial g} > 0$ with $g = (1 - \eta)y$, where $\frac{\partial u}{\partial g} = (1 - \alpha)\frac{y}{g} - 1$, and $\frac{\partial u}{\partial t} < 0$ with $t = \frac{g}{y}$. These first-order conditions imply:

$$g = \min[(1 - \alpha)^{1/\alpha}, (1 - \eta)^{1/\alpha}] \qquad (5)$$

and:

$$t = \min\ (1 - \alpha, 1 - \eta). \tag{6}$$

Given these choices for g and t, the values of the remaining variables are: $\ell = 1$, $z = 0$, $u = y - g = \min[\alpha(1 - \alpha)^{\frac{1-\alpha}{\alpha}}, \eta(1 - \eta)^{\frac{1-\alpha}{\alpha}}]$, and $ty = g$.

Equations (5) and (6) indicate that, under a welfare-maximising policy, the tax rate does not exceed $1 - \eta$, with the result that all production is legal, and the state's budget constraint is satisfied as an equality, with the result that the state extracts zero political rent. Moreover, if $\alpha \geq \eta$, then the constraint that the tax rate not exceed $1 - \eta$ is not binding, and the state expands the provision of state services until the marginal product of state services equals unity. In this case, net production, $y - g$, equals its technically feasible maximum.

Alternatively, if $\alpha < \eta$, then the constraint that the tax rate not exceed $1 - \eta$ is binding and the state cannot raise enough tax revenue to expand the provision of state services until the marginal product of state services equals unity. With the marginal product of state services greater than unity, net production is less than its technically feasible maximum. In this case, the ability of producers to use state services in extralegal production prevents an optimal allocation of resources and reduces welfare, even though all production is actually legal.

4   Kleptocratic policy with a monopoly state

The objective of a proprietary or kleptocratic state is to maximise political rent, rather than to maximise the welfare of the representative producer. Political rent, denoted by r, is equal to tax revenue, ty, minus provision of state services, g. Thus, the problem for the kleptocratic state is to choose g and t to maximise

$$r = ty - g \tag{7}$$

subject to the production technology, given by equation (1), and subject to the behaviour of the representative producer, given by equation (4). The solution to this problem satisfies the first-order conditions $\frac{\partial r}{\partial g} = t(1 - \alpha)\frac{y}{g} - 1 = 0$ and $\frac{\partial r}{\partial t} > 0$ with $t = 1 - \eta$. These first-order conditions imply:

$$g = [(1 - \eta)(1 - \alpha)]^{1/\alpha} \tag{8}$$

and:

$$t = 1 - \eta. \tag{9}$$

Given these choices for g and t, the values of the remaining variables are:
$\ell = 1$, $z = 0$, $y - g = [1 - (1 - \eta)(1 - \alpha)][(1 - \eta)(1 - \alpha)]^{\frac{1-\alpha}{\alpha}}$, $u = \eta[(1 - \eta)(1 - \alpha)]^{\frac{1-\alpha}{\alpha}}$, and $r = y - g - u = \alpha(1 - \eta)^{\frac{1}{\alpha}}(1 - \alpha)^{\frac{1-\alpha}{\alpha}}$.

Equations (8) and (9) indicate that, under a political-rent-maximising policy, the state sets the tax rate equal to the maximum tax rate at which all private resources and all state services are used in legal production. This tax rate is either as high as or higher than the tax rate under a welfare-maximising policy. Also, the state provides less state services than under a welfare-maximising policy. Consequently, although all production is still legal, net production as well as the utility of the representative producer are less than under a welfare-maximising policy. But now political rent is positive.

In addition, the tax rate, the provision of state services, net production and the amount of political rent all are negatively related to η. But the net income and utility of the representative producer is positively related to η for $\eta < \alpha$ and negatively related to η for $\eta > \alpha$. In other words, up to a point, the ability of producers to use state services in extralegal production increases the equilibrium net income of the representative producer, although it decreases political rent as well as net production, but after a point the ability of producers to use state services in extralegal production causes the state to decrease the provision of state services so much that even the net income of the representative producer is decreased.

5   The mafia as an alternative provider of public services

> The distinction between robber and cop, between extortion and taxation, has been blurred at many times in human history. Robert Claiborne, *Climate, Man, and History* (1970), pp. 266–7

> Palermo's chief prosecutor, Giancarlo Caselli, describes the Mafia ··· as a state within the state, 'with its own territory, population and laws' ····. 'The Mafia's determination to establish itself as a state within the state is what makes it unique,' says Roberto Scarpinato, one of 13 Palermo prosecutors committed full-time to Mafia enquiries. And the would-be state not only imposes its own laws – at gunpoint – but levies its own taxes. *The Economist*, April 24, 1993, pp. 21–2

In the preceding analysis, the state had a monopoly over the provision of public services, but the ability of producers to use state services in extralegal production constrained the tax rate as well as the amount of political rent that the state could extract from producers. This section introduces the mafia as an alternative provider of public services for extralegal production. The analysis distinguishes the mafia as a provider of public services from the representative producer who uses mafia services in extralegal production. [This set-up abstracts from the recent tendency, documented by Pino Arlacchi (1986), for the mafia to expand its role from the provision of public services for extralegal production to direct involvement in extralegal production.]

The mafia provides the representative producer with h units of public services, $h \geq 0$. These mafia services are not useful in legal production, but are fully available for use in extralegal production. Accordingly, the quantity of extralegal production becomes:

$$z = (1 - \ell)^{\alpha}[\gamma(1 - p)g + h]^{1-\alpha}. \tag{10}$$

Equation (10) generalises equation (2).

But the mafia is not Santa Claus. For one thing the mafia extorts revenue from extralegal production at the rate x, $0 \leq x \leq 1$. [For simplicity, the analysis abstracts from the possibility that the mafia might try to extort revenue from legal production, to which it provides no services.] The mafia chooses h and x to maximise its net revenue, denoted by q, where:

$$q = xz - h \tag{11}$$

Accordingly the net income and utility of the representative producer becomes:

$$u = (1 - t)y + (1 - x)z. \tag{12}$$

Equation (12) generalises equation (3). In addition, mafia services can be disruptive to the provision of state services and, hence, disruptive to legal production. This effect is analysed in a subsequent section.

The representative producer's problem now is to choose ℓ and p to maximize u, as given by equation (12), subject to the production technology given by equations (1) and (10), taking t, g, x and h as given. The solution to this problem satisfies the following first-order conditions: either $\frac{\partial u}{\partial p} \geq 0$ with $p = 1$ or $\frac{\partial u}{\partial p} < 0$ with $p = 0$, where $\frac{\partial u}{\partial p} = (1 - t)(1 - \alpha)\frac{y}{p}$ $-(1 - x)(1 - \alpha)\frac{\gamma gz}{\gamma(1-p)g+h}$, and $\frac{\partial u}{\partial \ell} = (1 - t)\alpha\frac{y}{\ell} - (1 - x)\alpha\frac{z}{1-\ell} = 0$. These first-order conditions imply:

$$\frac{\ell}{1-\ell} = \left(\frac{1-t}{1-x}\right)^{\frac{1}{1-\alpha}} \frac{pg}{\gamma(1-p)g+h} \tag{13}$$

and

$$p = \begin{cases} 1 \text{ for } 1-t \ge \eta(1-x) \\ 0 \text{ for } 1-t < \eta(1-x) \end{cases} \tag{14}$$

Equation (13) indicates that the representative producer allocates a larger fraction of his resources to legal production, and a smaller fraction to extralegal production, the lower is the state's tax rate, the larger is the provision of state services, the higher is the mafia's extortion rate, and the smaller is the provision of mafia services. Equation (14) indicates that, if and only if the tax rate is low enough that $1-t \ge \eta(1-x)$, then the representative producer allocates all of his state services to legal production.

In attempting to maximise political rent, the state now faces a situation in which, the higher the tax rate on legal production relative to the extortion rate on extralegal production and the smaller the provision of state services relative to the provision of mafia services, the smaller the fraction of private resources that are allocated to legal production and the larger the fraction allocated to extralegal production. The mafia, in attempting to maximise its net revenue, faces an analogous situation.

Consider a Nash equilibrium in which the state and the mafia each take the behaviour of the other as given. [In assuming a Nash equilibrium, the model abstracts from the possibility of collusion between the mafia and the state, also documented by Arlacchi (1986).] In a Nash equilibrium the state's problem is to choose t and g to maximise r, as given by equation (7), subject to the production technology for legal production, given by equation (1), and subject to the behaviour of the representative producer, given by equations (13) and (14), taking x and h as given. The solution to this problem satisfies the following first-order conditions:

$$\frac{\partial r}{\partial g} = t\left[(1-\alpha)\frac{y}{g} + \alpha\frac{y}{\ell}\frac{\partial \ell}{\partial g}\right] - 1 = 0 \tag{15}$$

and

$$\frac{\partial r}{\partial t} = y + t\alpha \frac{y}{\ell} \frac{\partial \ell}{\partial t} = 0, \tag{16}$$

where $\frac{\partial \ell}{\partial g}$ and $\frac{\partial \ell}{\partial t}$ are derived from equation (13).

The mafia's problem is to choose x and h to maximise q, as given by equation (11), subject to the production technology for extralegal production, given by equation (10) and subject to the behaviour of the representative producer, given by equations (13) and (14), taking t and g as given. The solution to the mafia's problem satisfies the following first-order conditions:

$$\frac{\partial q}{\partial h} = x\left[(1-\alpha)\frac{z}{h} + \alpha \frac{z}{1-\ell}\frac{\partial \ell}{\partial h}\right] - 1 = 0 \tag{17}$$

and:

$$\frac{\partial q}{\partial x} = z - x\alpha \frac{z}{1-\ell}\frac{\partial \ell}{\partial x} = 0, \tag{18}$$

where $\frac{\partial \ell}{\partial h}$ and $\frac{\partial \ell}{\partial x}$ are derived from equation (13).

6   Nash equilibrium

To compute the Nash equilibrium outcome of the competition between the mafia and the state, we solve equations (13)–(18) simultaneously for t, g, x, h, p and ℓ. The solution to this system of equations is:

$$g = h = \frac{1}{2}(1-\alpha)^{\frac{1}{\alpha}} \tag{19}$$

and:

$$t = x = \frac{1-\alpha}{1-\frac{\alpha}{2}}, \tag{20}$$

as well as $p = 1$ and $\ell = 1 - \ell = \frac{1}{2}$. Further, these values for t, x, g, h, p and ℓ imply: $y - g = z - h = \frac{\alpha}{2}(1-\alpha)^{\frac{1-\alpha}{\alpha}}$, $u = \frac{\frac{\alpha}{2}}{1-\frac{\alpha}{2}}(1-\alpha)^{\frac{1-\alpha}{\alpha}}$, and $r = q = \frac{1}{2}\frac{\frac{\alpha}{2}}{1-\frac{\alpha}{2}}(1-\alpha)^{\frac{1}{\alpha}}$.

Equations (19) and (20) indicate that competition between the mafia and the state causes the tax rate on legal production to equal the extortion rate on extralegal production and also causes the provision of mafia services to equal the provision of state services. Consequently, the representative producer uses all of his state services in legal production and, in this simple model, divides his own resources equally between legal production and extralegal production. As a result, legal production and extralegal production are equal.

More importantly, both the marginal product of state services and the marginal product of mafia services equal unity. Consequently, net total production, which is the sum of net legal production, $y - g$, and net extralegal production, $z - h$, equals its technically feasible maximum. Thus, net total production is higher than net total production would be under a political-rent-maximising policy with a monopoly state and it is as high as or higher than net total production would be under a welfare-maximising policy with a monopoly state.

Furthermore, the net income and utility of the representative producer is higher than it would be under a political-rent-maximising policy with a monopoly state. Competition between the mafia and the state benefits the representative producer. More surprisingly, the net income and utility of the representative producer can be even higher than it would be under a welfare-maximising policy with a monopoly state. This result would obtain if the parameter η were sufficiently larger than α for the maximum tax rate that a monopoly state could impose to be much less than $1 - \alpha$. In addition, although the state's political rent and the mafia's net revenue are positive and equal, each is less than the maximum political rent of a monopoly state. But if η is sufficiently large, then the sum of the state's political rent and the mafia's net revenue is larger than the maximum political rent of a monopoly state.

In sum, given a Nash equilibrium, competition between the mafia and the state reduces political rent, and it increases net total production to its technically feasible maximum, which may not be achievable even under a welfare-maximising policy with a monopoly state. In addition, competition between the mafia and the state increases the net income of the representative producer, perhaps even relative to a welfare-maximising policy with a monopoly state, and it can even increase the excess of net total production over the net income of the representative producer. According to this analysis, the existence of the mafia harms only the members of the ruling class or political establishment whose main source of income is political rent.

The critical factor underlying the beneficial effects of competition between the mafia and the state is that, because the mafia provides services for use in extralegal production and imposes an extortion rate on extralegal production equal to the tax rate on legal production, the representative producer uses all of his state services in legal production.

Thus, in choosing t and g the state behaves as if the parameters γ and η were equal to zero. At the same time, with an active mafia, the state is concerned about the mafia's efforts to attract private resources into extralegal production, and the state both reduces its tax rate and increases its provision of state services, to meet this competition.

7   Disruptive effects of the mafia

The preceding sections analysed the effect of the mafia as an alternative provider of public services under the assumption that mafia services are as socially productive as state services. This section considers the possibility that mafia services are disruptive to the provision of state services and, hence, disruptive to legal production. Specifically, we assume that, with the mafia in action, the net provision of state services is G, where:

$$G = g - \beta h, \quad \beta \geq 0. \tag{21}$$

The parameter β measures the disruptive effect of mafia services. The previous analysis dealt with the case of $\beta = 0$.

[Another way to introduce a negative effect of mafia activity would be to assume that extralegal production, perhaps like the drug trade, generates negative externalities for legal production. Yet another possibility would be to assume that extralegal activity is appropriative, like theft, rather than productive. Either of these models would be similar, but not fully isomorphic, to the model analysed here.]

Given equation (21), the quantities of legal production and extralegal production are still as given by equations (1) and (10), but with G appearing in place of g. Accordingly, the first-order conditions for the representative producer's maximisation of utility, for the state's maximisation of political rent, and for the mafia's maximisation of net revenue are unchanged from equations (13)–(18), except that G now appears in place of g. [This set-up assumes that the mafia now takes G, rather than g, as given. This assumption involves a slight departure from a strict Nash equilibrium, but it simplifies the analysis without affecting the main results.]

Accordingly, as long as maximum political rent remains non-negative, the Nash equilibrium is exactly as given in the preceding section except for two differences. First, G appears in place of g in equation (19). In other words, the state responds to any disruptive effect of the mafia by increasing the provision of state services by the amount βh. Solving for g, we now obtain $g = \frac{1+\beta}{2}(1-\alpha)^{\frac{1}{\alpha}}$. Second, because g is increased, both net legal production and political rent are reduced. Specifically, we now have $y - g = \frac{1}{2}[\alpha - \beta(1-\alpha)](1-\alpha)^{\frac{1-\alpha}{\alpha}}$ and $r = \frac{1}{2}(\frac{\frac{\alpha}{2}}{1-\frac{\alpha}{2}} - \beta)(1-\alpha)^{\frac{1}{\alpha}}$.

In this case, because the equilibrium values of t, G, x and h are independent of β, the net income of the representative producer as well as the net revenue of the mafia are also independent of β. Although the disruptive effect of the mafia reduces net legal production and net total production, this entire reduction shows up as reduced political rent for the state.

As we see from the above expression for r, the necessary and sufficient condition for political rent to be non-negative is $\beta \leq \frac{\frac{\alpha}{2}}{1-\frac{\alpha}{2}}$. This condition says that the disruptive effect of mafia services cannot be too large. If this condition is not satisfied, then the state cannot pay its way and is not viable. In this event, competition between the mafia and the state would leave the mafia as the monopoly provider of public services. In other words, the mafia would 'take over'. For the representative producer, a mafia monopoly would be at least as undesirable as a monopoly state. [Whether or not the mafia would be able to preserve its monopoly in the long run would depend on its ability to disrupt the provision of public services by all potential competitors.]

8   Conclusions

This paper has developed a model of the mafia as a competitor to the state in the provision of public services and has analysed the effect of competition between the mafia and the state on the allocation of resources and the distribution of income. The model implies that, as long as the state remains viable, competition between the mafia and the state increases the provision of public services and, thereby, also increases the net income of the representative producer. In fact, the net income and utility of the representative producer can be higher if a kleptocratic state faces the competition of the mafia than it would be if the state were a benevolent monopolistic provider of public services. Accordingly, as long as the state remains viable, the representative producer should support the continued existence of the mafia.

Furthermore, as long as the state remains viable, the existence of the mafia reduces the income only of members of the ruling class or political establishment whose main source of income is political rent extracted by the state. Accordingly, this group should be the only source of opposition to the mafia. Opposition to the mafia would be widespread only if this group is large.

If the activities of the mafia are so disruptive as to threaten the viability of the state, however, – that is, if the mafia threatens 'to take over' – then the representative producer faces the prospect of the mafia as the monopoly provider of public services. In this event, the representative producer would have reason to oppose the mafia and to support the political establishment in taking actions that preserve the state as a competitor of the mafia. Nevertheless, although the representative producer should want to weaken the mafia enough to prevent a mafia monopoly, it would not be in his interest for the mafia to be destroyed and for the state to be a monopoly provider of public services.

Competition between the mafia and the state for the market for public services is not the only phenomenon that can limit the ability of the incumbent political establishment to extract political rent. In practice, competition between the mafia and the state as alternative providers of public services can be either a substitute for or a supplement to political competition among different potential ruling groups for control of the state. Why at certain times and places competition between the mafia and the state has been more or less important relative to political competition for control of the state remains an intriguing question for future research.

REFERENCES

Anderson, A. G. (1995), 'Organised Crime, Mafia and Governments', Ch. 2, this volume.

Arlacchi, P. (1986), *Mafia Business: The Mafia Ethic and the Spirit of Capitalism* (translated by Martin Ryle), London: Verso.

Auster, R. and M. Silver (1979), *The State as a Firm: Economic Forces in Political Development*, Boston: Martinus Nijhoff.

Bardhan, P. (1990), 'Symposium on the State and Economic Development', *Journal of Economic Perspectives*, 4, Summer, pp. 3–7.

Claiborne, R. (1990), *Climate, Man, and History*, New York: W. W. Norton & Co.

Findlay, R. (1990), 'The New Political Economy: Its Explanatory Power for LDC's', *Economics and Politics*, 2, July, pp. 193–221.

Gambetta, D. (1988), 'Fragments of an Economic Theory of the Mafia', *Archives Européennes de Sociologie*, 29, pp. 127–45.

Gambetta, D. (1993), *The Sicilian Mafia: The Business of Private Protection*, Cambridge MA: Harvard University Press.

Gambetta, D. and P. Reuter (1995), 'Conspiracy among the Many: The Mafia in Legitimate Industries', Ch. 5, this volume.

Grossman, H. I. and S. J. Noh (1990), 'A Theory of Kleptocracy with Probabilistic Survival and Reputation', *Economics and Politics*, 2, July, pp. 157–71.

Grossman, H. I. and S. J. Noh (1994), 'Proprietary Public Finance and Economic Welfare', *Journal of Public Economics*, 53, February, pp. 187–204.

156 Discussion by Marco Celentani

Lal, D. (1988), *Cultural Stability and Economic Stagnation*, Oxford: Clarendon Press.
Lane, F. (1958), 'Economic Consequences of Organized Violence', *Journal of Economic History*, 18, December, pp. 401–17.
Mills, E. (1986), *The Burden of Government*, Stanford CA: The Hoover Institution.
Zamagni, S. (ed.) (1992), *Criminalità organizzata e dilemmi della mutua sfiducia: sulla persistenze dell'equilibrio mafioso*, unpublished, October.

Discussion

MARCO CELENTANI

1 Competition between mafia and the government

The presence of a criminal organisation affects the allocation of resources and the surplus they produce in several different ways. The most obvious way in which criminal activity affects the economic decisions of other agents is through the imposition of externalities of different kinds. Many times, however, criminal organisations carry out production activities that can actually generate surplus. This production activity can take the form of direct production of a consumption good or production of inputs that are used in turn for the production of consumption goods.

Grossman's purpose is to study how the production of input services by the mafia affects the government's fiscal policy, i.e. how the amount of production services produced by the government and the tax rates it sets are affected in equilibrium when another organisation can produce alternative production services and can impose 'taxes' on the people that use such services.

The model employed in the paper is a static representative agent model in which a government produces 'public services' that are an input for the private sector that can engage in the legal or extralegal production of a final good.

Grossman first deals with the case in which the government is a monopolistic supplier of the public services needed for legal production. In this case, if the tax rate is too high, private agents will use all their labour inputs and all government-produced public services in extralegal production even though marginal productivity in extralegal production is lower. Grossman shows that this constraint can be binding even if the government's objective is to maximise social welfare and is always binding for a 'kleptocratic government', i.e. for a government that seeks to maximise its 'political rent'. The remarkable aspect of the latter case is the underprovision of public services on the part of the government compared with the welfare maximisation case, and the consequent efficiency loss.

The fact that a criminal organisation can provide alternative public services to the ones produced by the government introduces some degree of competition to the government. The mafia, like the government, is assumed to be able to finance its production of public services by income tax, or income 'extortion'.

Competition between mafia and the government leads in equilibrium to the striking result that net total production is the optimal one, so that the utility of the representative private agent is higher than in the case with a monopolistic government and can even be higher than his utility with a welfare-maximising government if the government is constrained by the possibility of extralegal production.

2   Free riding

The important implication of the previous result is that competition between mafia and the government leads to an efficient allocation of resources. As is clear, such a result depends on the fact that in equilibrium no portion of government-produced public services is used in extralegal production, so that no free riding occurs. It seems interesting to find out how such a result is modified when some portion of government-produced public services is used in extralegal production in equilibrium.

To do this it will be assumed that the government-produced public service is a pure public good, which means in particular that it is non-rival in use for production. Making this assumption is equivalent to shifting the focus of the problem to address the question of how the fact that a criminal organisation can provide a free-riding technology affects the allocation of resources in an economy.

Suppose that legal and extralegal production are described by the following production functions: $y(\ell, g) = \ell^\alpha g^{1-\alpha}$, and $z(\ell, g, h) = (1 - \ell)^\alpha g^{1-\alpha} h$, where $h \in \{0, 1\}$ and $0 < \alpha < 1$. This means that a representative producer can use its labour input and the government-produced public good in extralegal production, provided that $h = 1$, i.e. provided that the mafia provides a free-riding technology.

Suppose that, as above, both the government and the mafia can only finance the production of the public good through income taxation (extortion), and that the representative producer chooses an allocation of labour inputs that maximises the utility of its net income. In this case the solution to his utility maximisation problem will be:

$$\ell = \frac{(1-t)^{\frac{1}{1-\alpha}}}{(1-x)^{\frac{1}{1-\alpha}} + (1-t)^{\frac{1}{1-\alpha}}} \tag{1}$$

Suppose that the mafia's public good production cost is low enough, so that in equilibrium the free-riding technology will be provided $(h = 1)$. Then the equilibrium is given by a tax rate and an amount of the public good that maximises the government's political rent, and by an extortion rate that maximises the mafia's net revenue. These are given by the solution to the following system of equations:

$$\frac{\partial r}{\partial t} = 0, \quad \frac{\partial r}{\partial g} = 0, \quad \frac{\partial q}{\partial x} = 0. \tag{2}$$

Since the government-produced public good can be used for both legal and extralegal production, the allocation of labour inputs is not affected by its level (see equation (1)) and the solution to (2) is one in which the tax rate and the extortion rate will be equal to each other:

$$t = x = \frac{1 - \alpha}{1 - \alpha/2}. \tag{3}$$

Given these tax and extortion rates, the level of the public good that maximises the government's political rent can be computed as the solution to

$$\frac{\partial r}{\partial g} = t \left[(1-\alpha)\frac{y}{g} + \alpha \frac{y}{\ell}\frac{\partial \ell}{\partial g} \right] - 1 = 0 \tag{4}$$

which simplifies to

$$t(1-\alpha)\frac{y}{g} = 1 \tag{5}$$

since $\partial \ell / \partial g = 0$ as argued above.

The solution is therefore

$$g = \frac{1}{2}\frac{(1-\alpha)^{\frac{2}{\alpha}}}{(1-\alpha/2)^{\frac{1}{\alpha}}} \qquad (6)$$

which is always smaller than the equilibrium amount of the public good in the case discussed in the previous section. Even though the use of the public good for extralegal production does not disrupt its marginal productivity in legal production, and even though the equilibrium tax and extortion rates are the same as in the previous case, the amount of government-produced public good is lower, so that in particular the equilibrium allocation of resources is no longer efficient.

This surprising result arises because the government-produced public service is a pure public good. As a consequence of this, the allocation of labour inputs does not depend on its level, so that $\partial \ell / \partial g$ in (4) is equal to zero whereas it was positive in the case in which the government-produced public service was rival in use for production.

In other words when the government-produced public good is rival in use for production (as in Grossman), the government (as well as the mafia), in order to skew the use of labour inputs in their favour, have an additional incentive to provide more public services. When the government-produced public service is a public good, however, this additional incentive is missing and in equilibrium underprovision of the public good will occur.

3   Conclusions

Grossman introduces the challenging idea that to the extent that the mafia is an alternative provider of production services to the private sector and that it competes with the government in terms of tax rates and provision of production services, its existence can have a beneficial effect to society because it moderates the kleptocratic tendencies of the government.

A possible interpretation of this result is that an institutional reform that introduced competition among competing government agencies could dramatically reduce the distortions of a monopolistic government.[1]

This introduces the question of why the mafia is not institutionalised. The last part of Grossman's paper answers this question by pointing out that mafia activity usually generates externalities, so that the net effect of its existence can be positive or negative, depending on whether the beneficial effects of dampening the government's kleptocracy through the introduction of possible tax evasion are outweighed by the negative externalities the mafia imposes on society.

Since free riding (or tax evasion) appears to be a significant way in which a criminal organisation affects the allocation of resources, the previous section used a modified version of Grossman's model to study how free riding affects the government's fiscal policy. It was shown that in contrast to Grossman's model, even though competition makes tax rates lower, government's provision of a public good can be negatively affected by the fact that a criminal organisation can provide a free-riding technology therefore leading to an inefficient outcome.

NOTE

1   This is true as long as the production technology is constant returns to scale, which implies that there is no natural monopoly.

7 Corruption: arm's-length relationships and markets

VITO TANZI

1 Introduction

On 8 May 1993 *The Washington Post* carried a front-page story about a division of the US National Institute of Health in Bethesda 'in which some female employees were promised promotions and raises if they agreed to have sex with their male managers ...' (Jennings, 1993, p. 1). On the same day, an article in *The New York Times* reported that in China, in the process of privatisation of land, 'individuals seem to be expropriating the state's property at bargain prices.' (Dunn, 1993, p. 3). The article goes on to state that '... today's real estate boom raises troubling questions about land that is allocated not [so much] by prices but by *guanxi*. The deals ... say less about market economics than about simple corruption'[1] (*ibid.*). *Guanxi* is the Chinese word for 'connections'. The article cites a Chinese businessman to the effect that: 'if you have *guanxi*, it is the time to make big money.' Thus, according to this article, in today's China, 'connections' have great economic value and smart people can capitalise on them to earn large 'incomes'. On 8 May 1993 French newspapers were still carrying stories about the suicide of former Prime Minister Pierre Bérégovoy, attributed in part to the accusation that he had received an interest-free loan from a friend. And Italian newspapers were providing further details about private entrepreneurs who had paid large bribes to well-placed politicians in order to get lucrative contracts with the Italian public sector.

What is the unifying thread of all of these stories? Essentially, it is the lack of the application of the 'arm's-length principle' to economic decisions. This principle requires that personal or other relationships should play no role in economic decisions that involve more than one party. Equality of treatment for all economic agents is essential for a well-working market economy. In the examples provided above, economic decisions – in land markets, in labour markets, in financial

161

markets, and in the market for government contracts – were apparently not guided by arm's length.

A few years ago the *Financial Times* reported on a survey of individuals working in the business sector of several industrial countries. They were asked whether personal and family connections played a role in hiring and promotion decisions in the companies in which they worked. The answers were striking: in several countries as many as two-thirds of the respondents answered that these relationships did indeed play a major role. The countries in which they were least important were Australia and the United States. Even in these countries, however, the proportion of the respondents who answered that connections mattered was significant. Thus, according to the results of this survey, decisions about hiring and promotions are often not based on neutral, objective, or arm's-length criteria. This result would not come as a surprise to anyone familiar with the Italian situation.[2] But it would be a mistake to think that Italy is unique. In France, the United Kingdom, and even in the United States, for example, the economic and social benefits derived from going to Ivy League (Harvard, Yale, etc.) or other prestigious schools (ENA, Eton, Oxford) may have as much to do with connections made there as with the quality of the education received. It is the thesis of this paper that these connections, under particular social circumstances, can create a fertile ground for corruption.

2   Markets and government

Economic theory tells us that if markets were perfect, there would be no need for the government to play an economic role. Furthermore, almost by definition, these markets would be guided by the extreme version of arm's-length relationships among market participants implied by perfect competition. Decisions concerning the selling and buying of goods; the hiring, retention and compensation of workers; the lending and borrowing of money; the timing, size and location of investment projects, and so forth would be determined by economic considerations and profit opportunities alone. Relationships among the parties would play no role.

However, markets are not perfect; the existence of public goods, of externalities in production and consumption, of informational deficiencies, and of monopolistic practices, justifies and requires that the state play a corrective role in the economy.[3] The work of Lindahl, Wicksell, Samuelson and others has been influential in determining the optimal *theoretical*, or normative, role of the state.

A fundamental but unstated assumption in the theoretical work on the role of the public sector is that public sector officials (both policy-makers *and* civil servants) know what they are doing and are neutral and impersonal in their pursuit of social welfare.[4] When these officials make mistakes, they are honest mistakes. This assumption, though of fundamental importance, is hidden in the pure theory of public expenditure.[5]

Although, to my knowledge, this has not been recognised, the theoretical work on how the public sector should pursue its corrective role owes a great deal to Max Weber's *ideal* or *normative* type of rational-legal bureaucracy. As Robin Theobald has put it: Weber's bureaucrats would operate '... according to rational procedures and universalistic principles in which there is no place for personalism, cronyism, and, most of all, the confusion of public and private interests.'[6] This bureaucracy '... is run by hierarchically ordered corps of officials who are recruited and promoted according to objective criteria such as educational qualifications and professional experience; who are paid a regular salary which is graded according to rank and qualifications; and who are allocated fixed jurisdictional areas governed by clearly laid down rules and procedures' (see Theobald, 1990, p. 56). Weber was aware that 'Bureaucracy, thus understood, is fully developed ... only in the modern state, and in the private economy only in the most advanced institutions of capitalism.' (See Weber, 1978, p. 56.) In other words he was fully aware that he was presenting an ideal type of bureaucracy rather than describing reality.[7]

The extent to which the real world approximates the Lindahl–Samuelson–Weber ideal is, of course, an open question. The Italian *Scienza delle Finanze*, which had a lot of influence on James Buchanan's work and, through him, on the development of public choice, would have been sceptical on various grounds about the realism, and, indeed, about the usefulness of the theoretical approach.

In practice, the economic role of the state is exercised through the use of various instruments such as: (a) public spending for government consumption and transfers; (b) taxation and borrowing; (c) various forms of regulation; (d) lending activities; and (e) occasionally, less orthodox governmental actions such as expropriation, conscription, nationalisation, privatisation, exhortation and so forth. Depending on the level of development of a country and on its sophistication, some of these instruments are used more than others. For example, poorer countries are less able to raise large shares of their national incomes in taxes; as a consequence, they tend to abuse the instruments listed under (c), (d) and (e).[8]

If the behaviour of real world bureaucracies (and policy-makers) departs significantly from the Weberian ideal, the reasons can be several. Some of these reasons have provided the basis for the public choice literature.[9] In this paper the focus is on the economic role of 'corruption'. An important conclusion will be that the more real-life bureaucracies diverge from Weber's ideal, the less control the government will have over its policy instruments and the less correction it will be able to apply through its actions to the imperfections of the market. In other words, the less legitimate and justified will be the corrective role of the government.

The divergence between the optimum of the Samuelson solution and the real outcome of the public sector's action may be due either to the policy-makers' pursuit of policies that are not consistent with the achievement of the social welfare function, or to the bureaucrats distorting, in various ways, the signals they get from the policy-makers. The issue of corruption obviously concerns both. We thus have what could be called administrative and political corruption (see Rose-Ackermann, 1978). This paper deals mostly with administrative corruption. However, some limited references will be made to the forms of 'corruption' implied by the lobbying of legislators and by the 'buying' of prestigious public positions (i.e. ambassadorships) in some countries through large monetary contributions to candidates running for high office. The issues discussed in this paper transcend the political configuration of the country. In other words, they are not limited to whether a country has democratic or authoritarian institutions. Political corruption is likely, however, to be more closely linked to the country's political system.

3   Arm's-length relationships and cultures

On 25 January 1992, *The Economist* reviewed a paper by Prakash Reddy, an Indian social anthropologist who, reversing the common pattern of Western scholars going to study developing countries' social behaviour, obtained a research grant to study a village in Denmark. He spent a few months in this village – Hvilsager – and registered his impressions of the relations among its inhabitants.[10] These impressions formed the basis of the paper reviewed by *The Economist*.

Professor Reddy had been amazed to observe that the villagers hardly knew one another. They practically never exchanged visits and had very few other social contacts. They had little information on what other villagers, including their neighbours, were doing and apparently little interest in finding out. Even the relationships between parents and children were not very close. When the children reached adulthood they moved out and, after that, they visited their parents only occasionally. They just telephoned.

Professor Reddy contrasted this behaviour with that prevailing in a typical Indian village of comparable size. In the latter, daily house visits would be common. Everyone would be interested in, and getting involved in, the business of the others. Family contacts would be very frequent and the members of the extended families would support one another in many ways. Relations with neighbours would also be close.

This story has implications for the concept of arm's length and, in turn, for the role of corruption. Arm's-length relationships in economic exchanges would be much more likely to prevail in the Danish village than in the Indian village. In the latter, the concept of arm's length would seem strange and alien. It might even seem immoral. The idea that, economically speaking, one should treat relatives and friends in the same way as strangers would appear bizarre. Relatives and friends would simply expect preferential treatment whether they were dealing with individuals in the private or in the public sector.

If a government were established in each of the two villages, with a bureaucracy charged with carrying out its functions through the instruments described earlier, it would be far easier for the Danish bureaucrats to approximate Weber's ideal in their behaviour than for the Indian bureaucrats. In the Indian village the attempt to create an impersonal bureaucracy that would operate '... according to ... principles in which there is no place for personalism, cronyism, etc.' would conflict with the accepted norm that family and friends come first. In this society the government employee, just like any other individual, would be expected to help relatives and friends with special treatment or favours even if, occasionally, this behaviour might require bending, or even breaking, administrative rules and departing from 'universalistic principles'. The person who refused to provide this help would be seen as breaking the prevailing moral code and would not be popular.

Once civil servants begin to make distinctions among the people they deal with according to the degree of family relationship or friendship, they have abandoned the arm's-length principle. It might consequently be a small step to begin to expect some compensation from more distant members of the community for performing tasks for them that should be the duty of the civil servants to perform or for treating them in the same way as others. Without such compensation, those who required particular permits or legal documents or other services might have to wait a long time to get them.[11] Thus, 'speed money' may be required to accelerate the process and bribes to get a positive response in cases where the bureaucrat has the power of refusal.

The Indian and Danish villages described above represent polar or extreme cases of how individuals interact within a community. Most societies would probably find themselves somewhere between these two poles, with North European and Anglo-Saxon countries probably closer to the Danish village model and many other countries closer to the Indian village model. The Anglo-Saxon concept of 'privacy' is probably just a manifestation of arm's-length relationships.[12] Many developing countries would probably be closer to the model represented by the Indian village. Some industrial countries, such as Italy and possibly Japan, would also come closer to the latter than the former. In a way, the very features that may make a country a less cold and indifferent place are the same that increase the difficulty of enforcing arm's-length rules.

In this connection, the concept of 'social capital' as used by Coleman (1990) is of relevance. Coleman criticised the economic theory of perfect competition in a market since it accepts '[the] fiction ... that society consists of a set of independent individuals, each of whom acts to achieve goals that are independently arrived at, and that the functioning of the social system consists of the combination of these actions of independent individuals' (p. 300). He argues that '... individuals do not act independently, goals are not independently arrived at, and interests are not wholly selfish' (p. 301) and that 'personal relations and networks of relations' are important to achieve personal goals. He considers these relations and networks as a capital asset for the individual, a kind of personal *social capital*. This social capital is not tangible and is not completely fungible but is '... productive, making possible the achievement of certain ends that would not be attainable by the individual in its absence' (p. 302).

Social capital is an asset to the individual who possesses it. It is in essence a summation of all the 'I owe yous' that the individual has accumulated *vis-à-vis* others. Some of these may come from his family background, some from connections developed in school or at work, some from past favours made, and so forth. But, of course, the social capital of an individual does not represent a one-way street in obligations. While the individual can use this capital to ask others to do things for him, others can draw from *their* social capital to ask him to perform tasks or do things for them. One could, thus, distinguish a *gross* from a *net* concept of social capital. The obligations that others have towards the individual might be largely balanced by the obligations that he has towards them. The existence of social capital links individuals in a network of obligations that both increases and reduces their individual freedom.

In some societies (those closer to the polar case of the Indian village) the social capital of individuals will be particularly large. The examples of the *guanxi* in China, the family connections as reported in the survey in the *Financial Times*, and the relations in the Indian village all reflect the existence of social capital. This existence is likely to interfere with arm's-length relationships and, in particular circumstances, it may lead to corruption. At the end of this paper, I will speculate that it is also likely to play a role in the development and the persistence of particular types of organised criminal activities.

4   On corruption

Not long ago the word 'corruption' was infrequently used although the problem reflected by its existence is obviously a very old one.[13] The word did not often appear in newspapers and it was rarely mentioned by economists even though sociologists, political scientists and a few economists did pay attention to it. Very few economists spent much time assessing its economic significance.[14] Recent newspaper articles indicate that this phenomenon is far more widespread and universal than previously thought. Evidence of it is everywhere, in developing countries and, with growing frequency, in industrial countries. A perusal of recent daily newspapers would show that this problem has attracted a lot of attention in France, Germany, Greece, Italy, Japan, Russia, Spain, Brazil, India, South Korea, Venezuela and many other places.[15] Prominent political figures, including presidents of countries and ministers, have been accused of corruption and, as a consequence, some have resigned or have been forced out of office.

Corruption comes in many shapes and forms. It is very difficult to define and at times it is difficult to identify. Several definitions have appeared in the literature but none seems to be fully satisfactory.[16] Here we will simply define it as the intentional non-compliance with the arm's-length principle aimed at deriving some advantage for oneself or for related individuals from this behaviour. In the Danish village described by Professor Reddy, if corruption existed, it would reflect the isolated acts of particular individuals who would try to take advantage of their positions for personal gain. In other words it would reflect clearly unwarranted and anti-social behaviour not induced by social pressures. In this case its identification might be easier since the victims of this corruption would be more likely to identify the perpetrators. Its punishment would also be easier since it would conform with generally accepted norms. In societies with close social relationships, however, its frequency is likely to be greater, its identification much more difficult, and its punishment more problematic. This implies that models of criminal or illegal behaviour of the type pioneered by Becker (1968) and by Allingham and Sandmo (1972) will be of limited applicability.

The term 'corruption' comes from the Latin verb to break, *rumpere*. It, thus, implies that something is broken. This something might be a moral or social code of conduct or an administrative rule.[17] If it is the latter, a requirement must be that the rule that is broken is precise and transparent. Another is that the official who breaks it derives some recognisable benefit for himself, his family, his friends, his tribe or party, or some other relevant group. Additionally, the benefit derived must be seen as a direct *quid pro quo* from the specific 'corrupt' act. This simple description reveals several potential difficulties.

There must be evidence that a precise rule is broken. This requires that all the rules must be precisely stated, leaving, thus, no doubts about their meaning and no discretion to the public officials. But what about cases where the rules are not precise or where the bureaucrats are specifically given some discretion? For example, in many countries legislation related to the granting of tax incentives or import licences has often left a lot of discretion in the hands of the officials who must make the decisions to grant them. They must decide whether an investment or an import is 'essential' or 'necessary' to the country. These officials are often the sole interpreters of what those terms mean. Thus, in a way, they are in a position of monopoly since they can grant or deny these permits. Or, taking a different example, what about the selection of a tax return for an audit or the selection of an enterprise for a site-inspection when there are no precise rules for making these choices? Or the hiring of a new employee when there are no precise objective and honest tests for the selection?

Over the years there has been a lot of controversy among economists on whether economic policy should be guided by precise rules or should have an element of discretion.[18] It is evident that the greater is the element of discretion, the greater is the possibility that it will be used to someone's (rather than the public's) advantage. Thus the possibility of corruption would seem to create a presumption in favour of precise and rigid rules.[19] But, of course, the creation of such rules can itself reflect an attempt on the part of some officials to benefit in a large way from that creation. In many cases it is precisely the excess of rules that creates a fertile ground for corruption. Furthermore, the lack of discretion can make the rules too rigid and this could create obstacles to the proper functioning of the economy or the particular organisation. At times workers who have wanted to embarrass an organisation have complied rigidly with the existing rules to bring the organisation to a standstill.[20]

When social relations are very close, it may be difficult to establish a direct link between an act that could be assumed to reflect corruption and a particular payment for it. An employee who, using his official position, does a special favour to an acquaintance – say helps him or her get a valuable licence, a government contract, or a government job – may be compensated with an immediate or explicit payment (clearly a bribe); alternatively, he may be compensated, at a much later time, with a generous gift to his daughter when she gets married; or with a good job offer for his son when he completes his studies. In other words, there may not be any direct, explicit and immediate compensation for the favour. The payment may be delayed in time and, when made, to outsiders it may appear completely unconnected with the favour received.[21] In many cases the 'corrupted' and the 'corruptor' may never even have discussed the payment. It would simply be understood that a favour today creates a presumption or even an obligation for a reciprocal favour later. In other words, it contributes to the growth of the giver's 'social capital'. One is reminded of the scene in *The Godfather*, the most famous book and movie on the mafia, when the funeral parlour operator asks Don Corleone to punish the guys who have raped and beaten his daughter. He gets his request and he understands that one day he will have to reciprocate the favour. A credit entry has been made to the social capital of Don Corleone and a debit entry to the social capital of the funeral parlour operator. In some societies there is a shadow market for favours with demand and supply and with implicit prices. This market could lend itself to economic analysis.

This takes us to the final difficulty. In societies where family or other kinds of relationships are very strong, and especially where existing moral or social codes require that one helps family and friends, the expectation that the public employee will routinely apply arm's-length principles in his relations with friends and relatives is unrealistic. In these societies the Weberian type of ideal bureaucracy will prove very difficult to install. Century-old and widely-accepted social norms will often prove more powerful as guides to behaviour than new and often imported rules based on arm's-length principles. When this reality is ignored, disappointment is likely to follow.

In these societies, the cost of the corrective role of the government in the market is likely to rise and to affect economic relationships within the private sector as well, thus rendering more difficult the establishment of a true market economy.[22] To argue that the personal relationships that come to be established between public sector employees and individuals who deal with them reflect a 'corrupt' society is correct in a legalistic sense but misses the point that these relationships simply reflect different social and moral norms.

The instruments that make corruption possible are many. Important examples would include: (a) regulations (such as the issue of licences of various kinds; zoning and other sorts of regulations which may have great economic value; permits of various kinds); (b) fines for alleged or actual violations of existing legal norms; (c) control over procurement contracts; (d) control over public investment contracts (roads, airports, bridges) which can benefit some areas over others, and some contractors over others; (e) programmes related to the provision of tax incentives, subsidised credit, overvalued foreign exchange; (f) controls over hiring and promotion; (g) controls over the assignment of entitlements and other benefits (pensions for disability, scholarships, subsidies); (h) controls over access to underpriced public services (electricity, telephone, water); and (i) tax administration decisions (auditing, determination of presumptive income, etc.).

These examples are not exhaustive. The greater is the use of these instruments, the greater will be the potential for corruption. Control over these instruments can give government employees great power which, given the right social environment, the right incentive systems and weak and uncertain penalties, may allow them to extract large rents for themselves or for their families and friends. Gary Becker's (1968) analysis of crime, or Allingham and Sandmo's (1972) analysis of tax evasion, can be applied to the analysis of corruption when it occurs in an environment more like that of the Danish village than that of the Indian village. In the latter case, the difficulty of identifying many acts of corruption, of proving that a bribe has actually been paid, and of inducing society to apply significant penalties to these acts is likely to reduce the value of that analysis.

5   Economic consequences of corruption

When civil servants appropriate for their own use the instruments that the government has at its disposal to influence the economy and to correct the shortcomings of the private market, they reduce the power of the state and its ability to play the intended and presumably corrective role. In a way this represents a privatisation of the state in which its power is not shifted to the market, as privatisation normally implies, but to government officials and bureaucrats.

Assuming that government policies had been or would have been guided by the objective of correcting for the shortcomings of the market,[23] corruption distorts the end result in several ways. It distorts the *allocative role* in several ways:

First, by favouring taxpayers who, because of the special treatment they receive from tax inspectors, are able to reduce their tax liabilities. If the statutory tax system had been designed to be neutral, corruption would destroy its neutrality by giving a competitive advantage to some producers over their competitors.

Second, through the arbitrary (i.e. non-arm's-length) application of rules and regulations, thus giving preferences to some individuals over others. This may be particularly important in the allocation of import permits, subsidised credit, zoning permits and permits related to particular activities. If, for example, these instruments had been developed to assist genuine 'infant industries' but ended up assisting others, the corrective role of the governments would be distorted.

Third, through the allocation of public works, or procurement, contracts to enterprises that win the competition not because they can do the job at the least cost but because of their connections and the bribes they pay.[24]

Fourth, through the arbitrary hiring and promotion of individuals who would not have been selected or promoted on the basis of fair and objective criteria. The selection of these individuals will damage the economy not only by lowering the quality of the decisions made by these individuals and by increasing the frequency of mistakes but also by discouraging more able but less well-connected individuals from pursuing particular careers if they feel that the decks are stacked against them. In societies where the best jobs are seen to be in the public sector and where these jobs go predominantly to those with special connections,[25] the incentives to work hard in school and to get a good education for those without these connections will be reduced, thus lowering the growth potential of the economy.

Fifth, some individuals will try to get jobs not in the areas in which they have particular abilities but in the areas which provide more scope for higher rents. In other words, the official wage will not play a significant role in attracting individuals to particular jobs if it comes to diverge much from the total earnings that a particular position allows. In a South East Asian country, for example, over the years the number of individuals taking the exam to become income tax inspectors has increased remarkably, in spite of the low wages that these jobs pay. The reason seems to be that individuals have sensed that these low-paying positions can generate substantial extra earnings. More important and better-paying jobs that do not provide such opportunities have been shunned. There have even been reports that at times, in particular countries, some jobs with clear potential to earn high rents have been auctioned by those with the power to assign them. Baumol (1990) and, independently, Murphy, Shleifer, and Vishny (1991) have argued that in any society the few individuals with significant managerial skills, and thus with the greatest potential to contribute to growth, will gravitate towards activities likely to generate the highest rates of return *regardless of whether these are productive or rent-seeking activities*. If corruption allows some of them to gain more by pursuing rent-seeking rather than productive activities, they will pursue the former. The loser will be the performance of the economy.[26]

Corruption distorts the *redistributive role* of the government in myriads of ways. If the well connected get the best jobs, the most profitable government contracts, the subsidised credit, the foreign exchange at the overvalued rates and so forth, and if they are able to reduce their tax payments by bribing officials, it will be less likely that the activity of the government will improve the distribution of income and make the economic system more equitable.[27]

Finally, in all its ramifications, corruption is likely to have negative implications for the *stabilisation role* of the government, if that role requires, as is often the case, a reduction of the fiscal deficit. This will occur because corruption will most likely raise the costs of running the government while reducing government revenues. For example, the allocation of disability pensions to people who are not disabled; of unemployment benefits to people who are not unemployed; of government contracts to people who pay bribes for the contracts and thus raise their costs; the increase in unproductive capital spending often promoted by those who benefit from the capital project; and the many other ways in which corruption distorts spending decisions must very likely raise total government spending in relation to the benefits that the economy receives from that spending.[28] By the same token, government revenue falls when some of the potential tax payments to the government are diverted or are never collected. In some developing countries, the *effective* tax burden (i.e. the ratio of all tax-related payments by taxpayers to national income) may be significantly higher than the *official* tax burden because some payments end up in the pockets of the tax inspectors.

6   Policy implications

Several factors are likely to determine the extent to which corruption will play a significant role in a country. These are: (a) the role of the state and the instruments it uses to pursue that role; (b) the social characteristics of the society, i.e. the extent to which arm's-length relationships are prevalent in social relations; (c) the nature of the political system; and (d) the penalty system for acts of corruption that are uncovered.

In some countries corruption is prevalently an activity of the political leaders. In others, it is prevalently an activity of the civil servants. In still others, it is an activity of both. In a truly democratic system, with checks and balances exercised through elections, through the Parliamentary process, and through a vigorous free Press, the extent of corruption by the political leaders will generally be checked or at least it will eventually be discovered and hopefully checked. This kind of corruption will exist but it will rarely reach the extreme levels attained by some authoritarian governments (see Harsch, 1993). Therefore, if, as it has been argued in a recent best-seller, the inevitable course of history is to transform authoritarian into democratic governments, because of this change, the future should experience less corruption than the past or even the present (see Fukuyama, 1992). But let us consider the other factors that determine corruption, focusing mainly on the role of the state and on the social characteristics of the countries' citizens.

Especially in societies where arm's-length relationships are unlikely to be enforceable (because of the close and continuous contacts among closely-knit groups of citizens who tend to personalise most relations), the larger is the role of the state, the greater is the probability that its instruments will be used by public officials and civil servants to favour particular groups in addition to themselves. When this happens, the cost of government rises and its ability to correct the shortcomings of the market falls. In other words, the effective control that the government has over the economy is reduced.[29] In this situation the best policy to reduce corruption will be a reduction of the opportunities to engage in it by scaling down the government's role in the economy. Corruption can be contained by a sharp reduction of that role in all its aspects, i.e. spending and taxing activities and, especially, in economic regulations. It is no accident that in centrally planned economies, where regulation of economic activity has been most widespread, corruption seems to be everywhere.[30] Unfortunately, in these countries, the process of reducing the role of the state in the economy (by freeing prices, by privatising state enterprises, etc.) may itself produce enormous opportunities for corruption during the transition.

When corruption in the Weberian sense characterises modern states, it can be reduced by increasing penalties on those who engage in it, by increasing the transparency of the rules, regulations and laws, and by strengthening audits, checks and other controls on the civil servants. In this environment, the analysis suggested by Becker (1968) will be particularly relevant. However, when it characterises more traditional societies, this option, while still worth pursuing, is not likely by itself to give very positive and, especially, permanent results. History is full of examples of campaigns against corruption which started with great fanfares but which, over the long run, did not accomplish much. One should therefore be sceptical about the end result of well-intentioned initiatives such as the very recent one by Transparency International, an anti-corruption organisation based in Germany, that aims at reducing corruption by having enterprises agree to a code of conduct for business. By the same token, one should not officially sanction corruption by, for example, reducing the wages of the civil servants on the assumption that they are getting payments under the table. In an African country, for example, three years ago, the government reduced the wages of customs officials to zero for six months under the assumption that 'they could take care of themselves.'[31] Unrealistically low wages always invite corruption.

Because it is social intimacy that creates the environment that promotes corruption, a policy that has been effective in some cases (for example in tax administration) in reducing corruption is that of forced and periodic geographical mobility for civil servants, in order to remove them from the region where they have their closest social or family relations and to prevent the formation of new relations. Some forms of social relations take time to develop so that for a while, after a bureaucrat has moved to a new region, they will not play a large role in the contacts between the bureaucrats and the citizens who depend on them. Thus, periodic mobility, especially in a large country, will be an effective policy to reduce bureaucratic corruption. It is no accident that in large countries, such as the United States, corruption is more of a problem for local governments where bureaucrats and citizens often know each other and where arm's-length relationships are less likely to prevail. In general, one can speculate that the larger a country is and the more mobile its population, the less of a problem corruption will be.

7   Corruption and organised crime

In view of the focus of the present volume on the activities of criminal organisations, I should perhaps conclude this paper by relating in a rather casual way my discussion of administrative corruption to these organisations.

In societies typified by the social environment attributed to the Danish village, a criminal group – say a gang bent on pursuing criminal activities – would, most likely, be made up of inherently anti-social and socially unrelated individuals brought together by the specific objective of committing particular crimes. These individuals are more likely to have met in gaol than in their neighbourhood. Without this objective, these individuals would probably have no social contacts among themselves. These individuals are likely to be largely marginalised from the society in which they operate. They would be outcasts and their links to that society would be tenuous. Their social capital, using Coleman's expression, would be almost non-existent. They would neither ask for favours from non-gang members nor would they do them favours. The corruption of public officials would bear little or no relation to their criminal activities. A determined government intent on controlling these activities would have a good chance of success. These gangs would have a limited time-horizon.

In societies with characteristics similar to those attributed to the Indian village, criminal organisations that did not direct their activities exclusively or predominantly against the society in which they operate, could exploit their links to that society to facilitate their illegal activities and to perpetuate their existence. Take, as an example, organisations such as those which characterise the Sicilian mafia.[32] The members of these organisations (a) come from the same region, and often even from the same small towns; they have known one another all their lives; (b) speak the same language (i.e. the same dialect); (c) often intermarry; (d) direct some of their criminal activities (drug trafficking) outside the areas where they live;[33] and (e) rather than being completely marginalised from the society in which they operate are often an integral part of it. Because their links with the society in which they operate are strong, they possess considerable 'social capital' made up of obligations from and obligations to many individuals who, strictly speaking, are not members of the criminal organisations.

This social capital and these links are exploited: (a) to hold mafia members together in the absence of legal contracts; (b) to extend mafia power into legitimate businesses; (c) to corrupt public employees to induce them to provide special favours to mafia members or to individuals who ask the mafia for assistance in various areas (getting permits, loans, jobs, disability pensions, etc.). The corruption of bureaucrats is often the instrument through which the mafia gets favours in the justice system, in the allocation of government contracts, in zoning decisions, in the ability to violate existing rules and regulations with impunity, in the exploitation of various government programmes, and in many other ways.

The closeness of the links between the mafia and the society in which it operates can be glimpsed from a few anecdotes. According to a recent book (Deaglio, 1993), in Torretta, one of the small towns surrounding the airport near Palermo '... 40 per cent of the local families ... had made at least one trip to New York carrying heroin; ... the same situation prevailed in other towns near the airport' (p. 42). These couriers were not mafia members but just ordinary citizens attracted to this occasional illegal activity by the large financial rewards, by the low risk of the operation, and by the social vicinity to the mafia members. Deaglio reports that these individuals, mostly women, themselves volunteered for these activities. He comments that in these towns everyone knows about these activities. He also reports that when the head of the Riesi mafia family was killed, the municipal council closed the local schools as a sign of public mourning for the important fallen citizen (p. 96). In Palermo when someone has his/her automobile stolen, he/she always knows whom to contact to have them returned (p. 95).

The corruption of bureaucrats who hold power in local decisions allows the mafia to operate with relative impunity and to expand its power, especially if that power brings a lot of money with which to compensate the bureaucrats (and sometimes the local politicians) for their assistance. These officials may be useful in allowing mafia members to ignore local building-codes and zoning regulations, thus allowing them to make enormous profits in construction activities; to control the allocation of government contracts; to control some forms of public hiring; to control or at least regulate the allocation of public entitlements such as 'disability' pensions; to control the taxes they pay; and to do many other illegal actions.

Although the mafia has often transplanted itself to areas outside Sicily, such as northern Italy, the United States and some other places, in these other areas it generally does not have the same close relationship with the society in which it operates as it has in Sicily. It is, thus, much more exposed to concerted attempts by the government at eradicating it. For this reason, it has often tried to become legal by investing in legitimate activities.

8   Concluding remarks

Many governments want to play an active role in the economy but find it difficult to pursue their traditional objectives through taxing and spending activities. Developing countries, for example, are not able to raise high shares of gross domestic products in taxes and are thus frustrated in their often ambitious spending activities. As a consequence, they often resort to what could be called quasi-fiscal regulations.[34] When these regulations are prevalent in an environment in which interpersonal relations are important, the ground for corruption will be fertile. In this situation, the most efficient way for the government to reduce corruption is to scale down its role in the economy.

NOTES

* The views expressed are strictly personal. They do not necessarily reflect official positions of the International Monetary Fund. Comments received from

Ke-Young Chu, A. Premchand, Partho Shome, Howell Zee and Vito Luigi Tanzi are much appreciated.

1 The process of price deregulation also seems to be creating opportunities for corruption. See Wong (1992).

2 As someone declared in Donald Pitkin's book, 'We know how things are in Italy. You cannot find a job without a recommendation.' See Pitkin (1990, p. 68). By the way, the word recommendation (*raccomandazione*) has a different connotation in Italian than in English. It essentially means a 'push' or at least a sponsorship rather than an objective assessment of someone's ability and character.

3 An economic role for the state may also be justified by concerns for equity and stabilisation. See Musgrave (1959) and Stiglitz (1989).

4 Without this assumption, one could not defend a corrective role for the state. The definitions of social welfare or the public interest raise difficult theoretical and practical questions ignored here. For the classic treatment of the theoretical difficulties, see Arrow (1951). See also the discussion of a social welfare function in Mueller (1989, pp. 384–407).

5 See Samuelson (1954); and Musgrave (1938). See also Mueller (1989, pp. 144–7).

6 See Theobald (1990, p. 47). Max Weber's fundamental work is in *Economy and Society* (1978), in two volumes. For a discussion of the characteristics of a modern bureaucracy, see especially Chapter XI, Volume 2, pp. 956–1005.

7 See also Weber (1947).

8 For this reason, the fact that developing countries have tax levels much lower than industrial countries does not imply that the government plays a smaller role in them.

9 Mueller (1989) is probably the best source on that literature. Issues such as voting rules, multi-party systems, rent-seeking activities and so forth are the essence of the public choice literature.

10 The title of the unpublished English manuscript is 'Danes are Like That'. The published version is in Danish.

11 For example, tips or bribes may become necessary to get a telephone connection, to get the results of blood tests quickly, to get admission to schools or hospitals, to clear goods speedily at customs, to get import licences and so forth.

12 Interestingly enough the word 'privacy' is very difficult to translate into other languages. Translations generally do not render the precise English meaning.

13 Writing more than two thousand years ago, Kautilya (Prime Minister of a state in northern India) wrote in the *Arthashastra* (New Delhi: Penguin Books) that 'just as it is impossible not to taste honey or poison that one may find at the tip of one's tongue, so it is impossible for one dealing with government funds not to taste, at least a little bit, of the King's wealth.' The quotation is on p. 281.

14 There is, of course, some economic literature on it but much less than one would have expected from the importance of the phenomenon.

15 In countries without a free Press, of course, newspapers may have been prevented from reporting on it. In October 1993 several were executed in China for crimes of corruption.

16 See, for example, the various definitions given on p. 2 of Theobald (1990) or in Flitgaard (1988, pp. 21–4). A famous definition is the one given by the

Indian Penal Code and reported in Goode (1984, pp. 310–11). According to that code, a person is guilty of corruption who 'being or expecting to be a public servant, accepts, or obtains, or agrees to accept, or attempts to obtain from any person, for himself or for any other person, any gratification whatsoever, other than legal remuneration, as a motive or reward for doing or forbearing to do any official act or for showing or forbearing to show, in the exercise of his official functions, favour or disfavour to any person or for rendering or attempting to render, any service or disservice to any person.'

17 This already points to the difficulty faced when the behaviour expected from the moral or social code conflicts with that from the administrative rule. Saying that the administrative rule should always prevail opens up a lot of other difficulties not discussed here.

18 This controversy has usually related to major macroeconomic decisions such as the growth of the money supply, the size of the fiscal deficit, and so forth. In recent years, however, the public administration literature has also shown a distinct preference for rule-based administrations.

19 Perhaps this explains why some countries apply strict objective criteria for promotions (years of service, specific educational achievements, etc.) while others rely on the judgement of supervisors as to the performance of their subordinates. In general, Anglo-Saxon countries seem to prefer the latter option while countries such as Japan, France, Italy and some others seem to prefer a system based on more objective criteria, such as seniority, education, etc.

20 Some writers have argued that corruption can contribute to growth when existing regulations are too rigid and too stifling. Presumably corruption is the equivalent of introducing discretion in the application of the regulations. The same argument has been made about the contribution of the underground economy to growth. By getting around the many government-imposed restrictions, underground activities are supposed to give the economy a dynamism that it would otherwise not have. See various papers in Tanzi (ed.) (1982).

21 It has also been reported that in some Asian countries Parliament members or other public sector employees are given envelopes with cash, not for immediate favours but for possible future favours (Pye, 1985).

22 It is worth while to reflect on why arm's-length relationships are not fully operative in Japan or why the privatisation of state enterprises is proving so difficult in previously planned economies. The role of personal relationships is clearly important.

23 This is, of course, a big assumption which is unlikely to reflect reality in many cases. The corrective role of the state relates to the allocation of resources, the redistribution of income and the stabilisation of the economy.

24 For the public works budget a key question is whether it is only its allocation that is affected or also its size. It is possible that more spending is allocated to investment projects because they allow for the transfer of large amounts through 'tangents'. There is a strong suspicion in some countries that capital spending is often inflated by kick-backs. (See Tanzi, 1991, Ch. 3.) It is now evident that a substantial share of Italy's public investment budget, which had been one of the highest among the OECD countries, was *de facto* made up of transfer payments to political parties and to individuals.

25 In Italy, these individuals are often referred to as *pacchi raccomandati*, i.e. registered packages which always reach their destination.
26 Although I cannot prove it, my impression is that this has happened in Italy, in general, and in southern Italy in particular.
27 This may explain why some countries have at times introduced quotas for the less privileged.
28 In other words, corruption is likely to increase the capital/output ratio or the total cost of providing government services. It should probably enter as a variable in production functions, especially when its impact is changing over time.
29 In a powerful book, MacMullen (1988) has argued that the Roman Empire declined because, due to widespread corruption, the government lost control over its instruments of policy.
30 Campbell (1991, p. 71) has reported that, 'In the USSR at the end of the eighties about 18 million households had telephones, while there were 15 million households on the waiting list for them. The people who finally get a telephone installed tend to be those with special political influence or those who can offer bribes.' *South China Morning News* (October 26, 1993, p. 1) has reported the government announcement of an active corruption crackdown 'to halt the collection of illicit payments from among the mainland's staggering 1.11 million categories of government fees.' See also the chapter by Grossman on the USSR in Tanzi (ed.) (1982).
31 Sandbrook has reported that President Mobuto Sese Seko advised Zairian civil servants that: 'if you want to steal, steal a little in a nice way.' (See Sandbrook, 1986, p. 95.)
32 The characteristics of these organisations have been described by Deaglio (1993) and by Gambetta (1993).
33 It should be recalled that in *The Godfather* those who lived in the neighbourhood where the mafia chiefs lived were happy to live there because their neighbourhood was crime free.
34 These are regulations that *de facto* or implicitly tax some activities and subsidise other. This result is normally achieved with high efficiency losses.

REFERENCES

Allingham, M. E and A. Sandmo (1972), 'Income Tax Evasion: A Theoretical Analysis', *Journal of Public Economics*, 1(3–4), November, pp. 323–38.
Arrow, K. (1951), *Social Choice and Individual Values*, New York: Wiley.
Baumol, W. J. (1990), 'Entrepreneurship: Productive, Unproductive, and Destructive', *Journal of Political Economy*, 98(5), pp. 893–921.
Becker, G. S. (1968), 'Crime and Punishment: An Economic Approach', *Journal of Political Economy*, 76(2), March/April, pp. 169–217.
Campbell, R. (1991), *The Socialist Economies in Transition*, Bloomington: Indiana University Press.
Coleman, J. S. (1990), *Foundations of Social Theory*, Cambridge MA: Belknap Press.
Deaglio, E. (1993), *Raccolto Rosso*, Milano: Feltrinelli.
Dunn, S. W. (1993), 'China Sells Off Public Land to the Well-Connected', *The New York Times*, May 8.

Flitgaard, R. (1988), *Comptrolling Corruption*, Berkeley: University of California Press.

Fukuyama, F. (1992), *The End of History and the Last Man*, New York: The Free Press.

Gambetta, D. (1993), *The Sicilian Mafia: The Business of Private Protection*, Cambridge MA: Harvard University Press.

Goode, R. (1984), *Government Finance in Developing Countries*, Washington DC: The Brookings Institution.

Grossman, G., 'The Second Economy of the USSR', in V. Tanzi (ed.) (1982).

Harsch, E. (1993), 'Accumulators and Democrats: Challenging State Corruption in Africa', *The Journal of Modern African Studies*, 31(1), pp. 31–48.

Jennings, V. T. (1993), 'Sex Drove Promotions at N.I.H. Unit, Report Says', *The Washington Post*, May 8, p. 1.

Kautilya (1991), *Arthashastra*, New Delhi: Penguin Books.

MacMullen, R. (1988), *Corruption and the Decline of Rome*, New Haven: Yale University Press.

Mueller, D. C. (1989), *Public Choice II*, revised edition, Cambridge: Cambridge University Press.

Murphy, K. M., A. Shleifer and R. W. Vishny (1991), 'The Allocation of Talent: Implications for Growth', *Quarterly Journal of Economics*, 106, May, pp. 503–30.

Musgrave, R. A. (1938), 'The Voluntary Exchange Theory of Public Economy', *Quarterly Journal of Economics*, 53(2), February, pp. 213–37.

Musgrave, R. A. (1959), *The Theory of Public Finance*, New York: McGraw-Hill.

Pitkin, D. (1990), *Mamma, Cassa, Posto Fisso: Sermoneta Revisited, 1951–1986*, Napoli: Edizione Scientifiche Italiane.

Pye, L. W. (1985), *Asian Power and Politics: The Cultural Dimensions of Authority*, Cambridge MA: Belknap Press.

Rose-Ackerman, S. (1978), *Corruption: A Study in Political Economy*, New York: Academic Press.

Samuelson, P. (1954), 'The Pure Theory of Public Expenditure', *Review of Economics and Statistics*, 36, November, pp. 336–9.

Sandbrook, R. (1986), *The Politics of Africa's Economic Stagnation*, Cambridge: Cambridge University Press.

Stiglitz, J. E. (1989), *The Economic Role of the State*, Oxford: Basil Blackwell.

Tanzi, V. (ed.) (1982), *The Underground Economy in the United States and Abroad*, Lexington MA: D. C. Heath & Co.

Tanzi, V. (1991), *Public Finance in Developing Countries*, Aldershot: Edward Elgar.

Theobald, R. (1990), *Corruption, Development, and Underdevelopment*, Durham NC: Duke University Press.

Weber, M. (1947), *The Theory of Social and Economic Organisation*, Glencoe IL: The Free Press.

Weber, M. (1978), *Economy and Society*, two volumes, Berkeley: University of California Press.

Wong, K-Y. (1992), 'Inflation, Corruption, and Income Distribution: The Recent Price Reform in China', *Journal of Macroeconomics*, 14(1), Winter, pp. 105–23.

Discussion

FLAVIO DELBONO

Corruption is an excellent example of issues which lend themselves to a multi-faceted approach, i.e. an analysis based on economic as well as historical, political and sociological roots. Vito Tanzi's paper probes the theoretical underpinnings of this fairly new methodology. This is no surprise given the well-known expertise of Tanzi in related issues (e.g. underground economies).

According to Tanzi, the weakness (or the absence) of arm's-length relationships – due to history and culture – makes corruption somehow endemic in some communities, and this undermines the traditional tasks assigned to public intervention in the economy: allocation, redistribution, stabilisation. Following Stiglitz's (1989) characterisation of the distinctive features of the state as economic organisation, one can also argue that corruption weakens the universal membership of citizens and represents an abuse of its power of compulsion.

In my comments I will try to cover briefly two issues. First, what can be done to eliminate, or at least mitigate, the size of corruption? Second, what do we know about the demand for corruption?

As for the first problem, we are aware that corruption exists also outside the state organisations (e.g. in the market system and within private organisations) and we also know that such practices are fairly established and firmly rooted in many screening mechanisms, as Tanzi convincingly argues. This seems to suggest that the state faces a twofold problem. On the one hand, it should minimise its presence wherever market forces work sufficiently well, i.e. where rankings are not based on significant degrees of corruption. On the other, it should protect individuals that would be damaged in biased (via corruption) organisations (schools, hospitals, firms and so on). The latter task justifies the presence of public organisations, as they could assure talents and efforts the treatment they deserve. In other words, privatisation and deregulation are not the obvious way of reducing the extent of corruption in a society, whatever is the diffusion of arm's-length relationships.

Incidentally, I would like to note that I find hard to endorse Tanzi's statement that 'Economic theory tells us that if markets were perfect, there would be no need for the government to play an economic role.' Indeed, later on, Tanzi himself looks at how corruption distorts the redistributive role of the government in myriads of ways. That is to acknowledge that there is a non-negligible fraction of economic theory which does not confine the economic role of the state to a purely (Pareto) efficiency-improving role. If redistribution matters, then, it is worth observing that corruption might entail a redistribution of resources which results in a more egalitarian allocation, as it is not based only on initial endowments, but on other (socio-cultural and political) variables.

As for my second point, it is worth noting that Tanzi's paper seems more concerned with the supply side of corruption, i.e. the behaviour of corrupted people. What can we guess about the corrupting ones?

Easily enough, it can be argued that this is an issue of incentives. One can possibly outline a framework in which an agent faces a multi-level organisation (with many principals) and the outcome of such an interaction may or may not include corruption at some or all levels of the hierarchy. In this respect, an interesting question would be: which organisations (or institutional arrangements) would successfully compete against a system based on corruption?

To conclude on a purely speculative note, the previous remarks suggest that, even in relatively simple contexts, we need to ask many questions in the search for a better understanding of such phenomena in order to explain often observed behaviour. Perhaps the best we can hope for in some cases is to identify a set of logically consistent claims. In this respect the paper of Vito Tanzi is much more than a start.

REFERENCE

Stiglitz, J. E. (1989), *The Economic Role of the State*, Oxford: Basil Blackwell.

Part IV
Deterrence policies against legal firms involved in illegal activities

8   Auditing with 'ghosts'

FRANK A. COWELL and
JAMES P. F. GORDON

1   Introduction

This paper is about tax cheating by firms. Our aim is to compare the audit strategies available to a tax authority attempting to collect indirect taxes from sellers prone to evade. We model indirect tax evasion as follows: firms choose between taxable sales on the regular market and unreported sales in an informal market. The latter will typically be for cash.[1] There are three options open to each firm: specialising in legal sales (honesty), selling on both markets (diversifying) or specialising in informal sales (submerging). We call firms that choose the third option 'ghosts'.[2] Section 2 of the paper outlines our model.

As in Allingham and Sandmo (1972), tax evasion is a gamble. If a firm is audited and found to be making irregular sales, it is fined and made to pay back the evaded tax. Which firms should the authority audit? One possible strategy is to audit randomly, with some fixed probability that any firm is investigated. An alternative enforcement policy is to tailor the audit strategy to take into account what the authority knows about each firm. A simple form of this approach is where the authority conditions audit probability solely on reported turnover via a cut-off rule: those reporting less (no less) than a certain amount are always (never) audited. In Section 5 we compare this cut-off policy with random audit and investigate which is likely to yield the authority more revenue.

The authority may also have access to information which is likely to be correlated with a firm's turnover. Such information will define its audit class in the sense used by Scotchmer (1987).[3] This suggests a strategy of investigating only those firms who appear suspicious, i.e. those whose reported output appears low given their audit class. The exact interpretation of 'suspicious' depends on the type of information to which the tax authority has access. We investigate this issue further in Cowell and Gordon (1989).

Questions similar to the above have been addressed in the context of *income* tax evasion and it is important to explain how this paper relates to that literature. In common with Reinganum and Wilde (1985), Scotchmer (1987) and Border and Sobel (1987) we assume that the tax authority can precommit itself to an audit strategy. This implies working within the standard principal–agent framework.[4] In common with Reinganum and Wilde (1985) and Scotchmer (1987), we also take the tax-and-penalty system as given.

Both Reinganum and Wilde (1985) and Border and Sobel (1987) condition the audit probability solely on the income report. This is equivalent to assuming a single audit class. As noted we adopt this assumption in Section 4 where we consider the simple cut-off rule. Our analysis is thus directly comparable with Reinganum and Wilde (1985), who show that a cut-off rule dominates random audit given lump-sum taxation. Given that they simultaneously choose the tax system, the Border–Sobel paper is more ambitious in intent, but their finding that the optimal audit strategy is stochastic is worth noting.[5] We show in Section 5 that in our model neither the simple cut-off rule nor independent random audit is unambiguously superior. We identify conditions under which each in turn dominates the other.

The novelty of our approach over the literature on income tax auditing is that we recognise the possibility that taxpayers may become ghosts who will be unknown to the tax authorities. Ghosts file no report with the tax authorities (as opposed to a zero report). The important finding is that the number of ghosts is not invariant to the nature of the audit strategy adopted. If firms know that their income report affects the chances of being investigated, it may be optimal not to file at all. Thus the Reinganum–Wilde case for a cut-off rule must be balanced against the cost of deterring some firms from reporting altogether. This raises the possibility that it may sometimes be optimal for the tax authority *not* to use all available information.

2   The model

We consider an industry in which each firm has fixed production capacity, y, distributed over the interval (y_0, y^0) according to a distribution function $F(y)$. Costs of production are given by:

$$C(y) - cy \tag{1}$$

where c is constant and common to all firms. Each firm can sell in a regular market at a price P or in an informal market (for cash) at a price

p. By selling in the informal market the firm is able to evade sales tax. For obvious reasons, it is difficult to get reparation for defective cash purchases, so $p \leq P$: the cash discount of $P - p$ compensates for the extra product risk. The *regular* market is competitive and each firm takes P as fixed: we denote its sales in this market by X.[6] By contrast, in the *informal* market each firm can increase p without losing all its custom (provided $p < P$). This is because the riskiness of cash purchases is perceived to be lower the better the buyer knows the seller and buyers are best acquainted with the local seller. In fact, we make the strong assumption that buyers either buy for cash from their local seller or do not buy for cash. Each firm thus has a local monopoly in cash sales. If illicit sales are x – and all capacity is utilised – then $y = x + X$. For convenience, we assume the same linear relationship between each firm's cash sales and cash discount:

$$x = 2\frac{P - p}{\beta} \tag{2}$$

where β is an inverse measure of the strength of cash demand. Equation (2) incorporates the idea that if the firm attempts to extend its operations in the illicit sector it has to widen the circle of its customers: as it does so it encounters people who are progressively less trusting about the quality of the product, and who therefore require a progressively larger discount on the legitimate price. The larger is β, the deeper the degree of cash discounting necessary to generate a given volume of informal demand. So β can be considered to be an indicator of the perceived reliability of the product being offered for sale on the informal market: goods and services for which the quality can be easily checked at the time of sale will have a low value of β – in such cases the discount required to persuade strangers to buy is relatively small.[7]

As noted in the introduction, we distinguish between *honest* firms who make no illicit sales, *diversifying* firms who two-time the authorities by combining legitimate business with illicit sales, and *submerged* firms or 'ghosts', who operate only in the illicit market. The authorities know, at least, where to find the firms of the first two types, even though in the absence of an audit they do not know which are cheating; but firms of the third type – the ghosts – have to be discovered as well as investigated. Ghosts usually leave few traces in the legitimate economy: they pay no payroll taxes or social security contributions, transactions are normally done in cash, and advertising is discreet. The distinction between these three types of enterprise is important both from the point of view of the options facing any one firm, and from the point of view of the tax authority as it formulates its enforcement policy.

Let us now consider the tax structure and its enforcement. We suppose that the government has imposed an *ad valorem* tax t upon sales of the good. Each firm can evade this by switching sales to its informal market. However, it knows that it runs the risk of being audited by the tax authority and punished for any evasion. This risk depends on the enforcement strategy adopted. We turn now to the case of random audit which provides some useful general insights.

3   Random audit

As noted, the probability of an audit is likely to differ between firms who declare some legal sales (the honest and the diversifiers) and those who make no report. The tax authority does not know the identities of the latter (the ghosts). Suppose π_d is the fixed probability that a firm making any legal sales is investigated. If auditing is random, then π_d will also be the proportion of such firms investigated. By contrast, let π_g be the probability that a firm operating exclusively in the informal sector gets caught. Let the penalty for evasion be a surcharge s on the unpaid tax, which is the same for both diversifiers and ghosts and based on the tax payable on actual sales. Assume $\pi_d(1 + s) < 1$ (so that the evasion gambles are better than fair).

Assume that firms are *risk-neutral* profit maximisers.[8] A typical firm's problem can be stated generally as:

$$\left.\begin{array}{l} \max_{\{x, X\}} (1 - t)PX + \theta(P - \tfrac{1}{2}\beta x)x - cy \\[2mm] \text{subject to } x \geq 0, X \geq 0, x + X \leq y \end{array}\right\} \qquad (3)$$

where

$$\theta = \begin{cases} \theta_d = 1 - \pi_d(1 + s)t \text{ if } X > 0 \\ \theta_g = 1 - \pi_g(1 + s)t \text{ if } X = 0 \end{cases} \qquad (4)$$

To analyse the solution to this problem, consider the three special cases:

Honest behaviour   Given the restriction $x = 0, X > 0$, and assuming that $P(1 - t) > c$, the maximum of (3) may be written as:

$$\Pi_h = \theta_h P y - cy \tag{5}$$

where

$$\theta_h = 1 - t \tag{6}$$

Legal sales are of course $X = y$

Diversifying behaviour   If $x > 0$ and $X > 0$, the maximum of (3) is:

$$\Pi_d = \Pi_h + \tfrac{1}{2}\beta\,\theta_d\hat{x}_d^2 \tag{7}$$

with

$$\hat{x}_d^2 = \frac{1 - \pi_d(1 + s)}{\beta\,\theta_d}\,tP \tag{8}$$

and

$$\hat{X}_d = y - \hat{x}_d \tag{9}$$

Behaviour of Ghosts   Given the restriction $x > 0$, $X = 0$, the maximum of (3) is:

$$\Pi_g = \Pi_h + [1 - \pi_g(1 + s)]tPy - \tfrac{1}{2}\beta y^2 \tag{10}$$

with optimal (illegal) sales given by capacity output:

$$x_g = y \tag{11}$$

Figure 8.1 illustrates the sales decision of a diversifying firm. The intersection of the schedule of marginal revenue from illegal sales (a line with slope $\beta\theta_d$ and intercept $\theta_d P$ on the vertical axis) and the marginal revenue from legal sales (a horizontal line at $\theta_h P$) gives the division of the fixed total output between illicit sales, x_d, and legitimate sales, X_d.

It is immediately clear from (7) and (8) that if $\theta_d > \theta_h$, then $\hat{x}_d > 0$, so that $\Pi_d > \Pi_h$: in a world of random enforcement where evasion is a better-than-fair gamble, diversifying behaviour strictly dominates honest behaviour.

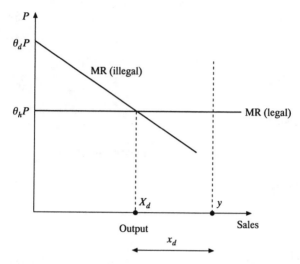

Figure 8.1   Sales decisions of a diversifier

By contrast, the result of comparing Π_g with Π_d is not so transparent. Becoming a ghost dominates diversification whenever:

$$\Pi_g > \Pi_d \qquad (12)$$

If we introduce the following quadratic function in y:

$$q(y) = \theta_g y^2 - \frac{2tP}{\beta}[1 - \pi_g(1 + s)]y + \theta_d \hat{x}_d^2 \qquad (13)$$

then, from (7) and (10) we see that (12) is equivalent to requiring that $q(y) < 0$. The roots of the equation $q(y) = 0$ are of interest in determining the set of y values for which (12) is satisfied.

$$y = [1 - \pi_g(1 + s)]\frac{Pt}{\theta_g \beta} \pm \sqrt{\left\{[1 - \pi_g(1 + s)]\frac{Pt}{\theta_g \beta}\right\}^2 - \frac{\theta_d}{\theta_g}\hat{x}_d^2} \qquad (14)$$

Consider the admissible values of y. First note that y must be positive. Second, we have assumed that all firms are large enough to produce $\hat{x}_d$. Thus from (9), we are only interested in values of y that are no smaller than $\hat{x}_d$. Using (13) and (14), it can be seen that diversifying may dominate submerging as long as:

$$\pi_g \geq \pi_d \tag{15}$$

The more interesting case occurs, however, when $\pi_g < \pi_d$ which, as mentioned before, seems most likely. Now inspection of (13) shows that firms with y less than the positive root of q will be ghosts, while firms whose capacity exceeds this level will diversify. Thus random enforcement with $\pi_g < \pi_d$ can be said to drive the smaller firms underground.

4 Conditioning audit probability on reported output

The random audit strategy examined in Section 3 makes very little demand on the tax authorities' knowledge and intelligence. In practice they have access to information which they are bound to use in enforcing tax payments. Since diversifiers conduct *some* of their operations openly, it is reasonable to suppose that something is known by the authorities about any particular diversifier. In Scotchmer's (1987) terminology, this information will determine its audit class. For example, since the authorities will have some familiarity with the workings of any particular industry, they will have some prior belief about what the fixed costs (rent, advertising expenditure, managerial salaries) of any firm in that industry should be. Does the firm at least appear to be covering these? If not, it is an obvious candidate for investigation. Alternatively, variable costs can be estimated on the basis of its other dealings with the tax authorities (national insurance contributions, income tax withheld from employees' salaries, etc.). Given estimates of both fixed and variable costs, the volume of sales reported by each firm will have to satisfy a different plausibility constraint – does the firm at least appear to be breaking even? If not, it is again a candidate for investigation.

To determine a firm's audit class will require information about costs in that industry and cross-checking with the information available from the payment of other taxes. This may be an expensive business. However, there is a source of 'free' information which may be very useful to the tax authority in designing its audit strategy. This is simply X, the level of legal sales recorded for tax purposes. In this section we examine how this might be used.

A simple version of a deterministic strategy is to audit intensively those reporting sales above that critical value. This is the audit cut-off rule analysed by Reinganum and Wilde (1985). The idea is to force an important sub-set of the firms into honest behaviour by making evasion a gamble which they can only lose. Of course in doing this the authorities will inevitably find themselves auditing small and honest inefficient firms and will miss some who are large and dishonest, but such a strategy may be justified on revenue grounds. There is, however, a further snag: the same type of snag encountered in Section 3. It is possible that some of those targeted for intensive audit will not be forced into honesty, but will instead become ghosts. This side-effect could evidently vitiate the carefully tailored audit strategy.

We investigate this possibility given the simple cut-off rule: investigate any firm selling less than an amount $\bar{X}$ on the legitimate market; ignore the others. For one class of firms – those with $y < \bar{X}$ – only Π_h and Π_g need now be compared (since evasion as a diversifier will always be detected). Inspection of (10) shows that honesty will dominate life as a ghost if:

$$y \geq \frac{2[1 - \pi_g(1+s)tP]}{\beta \theta_g} \tag{16}$$

and vice versa. Again the audit strategy drives the smallest firms underground. In order to determine the behaviour of firms with $y \geq \bar{X}$, we should also consider π_d and an expression representing a maximum of (4) subject to the equality constraint $X = \bar{X}$ (both with $\pi_d = 0$). The latter expression is given by:

$$\Pi_c(\bar{X}) - \Pi_h + [tP - \tfrac{1}{2}\beta(y - \bar{X})](y - \bar{X}) \tag{17}$$

with Π_c denoting profits from constrained diversification. Expression (17) can only be a solution if $d\Pi_c(\bar{X})/d\bar{X} < 0$, which implies:

$$y < \bar{X} + \frac{tP}{\beta} \tag{18}$$

for any y at which $\Pi_c(\bar{X})$ is a global maximum. Note that this is equivalent to $\bar{X}$ exceeding the solution to (8) with $\pi_d = 0$. Only those firms who would produce $X_d < \bar{X}$ (under the assumption that they would never be audited) find themselves constrained by the $\bar{X}$-rule. They must thus compare profits from constrained diversification, (17), with those from the alternative strategies open to them – honesty or submerging.

All other firms – those with $y \geq \bar{X} + tP/\beta$ – are unconstrained: for them X_d exceeds $\bar{X}$. They can choose between diversification (unconstrained and investigation free), honesty and submerging. Section 3 revealed that diversification (even with $\pi_d > 0$) always dominates honesty. Unconstrained firms thus need only compare (7), with $\pi_d = 0$, against (10). In general, becoming a ghost may dominate *uninvestigated* diversification (whether constrained or unconstrained by the $\bar{X}$-rule) because satisfying the $\bar{X}$ constraint necessitates paying *some* taxes. Those firms who find this price unacceptably high will prefer to disappear altogether, even though this reintroduces the possibility of being investigated (as a ghost).

5 Random audit versus the cut-off rule

Now compare the $\bar{X}$-rule with a random audit. Because of the possible existence of ghosts under both strategies, the comparison is extremely complex. We therefore begin by making the comparison in a world without ghosts.

We have seen that the smaller firms tend to find submerging most attractive. We therefore have to ensure that firms are all large enough to eschew submerging *even if ghosts were never detected* (or equivalently that β is large enough). From Section 3, there will be no ghosts under random audit even with $\pi_g = 0$, if:

$$y_0 \geq \frac{tP}{\beta} + \left[\left(\frac{tP^2}{\beta} \right)^2 - \hat{x}_d^2 \right]^{\frac{1}{2}} \tag{19}$$

On the other hand, from Section 4, there will be no ghosts under the $\bar{X}$-rule even with $\pi_g = 0$, if:

$$y_0 \geq \frac{2tP}{\beta} \tag{20}$$

Without ghosts, the authorities' expected tax revenue from random enforcement is:

$$R^R = tP \int_{y_0}^{y^0} y \, dF(y) - \beta \hat{x}_d^2 \tag{21}$$

while without ghosts, the authorities' expected tax revenue from the $\bar{X}$ rule is:

$$R^D = tP \int_{y_0}^{\bar{X}} y \, dF(y) + tP \int_{\bar{X}}^{\bar{X}+\frac{tP}{\beta}} \bar{X} \, dF(y)$$

$$+ tP \int_{\bar{X}+\frac{tP}{\beta}}^{y^0} \left(y - \frac{tP}{\beta} \right) dF(y) \tag{22}$$

For the costs of audit under both systems to be equal, requires an equal number of audits, i.e. that $\pi_d = F(\bar{X})$. Under this assumption, random audit dominates the $\bar{X}$ rule if $\Omega > 0$, where:

$$\Omega = \int_{\bar{X}}^{\bar{X}+\frac{tP}{\beta}} (y - \bar{X}) dF(y) + \left[1 - F\left(\bar{X} + \frac{tP}{\beta} \right) \right] \frac{tP}{\beta}$$

$$- [1 - F(\bar{X})(1 + s)]^2 \frac{tP}{\beta} \tag{23}$$

So a sufficient condition is that:

$$1 + s \geq \frac{F\left(\bar{X} + \frac{tP}{\beta} \right)}{F(\bar{X})} \tag{24}$$

i.e. that the penalty rate is large enough (or that the proportion of constrained diversifiers is small enough). This highlights the major weakness of the $\bar{X}$-rule: no-one who is investigated ever has to pay a fine (in fact, no-one ever pays a fine).

Conversely, the $\bar{X}$-rule is more likely to dominate, the smaller the number of unconstrained diversifiers (the closer $F(\bar{X} + tP/\beta)$ is to one) and the smaller the penalty rate.

So in a world without ghosts the sign of Ω depends on s, the shape of $F(y)$, and the level of $\bar{X}$ (i.e. the size of the audit budget).

Now relax assumption (20), but maintain (19):

If $\Omega > 0$ with (20) holding, the random audit will continue to dominate once (20) is relaxed. This is because the best the authorities can ever do with the administrative resources previously used to audit $F(2tP/\beta)$ firms who *initially* submerge is to get them all to become honest again (and the implied level of π_g may not be sufficient to do this).

If $\Omega < 0$, then relaxing (20) but keeping (19) can cause the $\bar{X}$-rule to become less attractive. Only $\pi_g = 1$ can ensure that the $F(2tP/\beta)$ firms resume their honesty and, by definition, the resources freed up will be insufficient to yield $\pi_g = 1$.

Thus, the possibility of ghosts, which appears *greater* under the $\bar{X}$-rule, can make this strategy inferior to random audit.

6   Conclusion

This paper has examined how a tax authority should audit indirect tax evaders. Our attempt to answer this question is novel in that we allow for the possibility that firms may make no tax return at all. In fact firms have three strategies open to them. They may specialise in regular sales (honesty), specialise in irregular sales (become ghosts) or sell in both markets (diversify). Only honest and diversifying firms file a tax return, so any attempt to condition audit probability on attributes of the firm thereby revealed runs the risk of creating ghosts. Consequently a policy as unsophisticated as random audit may sometimes dominate a deterministic strategy such as a cut-off rule. The optimal policy, however, is likely to be some combination of both.

There is also an added problem that we have not mentioned so far. If firms can skilfully and inexpensively disguise the scale of their operations, the information supplied to the tax authorities may in any case be worthless. The only firms which appear suspicious will be those with sloppy accountants. Moreover, the cost of the necessary dissimulation may be an extra incentive to go underground. This may provide another justification for a policy of random enforcement.[9]

NOTES

1 See Gordon (1990). See also Grossman, Ch. 6, this volume, for a similar framework where a tax-setting agency confronts the problem of firms shifting output between legal and illegal markets.
2 The term is used in this sense by the UK Inland Revenue.
3 Scotchmer (1987) notes that an income tax authority can condition audit probability on both reported income and various correlates of income: age, occupation, and the employer's report of gross income. Together these define 'audit class'. In the indirect tax context, reported income becomes reported output, while audit class is defined by information about type of business, location, technology and input usage (known to the authority if the firm complies with other taxes).
4 By contrast, Reinganum and Wilde (1986) and Chander and Wilde (1990) do not assume that the tax authority has the ability to precommit.
5 The Border–Sobel result rests on a tax system where *everything* is taken away from the poorest taxpayer. While this may maximise revenue for a given

investigative budget, such a system offends against even mild notions of vertical equity. We consider a less draconian tax-and-penalty system which corresponds more closely to those actually observed.

6 *P* will be determined in the long run by free entry to the industry. As will be evident from the model below, firms will enter as long as expected profits – including those made from illicit sales – are positive.

7 Gordon (1990) contains an explicit analysis of the consumer behaviour which would generate a demand for cash sales of the form shown in equation (2).

8 We make the assumption of risk neutrality to emphasise the role played in our model by the structure of markets rather than the preferences of individual agents. The case of risk aversion is discussed briefly in an appendix available from the authors.

9 As, of course, is risk aversion.

REFERENCES

Allingham, M. G. and A. Sandmo (1972), 'Income Tax Evasion: A Theoretical Analysis', *Journal of Public Economics*, 1(3–4), pp. 323–38.

Border, K. C. and J. Sobel (1987), 'Samurai Accountant: A Theory of Auditing and Plunder', *Review of Economic Studies*, 54, pp. 525–40.

Chander, P. and L. L. Wilde (1990), 'Corruption in Tax Administration', mimeo, California Institute of Technology.

Cowell, F. A. and J. P. F. Gordon (1988), 'Unwillingness to Pay: Tax Evasion and Public Good Provision', *Journal of Public Economics*, 36, pp. 305–22.

Cowell, F. A. and J. P. F. Gordon (1989), 'On Becoming a Ghost', *TIDI* Discussion Paper 127, (Taxation, Incentives and Distribution of Income Programme) STICERD, London School of Economics.

Gordon, J. P. F. (1990), 'Evading Taxes by Selling for Cash', *Oxford Economic Papers*, 42.

Grossman, H. I. (1995), 'Rival Kleptocrats: The Mafia versus the State', Ch. 6, this volume.

Reinganum, J. F. and L. L. Wilde (1985), 'Income Tax Compliance in a Principal-Agent Framework', *Journal of Public Economics*, 26, pp. 1–18.

Reinganum, J. F. and L. L. Wilde (1986), 'Equilibrium Verification and Reporting Policies in a Model of Tax Compliance', *International Economic Review*, 27, pp. 739–60.

Scotchmer, S. (1987), 'Audit Classes and Tax Enforcement Policy', *American Economic Review*, 77, pp. 229–33.

Discussion

DOMENICO SINISCALCO

The paper by Cowell and Gordon deals with tax evasion by firms. The model considers three kinds of firms: honest firms; diversifying firms, i.e. partial tax evaders who file unfaithful reports; and 'ghosts', i.e. firms that do not file any tax report and totally submerge in response to the auditing policy. The presence of endogenous ghosts is the novelty which reverses some of the conventional wisdom on tax auditing strategies. Under these circumstances, sophisticated cut-off rules can be dominated by simple random audit. As the authors suggest, this means 'that it may sometimes be optimal for the tax authority *not* to use all available information'.

I believe that the paper is empirically relevant and theoretically interesting, even if the analysis could be improved by taking into account more complex strategies.

Let us begin with the empirical relevance. Evidence from a large country like Italy suggests that ghosts are alive and kicking. The existing studies of the submerged sector show that ghosts can account for 10–20 per cent of GDP. They are particularly likely to proliferate in sectors with small firms in direct contact with consumers, and high fertility and mortality rates of firms. Whenever the national accounts have been revised, submerged firms accounted for a great part of the revision itself.

A recent, and most unfortunate, revision of the auditing strategy in Italy supports the view that ghosts are endogenous. In the 1992 fiscal year, to reduce partial evasion of small businesses, firms had to report at least a minimum income, pay taxes and then incur a long and tiresome bureaucratic effort to demonstrate their income was lower than the threshold. As a result, some 7 per cent of the firms in retail sectors, personal services, craftsmen etc. formally withdrew from economic activity. Such a high percentage looks suspicious *per se*. Subsequent controls by financial police showed that the withdrawal from economic activity was often false, and that firms simply had decided to submerge, becoming ghosts.

Accept now that ghosts exist. Under these circumstances, the model by Cowell and Gordon argues that a random strategy can dominate the optimal cut-off rules prescribed in the existing literature. This conclusion is fine, if one contrasts the cut-off rule with random auditing as 'extreme' models. But I would rather consider a 'convex' strategy, where the share of random audits depends on the expected distribution of firms in the three categories under review. One could begin by taking the number of ghosts as exogenous and then try to endogenise it.

Moreover, as the authors assume that tax authorities have access to the information which is likely to be correlated with a firm's turnover (e.g. electricity bills, which are successfully used by the authorities to unveil illegal activities by analysing the daily and weekly pattern of consumption), I believe that the authorities should actually use and combine all the information they can to identify the three kinds of firms analysed by the authors.

9 The reputational penalty firms bear from committing criminal fraud

JONATHAN M. KARPOFF and
JOHN R. LOTT JR

1 Introduction

Optimal penalties for corporate fraud require that firms face expected penalties equal to the total social costs of the crime. Yet formal court-imposed sanctions for committing fraud often represent a small fraction of the damage produced by the fraud. Sheer and Ho (1989), for example, estimate that the median and mean ratios of criminal fines to the private loss from private fraud were 0.14 and 0.73 in 1988. The corresponding median and mean ratios for government procurement fraud were 0.29 and 1.60. Including criminal restitution raises the median dollar sanction-to-loss ratio for private fraud to 0.84 and for government procurement fraud to 0.68. These ratios are for private parties *convicted* of fraud. The ratio of the *expected* court-imposed penalty to the social cost of the fraud is undoubtedly smaller. Particularly when compared to other crimes such as environmental pollution, where the median ratio of criminal fines to private loss is 3.71, the penalty for fraud seems surprisingly low.

The perceived underpunishment of corporate frauds has recently affected public policy. Reflecting popular opinion that existing penalties were too low, the US Sentencing Commission – the federal agency responsible for setting the penalty guidelines used by judges – established corporate sentencing guidelines in 1991 that raised median corporate fraud penalties by over twentyfold.[1]

This article criticises the conventional wisdom about corporate fraud in two ways. First, we explain that the typical optimal criminal penalty for private corporate fraud is small because the external effects of such frauds are usually small. An increase in criminal penalties for corporate fraud can do more harm than good because it encourages the substitution of criminal penalties for reputation as a mechanism to police fraudulent behaviour. Criminal penalties are unlikely to be perfect substitutes for reputation, and increased penalties will thus increase the total social costs of fraud control.

Second, we present evidence that the reputational cost of corporate fraud is large and constitutes most of the cost incurred by firms accused or convicted of fraud. Using data on 132 cases of alleged and actual corporate fraud from 1978 through 1987, we find that initial Press reports of allegations or investigations of corporate fraud against private parties correspond to an average decrease of 1.34 per cent, or $60.8 million, in the values of the common stock of affected companies. For frauds against government agencies, the loss in value is 5.05 per cent, or $40.0 million. These losses are too large to attribute to expectations of impending legal sanctions. For a sub-set of firms on which we obtained sufficient data, just 6.5 per cent of the loss represents court-imposed costs, with penalties and criminal fines accounting for 1.4 per cent.

Our investigation is related to several other papers that attempt to measure the value of lost reputation from changes in product quality.[2] Corporate frauds can provide more reliable estimates of reputational losses than events such as product recalls, however. Criminal frauds typically involve parties with whom the firm does business and who must be willing to press charges. Those cheated by frauds are therefore likely to believe they received a product quality different from that which was promised. In contrast, product safety recalls only require regulators' intervention. If government regulators value different attributes than consumers, government standards can force some customers to pay for safety characteristics or quality assurance to which they attach little or no value.[3] Regulations that force firms to increase product prices by more than they increase desired product quality can explain the decreases in firms' values that accompany product recalls.

Section 2 presents our argument that optimal criminal penalties for private frauds are small and discusses the costs of imposing too high a level of criminal penalties. Sections 3–5 provide evidence on the market and legal penalties associated with corporate fraud. Section 6 compares the expected penalties to estimates of the social costs of the crimes, and Section 7 examines the extent to which reputational losses are discernible in the firms' earnings data during the years surrounding the announcement of a fraud. Section 8 contains evidence on the aggregate market effects of recent proposals to increase criminal penalties for corporate crimes, including frauds. Section 9 summarises and concludes the article.

2   The theory of criminal penalties for frauds

2.1   Quality assurance through reputation

In this section we argue that optimal expected criminal penalties for corporate fraud are lower than the social cost of the fraud because market penalties for corporate fraud internalise many costs of the fraud. We assume throughout that fraud can occur because information is costly, and that the role of criminal penalties is to make criminals internalise the externalities they impose on others (Becker, 1968). Although the empirical results in Section 4 relate to several types of fraud, we focus here on consumer fraud. Similar arguments exist for frauds of other stakeholders, such as employees, franchisees and suppliers.

Consider a simple case in which a single firm is selling a product to consumers. Consumers value a reduction in the probability of being defrauded, but reducing that probability is costly. In the absence of government penalties, consumers can reduce the probability of fraud by having firms face larger reputational losses or higher civil penalties for fraud.[4] Reputational penalties are costly because they arise from the quasi-rents established when consumers pay high prices for high quality assurance.[5] Civil (and criminal) fines are also costly. In addition to administrative and enforcement costs, fines produce higher prices to customers of even legitimate firms because higher fines increase legitimate firms' returns from protecting themselves against false charges of fraud.

At some total penalty level, the cost to consumers of extra fraud deterrence exceeds the incremental expected cost of the fraud. When the cost of fraud is low or when customers have lower-cost alternative methods of insuring themselves against fraud, firms will invest less in reputation and provide little quality assurance. People who buy cars at flea markets are probably not making systematic mistakes – they simply value additional quality assurance less than do people who buy from new car dealers. Flea market customers are more likely to be defrauded, but they also pay lower prices for their cars.

This argument clarifies why the optimal amount of fraud is not zero: at some point the costs of reducing the probability of fraud exceed the expected benefits. Furthermore, and despite the presence of fraud, there is no externality in this case. Fraud deterrence is purchased until the marginal cost equals the marginal benefit.

A role for criminal penalties arises when a fraud imposes external costs on other parties. However, not all frauds that directly affect third parties represent *negative* externalities. Suppose a fraud committed by one firm causes the customers of other similar firms to invest more resources to assure quality and detect fraud. These extra costs *may* represent external costs of the fraud. But they *may not*. The fraud may simply reveal that the net gain to fraud is higher than the customers previously realised, and that greater investments in quality assurance and fraud detection are optimal. Such customers may demand greater investment in reputation to ensure quality. Learning that it paid for the firm to commit fraud represents an external benefit, not a cost, because the detection of the fraud has informed the customers that the probability of being defrauded was higher than they had realised. The external benefit is not produced by the fraud itself, but rather by the information that at least one firm considered fraud to be profitable. In fact, the sooner the information about the fraud is communicated, the shorter the period of time that consumers will be making purchases with less quality assurance than they would have purchased had they had the additional information.[6]

External costs arise when the firm committing the fraud has designed new methods that lower others' costs of committing frauds. The fraud may then motivate increased investment in quality assurance because it increases the likelihood that other firms will also engage in fraud. The external cost arises because one firm's fraud lowers other firms' costs of committing fraud.

For consumer fraud, externalities, and thus a role for criminal penalties, arise when the fraud represents an innovation in fraud technology. Even in these cases, however, it is the *innovation* that imposes the external cost, not the fraud itself. External costs of the fraud itself arise when the fraud corresponds to an innovation in fraud technology that changes the costs of other frauds. We do not know the fraction of frauds that also represent innovations in fraud technology. But these cases surely represent a sub-set of actual frauds. For all other consumer frauds, privately contracted penalties will optimally internalise the expected cost of the fraud.

2.2   Substitution of criminal fines for private quality assurance

Since private quality assurance mechanisms typically do not completely eliminate incentives to commit fraud, why not increase criminal penalties to deter fraud further? Can greater reliance on criminal penalties further reduce the incidence of fraud?

The answer depends on the substitutability of criminal penalties and reputation in deterring fraud. If criminal penalties and reputation are perfect substitutes, an increase in penalties will have no effect on the incidence of fraud. Increases in criminal penalties will simply reduce customers' reliance on reputation as a guarantor of quality.

We will argue, however, that criminal penalties are typically not perfect substitutes for reputation. As a result, an increase in the criminal penalty will cause a smaller decrease in reputational investments, causing an overall increase in firms' expected penalties. This will work to decrease the occurrence of frauds. But if there are no externalties for the criminal penalty to internalise, the penalty increase will also harm consumers and dissipate wealth.

One reason penalties and reputation are not perfect substitutes is that reputation relies on the threatened loss of supra-competitive prices and their associated (quasi) rents, while reliance on penalties does not. As Klein and Leffler (1981) point out, firms will compete to obtain those rents by providing additional goods and services (for example, information, comfort, etc.). A dollar increase in fines will deter fraud as much as a dollar of lost reputation, but customers will prefer reputation because the sunk investments that guarantee quality via reputation also yield other services.[7] As long as customers attach a positive value to the services lost from a reduction in sunk investments, a dollar increase in fines must result in less than a dollar reduction in sunk investments if consumers are to remain indifferent. An increase in criminal penalties will therefore result in smaller than dollar-for-dollar reductions in reputational investments.

Another reason reputation and criminal fines are not perfect substitutes in guaranteeing quality is that some types of fraud are very costly for a third party such as a court to arbitrate, for example, the taste of a hamburger.[8] Such frauds can be policed more efficiently by customers through the prospect of their repeat purchases. Therefore, criminal penalties can protect consumers from only a sub-set of the frauds from which reputation protects them.

Furthermore, the net costs of criminal penalties increase at an increasing rate because the marginal substitutability of criminal penalties for reputation decreases with higher penalties. Fines and reputation are most similar in their ability to protect customers when the frauds can be demonstrated to third parties. At low fine levels, a relatively large portion of the reputational investment protects consumers from the types of fraud for which fines are also effective; increasing fines will therefore cause a relatively large decrease in reputation. As the fine level gets larger, however, reputation and fines become progressively less close substitutes because reputation is increasingly relied on to prevent frauds that are costly to demonstrate to third parties. Further increases in fines therefore cause relatively small reductions in reputation and larger increases in the total penalty for fraud.

To illustrate, assume that expected criminal penalties increase to the point where the fines alone completely internalise those damages from frauds that can be demonstrated to third parties. At that point, further increases in fines are unlikely to reduce reputation to zero because only reputation and not fines would be useful in preventing frauds that cannot be readily proved to third parties. Still further increases in fines would result in little or no reduction in the use of reputation.

Even if reputation and fines were perfect substitutes over a broad range of criminal penalties, there would have to come a level of fines such that the optimal level of reputational bonding were zero. As long as firms could not make negative sunk investments in guaranteeing quality, further increases in fines would unambiguously result in higher total penalties. In fact, we show that the more extreme estimates of the US Sentencing Commission's recent penalty increases imply that this increase completely offsets our estimated value of the minimum reputational penalties firms suffer when they are accused of fraud.

Because reputation and criminal penalties are not perfect substitutes, an increase in penalties increases firms' total expected penalty of fraud. This works to deter some frauds, but it also increases the expected costs of all firms, as even innocent firms may have to defend themselves against fraud charges and will take extra measures to decrease the chance of being accused of fraud.[9] Some such measures will involve investing in production processes that provide a higher level of quality assurance. That is, firms will choose a higher level of quality assurance than consumers would otherwise prefer.

An increase in criminal fines will also decrease firms' abilities to meet demands for different levels of quality assurance. Different firms, or different product lines produced by the same firm, can meet the demands of different consumer clienteles by investing in different amounts of reputation. Criminal penalties that increase the total expected penalty discourage firms, however, from providing low-quality-assurance items. Flea markets may be hotbeds of fraud, but they satisfy a clientele of customers who attach a low value to buying additional quality assurance. Such consumers undoubtedly value not being cheated, but they are relatively unwilling to pay for quality assurance. For example, they may have alternative means of determining quality or may suffer relatively low costs from fraud. Large criminal penalties can eliminate the flea markets, but at a net cost to customers who prefer the low levels of quality assurance.

The effects on consumers of imposing high criminal penalties on firms are illustrated in the following comment by Robert Crandall, the chief executive officer of American Airlines:[10]

> Suppose [regulators] said, 'We don't want you guys to lose our bags anymore. And every time you lose a bag we're going to fine you a million dollars.' Well, I can fix that tomorrow morning! We will never lose another bag. But it will be very inconvenient to travel. Today you come into Dallas–Fort Worth from all these different places, and in 45 minutes you make your connection and you go out. But in the world of the future, where bags are never lost, I'm going to keep you there for three hours, because I'm going to make sure I get every bag.

Increased penalties will reduce the number of bags lost, but at a cost most consumers would not pay voluntarily.

These arguments imply that higher criminal penalties can reduce the incidence of fraud, but at a cost. At the very least, higher criminal penalties force some consumers to pay for a higher level of quality assurance than they would otherwise be willing to pay. It is also likely, however, that higher criminal penalties increase *all* consumers' costs, as *all* firms' costs rise. This latter conclusion is supported by observation. Criminal penalties could conceivably be lower-cost guarantors of quality. But the fact that we observe very little private arbitration or other third-party enforcement of quality indicates that the additional cost of third-party penalties exceeds the benefit.[11]

These conclusions directly contradict the current conventional wisdom on the topic, as represented by the US Sentencing Commission's guidelines that substantially increase criminal penalties for fraud. To this point, our argument has been based on the premise that private contracting controls and penalises firms that commit fraud. In the following sections, we present empirical evidence that supports this premise. The private wealth loss suffered by firms alleged, indicted or convicted of fraud is statistically significant and much larger than court-imposed penalties.

3 Data and empirical method

3.1 Fraud types

Press announcements of corporate fraud were collected from a search of entries under the 'Fraud' and 'Crime' listings in *The Wall Street Journal Index* from 1981 through 1987. Once a firm was identified as being accused of a fraud, we investigated all the listings under this firm's name to find additional information concerning this or other frauds. Several of the listings refer to cases that were initially publicised before 1981. For such cases, we searched previous issues of *The Wall Street Journal Index* to identify the initial Press announcements. Inclusion of these announcements extends our sample period to 1978–87. Our main concern is with cases in which the damaged party does business with the accused firm. For example, we consider frauds of customers, suppliers, employees and investors but do not consider damages to third parties such as pollution dumping. This allows us to focus on cases in which some or all costs of the fraud can be internalised by the firm through its repeat contracting with customers, suppliers, employees and investors. We further divide the types of fraud into four categories: fraud of stakeholders, fraud of government, financial reporting fraud and regulatory violations. Empirical tests are conducted for all fraud types aggregated and for each fraud type separately.

'Frauds of stakeholders' occur when the firm cheats or is accused of cheating on implicit or explicit contracts with suppliers, employees, franchisees or customers *other than governments*. The following are examples: Chrysler Corporation was indicted and eventually settled on charges that it sold 'as new more than 60,000 cars and trucks that company managers allegedly had used with the odometers disconnected;'[12] 'E. F. Hutton and two of its brokers were sued in Gainesville, Florida, by two clients who sought $27 million in damages stemming from allegedly improper securities trading in their accounts;'[13] and 'An Illinois couple was awarded $14 million in damages in a lawsuit accusing General Foods Corp. of fraudulent conduct toward Burger Chef franchisees.'[14] The discussion in Section 2 implies that the cost of defrauding stakeholders is internalised at least in part by the firm because it must deal with stakeholders on a continuing basis. The cost of contracting and the terms of contracts between the firm and its customers, suppliers, employees or franchisees determine and depend on the likelihood of fraudulent activity.

'Frauds of governments' are cases in which the firm cheats or is accused of cheating on implicit or explicit contracts with a government agency. Government frauds in our sample are either programme frauds or procurement frauds, and many involve defence contractors. For example, in 1985 General Electric Company was indicted and pleaded guilty to charges that it fraudulently overcharged the Defense Department more than $800,000 for labour cost overruns on Minuteman missile contracts. In another well-known case, Rockwell International was investigated in 1985 for improperly charging the Defense Department for 'overhead items such as entertainment and public relations' on military contracts. In other examples, River Oaks Industries Incorporated was accused and pleaded guilty in 1985 to charges that it padded invoices and overcharged the Veterans Administration for mobile homes, and Paradyne Corporation was accused in 1986 of overcharging the Department of Health and Human Services on a contract to supply equipment.

We separate government frauds from stakeholder frauds because the wealth effects may be different. Private customers, suppliers, employees or franchisees have incentives to consider the expected cost of doing business with the firm, including any cost that can arise from fraudulent behaviour by the firm. A firm that commits fraud against one of these parties suffers a wealth loss because stakeholders face increased costs of doing business with the firm. Government agents' incentives, however, may be totally different from private parties' incentives. On the one hand, a government agent can have negligible incentives to consider the expected cost of a firm's fraudulent activities, and a firm committing fraud may experience no loss in value. On the other hand, a government agent may demand contractual concessions that exceed the expected cost of any fraudulent activity by the firm, such as disqualifying the firm from bidding on future government projects. In this case, the firm can have a reputational loss that exceeds the loss it would have incurred if the fraud was committed against a private party.

'Financial reporting frauds' are cases in which agents of the firm misrepresent or are accused of misrepresenting the firm's financial condition. For example: 'A Charter Co. shareholder sued the firm and five of its top executives, alleging that Charter misrepresented its financial condition to inflate its stock price;'[15] and 'Two investors who recently purchased shares in the firm sued Cannon Group Inc. over its accounting policies; ... the suits allege that the firm's practice of amortizing film costs was "part of a scheme ... to inflate Cannon's earnings and the price of its securities." '[16] Financial reporting frauds may harm investors in the firm's securities and can affect the firm's value in two ways. The report of fraud can convey information about the firm's financial condition that previously was not public information. And the report of fraud can increase the firm's cost of obtaining new funds, as investors revise upward their expectations that the firm will act fraudulently in the future.

The fourth and last type of corporate fraud consists of actions labelled 'fraud' by the Press or by federal statutes, but which have ambiguous effects on parties that contract with the firm. These events are labelled 'regulatory violations' and typically involve violations of regulations enforced by federal agencies. Many of these events involve firms in the financial services industry. For example, Manufacturers Hanover Bank agreed to pay civil fines in 1985 for failing to report currency transactions; Interfirst Corporation was fined by the Treasury Department in 1986 for failing to disclose some large cash transactions. In a well-publicised case, E. F. Hutton pleaded guilty in 1985 to a large cheque-kiting scheme involving banks in New York state. In each of these cases, the firm was accused of fraudulent activities, but it is not apparent that the firm violated an implicit or explicit contract with an investor or stakeholder. For example, banks may have been knowingly involved in E. F. Hutton's cheque-kiting scheme, for which they may have been compensated through other business dealings with E. F. Hutton. (In fact, very few of the affected banks were willing to bring civil suits against E. F. Hutton.) The size of the reputational loss suffered by firms accused of regulatory violations seems likely to be negligible. Regulatory violations should thus provide a contrast to the other categories, in which some or all costs of the fraud can be internalised by the firm through its reputational losses.

To be included in the sample, the firm must be listed on the 1990 Center for Research in Security Prices (CRSP) Daily Returns tape and have returns data during the two-day announcement interval that consists of the initial Press day and the preceding day and must have returns data for at least 60 days during the estimation period, which is defined below.[17] The resulting sample consists of 132 fraud events from 71 firms. Table 9.1 reports the number of events for each fraud type in the sample. Table 9.1 also reports on the distribution of firms across industries. Each firm's two-digit Standard Industrial Classification (SIC) code was recorded from Dun and Bradstreet's *Million Dollar Directory* for the year before the year of the first Press report of fraud. The data indicate that the sample is distributed widely over many industries, although industry groups 37 (transportation equipment), 60 (depository institutions) and 62 (security and commodity brokers) are heavily represented.

3.2   Event date types

For each fraud event, we identified up to four distinct types of Press dates. The 'allegation date' (which we call 'date type 1') is the date allegations or investigations of alleged fraudulent activity were first reported in *The Wall Street Journal*. The 'charges filed date' (date type 2) is the first date of a report that charges or a law-suit claiming fraudulent activity were filed by a private party or government agency. The 'settlement date' (date type 3) is the date of the first report that the firm was convicted, found not guilty, agreed to a penalty, or otherwise reached settlement with at least one plaintiff in the case. The 'additional information date' (date type 4) is the date of the first report after the settlement date that contained any additional information about the settlement.

Table 9.1:   The distribution of the fraud sample by type of fraud and industry of accused firm, 1978–87[a]

	Type of Fraud				
	Frauds of Stake-holders	Frauds of Govern-ment	Financial Reporting Frauds	Regulatory Violations	Total[b]
Number of events in sample	57	40	11	24	132
Number of firms in sample	32	27	10	19	71
Firms grouped by two-digit SIC code:					
13 (Oil and gas extraction)	1			1	1
14 (Mining, non-metallic minerals)		1		1	1
15 (Building construction)	2	1			3
17 (Special trade contractors)		1			1
20 (Food and kindred products)	1		1		2
24 (Lumber and wood products)		1			1
27 (Printing and publishing)	1				1
28 (Chemicals and allied products)	3		1		3
29 (Petroleum refining)			1		1
35 (Machinery and computers)		2	1		2
36 (Electronic equipment)	2	5		1	5
37 (Transportation equipment)	2	9			10
38 (Medical and photo equipment)	1	1			2
48 (Communications)	1	1			2
49 (Electric and gas services)				1	1
50 (Wholesale – durables)				1	1
51 (Wholesale – non-durables)			1		1
60 (Depository institutions)	3			6	8
61 (Other credit institutions)	1		1		1
62 (Security and commodity brokers)	7		1	5	8
63 (Insurance carriers)	2				2
64 (Insurance agents and brokers)	1		1		1
65 (Real estate)		1			1
67 (Holding companies)	3	1	1	2	6
73 (Business services)		1			1
78 (Motion pictures)			1	1	2
79 (Recreation services)	1				1
89 (Miscellaneous services)		2			2

Notes: (a) The number of fraud events in the sample and the number of firms represented are broken down by Standard Industrial Classification (SIC) codes. The events are classified into four types of corporate fraud or alleged corporate fraud, as described in the text.

(b) The numbers in the total column may be less than the sum of the frauds listed for that row because some firms were involved in more than one type of fraud.

Only two of the fraud events have all four types of event dates. In 47 cases, the first Press date is an allegation date. For 55 cases, the first Press announcement indicates that charges of alleged fraudulent activity have been filed, that is, it is a charges filed date. In 30 other cases, the first Press announcement is a settlement date. It is very possible that news of alleged fraud is publicly available before it appears in *The Wall Street Journal*, especially if the first Press date is a charges filed or a settlement date. In the empirical tests reported below, we separate the events by type of initial event date. We also report average stock return forecast errors cumulated over different combinations of the available types of Press dates.

3.3   Empirical method

The empirical analysis has two parts. First, we estimate abnormal stock returns for the firms about which Press reports of corporate fraud appeared in *The Wall Street Journal*. These tests are designed to investigate whether firms accused of fraudulent activities experience wealth losses. Second, we compare the dollar size of the estimated wealth losses with estimates of the expected legal penalties incurred by firms accused of fraud. The difference between a firm's wealth loss and the amount of the loss attributable to legal penalties is an estimate of the loss imposed by the market.[18]

The forecast error for the common stock of firm j on day t is defined as:

$$FE_{jt} = r_{jt} - a_j - b_j r_{mt} \tag{1}$$

Here r_{jt} and r_{mt} are the continuously compounded returns on firm j's common stock and the CRSP value-weighted index of market returns on day t, assumed to be bivariate and normally distributed with independence across days. The coefficients a_j and b_j are estimated from an ordinary least squares regression of r_{jt} on r_{mt} using a 200-day period consisting of days -130 through -31 relative to the first *Wall Street Journal* announcement and days $+31$ through $+130$ relative to the last *Wall Street Journal* announcement concerning each fraud that we recorded. For example, if a given event has an allegation date and a settlement date, the estimation period for that event consists of days -130 through -31 relative to the allegation date and days $+31$ through $+131$ relative to the settlement date. Some firms have missing returns and have fewer than 200 observations during the estimation period.

Forecast errors are calculated for each firm over the 61-day period -30 through $+30$. For each day in the event period, the average forecast error is computed across firms:

$$AFE_t = \frac{1}{N_t} \sum_{j=1}^{j=N_t} FE_{jt} \tag{2}$$

where N_t is the number of firms over which forecast errors are averaged on day t. The cumulated average forecast error for days k through t is:

$$CAFE_{kt} = \sum_{\tau=k}^{\tau=t} AFE_\tau \tag{3}$$

The corresponding test statistic, denoted z_{kt}, is described in Appendix 1. Under the null hypothesis of no abnormal stock performance, z_{kt} is distributed approximately unit normal

4   Empirical results: stock return forecast errors

4.1   Overall stock price effects of fraud announcements

Table 9.2 contains the average and cumulated average forecast errors for the total sample when date $t = 0$ is defined as the day of the first *Wall Street Journal* announcement. Average abnormal stock returns during days -30 to -2 relative to the initial Press announcement are approximately zero, indicating that, on average, there is no unusual stock price movement during the period before the initial Press report of fraud. On the day immediately before the initial *Wall Street Journal* announcement about alleged or actual fraud, the average stock return forecast error is -0.54 per cent with $z_{-1,-1} = -2.07$. On the day of the Press report, the forecast error is -1.04 per cent with $z_{0,0} = -3.97$. Cumulated over both days, the average forecast error is -1.58 per cent with $z_{-1,0} = -4.38$. These results indicate that, on average, the initial Press reports of alleged or actual fraud correspond with statistically significant and economically meaningful losses in equity value.

The results are not the product of outliers and our underlying assumption that the forecast errors are distributed normally. As indicated in Table 9.2, just 40 per cent of the individual firm forecast errors are positive on day 0. Assuming the binomial distribution with a 50 per cent probability of a positive forecast error, the sign test z-statistic is -2.28. Although not reported in Table 9.2, 40.77 per cent of the individual two-day announcement period forecast errors over days -1 and 0 are positive, with an associated z-statistic of -2.10.

The average forecast errors are negative for 22 of the 30 days after the initial Press report. The cumulative stock return forecast error is 0.56 per

Table 9.2:   Average and cumulative average daily stock return forecast errors for all 132 events[a]

Event Day	Number of Events	Average Forecast Error (%)	z-statistic[b]	Per cent Positive[c]	z-statistic[c]	Cumulative Forecast Error (%)	z-statistic[b]
−30	132	0.00	0.63	49.24	−0.17	0.00	0.63
−20	132	0.02	0.67	46.21	−0.87	0.45	1.57
−10	132	0.10	0.76	58.33	1.91	0.53	1.08
−9	132	0.15	1.13	42.42	−1.74	0.68	1.29
−8	132	0.03	0.35	45.45	−1.04	0.71	1.27
−7	132	−0.12	−0.22	45.45	−1.04	0.59	1.19
−6	132	−0.21	−0.36	45.45	−1.04	0.38	1.08
−5	132	0.35	1.20	52.27	0.52	0.74	1.28
−4	132	−0.01	−0.18	50.76	0.17	0.73	1.22
−3	132	−0.05	−0.60	43.18	−1.57	0.68	1.09
−2	132	−0.12	−0.49	49.24	−0.17	0.56	0.97
−1	132	−0.54	−2.07	46.21	−0.87	0.02	0.60
0	130	−1.04	−3.97	40.00	−2.28	−1.02	−0.08
1	131	−0.26	−2.17	43.51	−1.49	−1.29	−0.43
2	132	−0.42	−2.27	43.94	−1.39	−1.71	−0.79
3	132	−0.50	−1.89	43.18	−1.57	−2.20	−1.07
4	132	0.12	1.13	50.00	0.00	−2.08	−0.88
5	132	−0.39	−1.67	43.94	−1.39	−2.48	−1.13
6	132	0.06	−0.35	42.42	−1.74	−2.42	−1.16
7	132	0.09	0.46	47.73	−0.52	−2.33	−1.07
8	132	−0.41	−1.82	42.42	−1.74	−2.74	−1.33
9	132	−0.12	−0.74	43.94	−1.39	−2.86	−1.41
10	132	0.34	1.95	58.33	1.91	−2.51	−1.11
20	132	−0.32	−1.29	51.52	0.35	−3.55	−1.47
30	132	0.10	1.08	51.52	0.35	−4.01	−1.51

Notes: (a) Average daily stock return forecast errors for 132 events from 71 firms for which allegations or charges of fraudulent activity, or settlements of charges of fraudulent activity, as were reported in *The Wall Street Journal*, 1978–87, are reported.
(b) The z-statistics are distributed approximately standard normal under the null hypothesis of zero abnormal stock price performance. The calculation of the z-statistic is described in Appendix 1.
(c) The per cent positive is the percentage of the forecast errors that are positive on the event day. The associated z-statistic is computed using the normal approximation to a binomial distribution.

cent on day -2 relative to the announcement, but it is -4.01 per cent $(z_{-30, +30} = -1.51)$ on day $+30$ relative to the announcement. A small part of this post-announcement drift is due to two firms with missing returns on days 0 and 1 whose stock price reactions are not picked up until days 1 and 2. Moreover, the post-announcement drift is sensitive to the model specification. The cumulated forecast error over days $+1$ through $+30$ is not significantly different from zero when the market model parameters are estimated over a post-announcement period that begins on day $+31$ and ends on day $+230$ relative to our last Press announcement about fraud.

We conducted several tests to examine the sensitivity of our results to the estimation procedure. Other than the post-announcement drift reported in Table 9.2, the important results remain virtually unaffected using the different estimation periods for the market model or different test statistics such as those discussed by Malatesta (1986). The results are also unaffected by the choice of market proxy. For example, using the equal-weighted CRSP index as the market proxy, the cumulated average forecast error for event days -1 and 0 is -1.5 per cent with $z_{-1,0} = -3.51$.

The most significant finding from the sensitivity tests occurs when events with contemporaneous announcements are deleted. For 28 of the 132 events in the sample, *The Wall Street Journal* contained at least one report about the firm other than about the corporate fraud on days -1, 0 or $+1$ relative to the initial fraud Press date. Most of these announcements appear to be routine, such as the award of a government contract or the announcement of a quarterly dividend. Deleting these 28 events changes the average two-day forecast error to -2.09 per cent with $z_{-1,0} = -5.08$. This deletion also changes some of the results reported in Tables 9.3–9.6, but towards findings of even larger market value losses than those we report here. The one contemporaneous event that appears to be significant is a report of a rumoured take-over bid for Gould, Incorporated on 4 October 1985, the same day of a report that Gould agreed to pay the federal government $3.7 million to settle procurement fraud charges. The two-day forecast error for Gould for this announcement is a positive 19.77 per cent. If this case is deleted from the sample, the average two-day forecast error is -1.75 per cent with $z_{-1,0} = -4.97$.

4.2   The wealth effects of different types of fraud announcements

The average forecast errors in Table 9.2 are disaggregated in Table 9.3 according to the type of fraud and the type of information contained in the initial Press report. The average two-day forecast errors for stakeholder fraud, government fraud and financial reporting fraud are negative and statistically significant. For the 57 stakeholder frauds the average forecast error is -1.22 per cent with $z_{-1,0} = -2.66$; for the 40 frauds of government, it is -1.67 per cent with $z_{-1,0} = -2.86$; and for financial reporting frauds it is -4.66 per cent with $z_{-1,0} = -2.80$. The average two-day forecast error for regulatory violations, however, is -0.93 per cent and is insignificantly different from zero ($z_{-1,0} = -0.58$), indicating that the value of lost reputation is smaller when firms are accused of violating regulations than when they are accused of other types of fraud. This is consistent with our prediction of small market value losses for frauds that have small reputational effects.

The earlier the Press report in the investigation of the fraud, the larger is the stock price reaction. Aggregating over all fraud types, the average two-day forecast error is -2.39 per cent with $z_{-1,0} = -3.93$ when the initial Press report is of an allegation or investigation of alleged fraud. When the initial Press report indicates that a formal charge or a law-suit has been filed, the average two-day forecast error is -1.98 per cent with $z_{-1,0} = -3.25$. When the initial Press report indicates that a verdict or settlement of the fraud charges has been reached, the average two-day forecast error is 0.36 per cent with $z_{-1,0} = 0.14$. It is likely that news of the fraud reaches financial markets before the settlement or verdict date. Stock price reactions on this date should therefore simply reflect new information about the amount of the settlement or penalty. The fact that the average forecast error on this date is insignificantly different from zero is consistent with the hypothesis that market prices before the settlement date contain unbiased estimates of the size of the settlement or penalty.

Table 9.4 reports on tests designed to investigate the effects of announcements *after* the initial Press report about the fraud. We identified a subsequent announcement in *The Wall Street Journal* for 58 of the 132 fraud events. For example, 47 cases have type 1 Press dates, that is, announcements that report allegations or investigations of fraud. Of these 47, 16 cases also have subsequent type 2 Press dates, that is, announcements that charges of fraud were formally filed. Of these 16, three cases also have type 3 Press dates, in which a settlement of verdict is reported, and two cases also have type 4 Press announcements, which report additional information about the monetary penalty paid by the firm. Thirteen cases have type 1 and type 2 Press announcements only. The second row of Table 9.4 reports that, for these thirteen cases, the average sum of the two-day forecast errors over these two dates is -2.93 per cent, with a t-statistic of -1.92. Likewise, ten cases have type 1 and type 3 Press announcements. The average sum of the two-day forecast errors over these two dates is -4.45 per cent, with a t-statistic of -2.66.

The results in Table 9.4 indicate that, on average, the stock price decline

Table 9.3:   Percentage changes in common stock market value by type of
fraud and event date[a]

	Type of Initial Press Announcement			
	Allegations or Charges or Investigations Law-suit Filed (Date Type 1)	Charges or Law-suit Filed (Date Type 2)	Settlement or Verdict (Date Type 3)	All Initial Press Announcements
Fraud of stakeholders:				
Number of events	19	25	13	57
Two-day forecast error (%)	−1.34	−1.67	−0.17	−1.22
Test statistic ($=cz_{-1,0}$)	−1.51	−2.35[b]	−0.49	−2.66[b]
Fraud of government:				
Number of events	13	17	10	40
Two-day forecast error (%)	−5.05	−0.93	1.48	−1.67
Test statistic ($=cz_{-1,0}$)	−4.77[b]	−1.14	1.20	−2.86[b]
Financial reporting fraud:				
Number of events	4	7	0	11
Two-day forecast error (%)	−4.60	−4.56	–	−4.66
Test statistic ($=cz_{-1,0}$)	−2.00[b]	−1.99[b]	–	−2.80[b]
Violation of regulations:				
Number of events	11	6	7	24
Two-day forecast error (%)	−0.11	−3.23	−0.24	−0.93
Test statistic ($=cz_{-1,0}$)	0.25	−0.99	−0.47	−0.58
All fraud types aggregated:				
Number of events	47	55	30	132
Two-day forecast error (%)	−2.39	−1.98	0.36	−1.58
Test statistic ($=cz_{-1,0}$)	−3.93[b]	−3.25[b]	0.14	−4.38[b]

Notes: (a) Average stock return forecast errors for the two-day interval consisting
of the day the first report of fraud or alleged fraud appears in *The Wall Street
Journal* and the immediately preceding day for 132 fraud events from 71 firms,
1978–87, are given.
(b) Significantly different from zero at the 5 per cent level. The calculation of the
test statistic is reported in Appendix 1.

observed on the initial *Wall Street Journal* report is not reversed when
new information about the fraud is published. For all 132 events, the
average sum of the two-day forecast errors over all available Press date
types is −1.77 per cent with a t-statistic of −4.78. This is not
significantly different from the average two-day forecast error for the
initial Press date of −1.58 per cent. Most of the results are similar when
the sample is divided into different fraud types and cases with different
combinations of date types. Exceptions occur when very few cases fall
into a category. For example, the sum of the two-day forecast errors for

Table 9.4: Summation of the two-day stock return forecast errors over date types[a]

	Stakeholder Fraud	Government Fraud	Financial Reporting Fraud	Violation of Regulations	All Fraud Types
All events, summation over available event dates:					
Number of events	57	40	11	24	132
Mean sum of forecast errors (%)	−1.67	−1.46	−5.04	−1.01	−1.77
t-statistic	−3.57	−2.66	−2.18	−1.05	−4.78
Frauds that have only Press date types 1 and 2:					
Number of events	5	3	1	4	13
Mean sum of forecast errors (%)	−2.52	−6.31	−7.72	1.76	−2.93
t-statistic	−1.45	−3.29	−0.67	1.08	−1.92
Frauds that have only Press date types 1 and 3:					
Number of events	–	6	1	3	10
Mean sum of forecast errors (%)	–	−4.66	−14.20	−0.92	−4.45
t-statistic	–	−2.07	−2.50	−0.34	−2.66
Frauds that have only Press date types 1, 2 and 3:					
Number of events	–	1	–	–	1
Mean sum of forecast errors (%)	–	3.25	–	–	3.25
t-statistic	–	0.93	–	–	0.93
Frauds that have only Press date types 1, 3 and 4:					
Number of events	2	–	–	1	3
Mean sum of forecast errors (%)	−0.26	–	–	−3.72	−1.42
t-statistic	−0.10	–	–	−1.22	−0.71

Table 9.4: *(contd)*

	Stakeholder Fraud	Government Fraud	Financial Reporting Fraud	Violation of Regulations	All Fraud Types
Frauds that have all Press date types 1, 2, 3 and 4:					
Number of events	1	1	–	–	2
Mean sum of forecast errors (%)	3.23	−20.75			−8.76
t-statistic	0.83	−3.18			−2.31
Frauds that have only Press date types 2 and 3:					
Number of events	7	5	3	1	16
Mean sum of forecast errors (%)	−5.33	−0.27	−4.19	0.61	−3.16
t-statistic	−3.16	−0.18	−0.78	0.052	−2.08
Frauds that have only Press date types 2, 3 and 4:					
Number of events	1	3	1	1	6
Mean sum of forecast errors (%)	−7.35	−1.41	1.53	−14.99	−4.18
t-statistic	−1.43	−0.67	0.39	−1.15	−1.58
Frauds that have only Press date types 3 and 4:					
Number of events	2	1	–	4	7
Mean sum of forecast errors (%)	−0.33	−6.47		−0.39	−1.24
t-statistic	−0.23	−2.40		−0.22	−1.07

Note: (a) Results are reported for all 132 corporate fraud events and for different combinations of available event dates, and for four different fraud types. The calculation of the *t*-statistic is described in Appendix 1.

the one case (involving General Dynamics) that has date types 1, 2 and 3 is a positive 3.25 per cent. Similarly, the sum of the two-day forecast errors for the single stakeholder fraud case that has all date types 1, 2, 3 and 4 (involving J. P. Morgan) is 3.23 per cent. Overall, however, the results indicate that the initial stock return forecast errors are unbiased estimates of the total stock price effects of the frauds.

We also examined the stock price reactions to the *second* announcement in *The Wall Street Journal* about the fraud for the 58 cases with at least two announcements. Consistent with the results in Table 9.4, the stock price reaction to the fraud is concentrated on the first announcement. The average two-day stock return forecast error for the second announcement is -0.60 per cent with $z_{-1,0} = -1.51$. There is no evidence that the initial stock price reaction is reversed upon later announcements.

As an additional sensitivity test, we examined the stock price reactions for a sample of 29 additional fraud cases that were carried on the Dow Jones News Retrieval Service (DJNRS). The DJNRS includes news stories carried on the Dow Jones News Service, often called the Broad Tape, many of which are not subsequently published in *The Wall Street Journal*. Our original sample would be biased if *The Wall Street Journal* editors' decision to publish correlates with the size of the anticipated stock price reaction to the news story.

The DJNRS sample was selected by identifying all 829 stories from 1981–3 containing the word 'fraud'. Of these, however, only 29 cases meet the criteria imposed on the original sample and are not already included in the original sample. Overall, the results from the DJNRS sample are consistent with those reported in Table 9.3, indicating that the empirical results reported in Table 9.3 are not sensitive to the sample selection procedure. For example, the announcement period forecast error average over all 29 events is -3.18 per cent, compared to -1.58 per cent for the main sample. When broken down by fraud type, the sub-sample results are also generally consistent with the results in Table 9.3.[19] These results do not support the conjecture that our sample of *Wall Street Journal* announcements is biased towards fraud events with large stock price reactions. The market reactions reflected in the DJNRS sample is, if anything, larger than that for the original sample.

5   The amount of lost reputation

5.1   The relative sizes of the market and legal penalties

To investigate the magnitude of the *dollar* losses involved, we computed the change in the market value of common stock for each of the fraud events. Table 9.5 reports the average changes in market value over the initial two-day announcement interval for the total sample and for sub-samples grouped by fraud type and the initial Press report type. To compute the change in market value, each firm's two-day forecast error for event days -1 and 0 was multiplied by the market value of the firm's outstanding common stock at the close of trading in the month before the initial *Wall Street Journal* announcement. To calculate the market value, the month-end closing stock price and number of shares outstanding were taken from the *Standard and Poor's Stock Guides*. For all 132 events, the median change in market value is $-\$5.540$ million and the mean change is $-\$6.418$ million. When divided into sub-samples, the results loosely parallel the results in Table 9.3. For frauds of stakeholders, the median and mean changes in market value are $-\$4.477$ million and $-\$37.847$ million. For frauds of government, the median and mean changes are $-\$9.457$ million and $\$0.029$ million.[20] For financial reporting frauds the respective values are $-\$10.984$ million and $\$5.280$ million, and for regulation violations they are $-\$0.552$ million and $\$52.122$ million.[21]

The largest losses occur when the initial announcement is of allegations or investigations of fraud. The median change is $-\$9.457$ million for these types of announcements, while it is $-\$0.924$ million for the 55 initial Press announcements that reported filings of charges or law-suits against the firm, and $-\$3.510$ million for the 30 initial Press announcements that reported a settlement or verdict.

These data indicate that, on average, the initial Press report of corporate fraud is associated with a large dollar loss in the market value of the affected company. Table 9.6 reports data we collected to investigate the portion of this loss that is attributable to the prospect of *legal* penalties. We were able to obtain detailed breakdowns of the criminal and civil penalties levied against 15 of the firms in our sample. The data on criminal fines and criminal restitution were available primarily from the Administrative Office of the US Courts' data set entitled the Federal Probation and Parole Sentencing and Supervision Research File (FPSSIS). In some cases the US Sentencing Commission augmented this file by including information on the Commission's estimates of the losses from the crime. The Commission defines the loss as 'the difference between the value paid and the value received by the victims.'[22] In the cases involving Dynalectric, Litton, Martin Marietta, Paradyne and Rockwell International, data on civil penalties and any court costs assessed against these firms were taken from the records of the cases when the verdicts were appealed. In other cases, information on civil penalties were obtained from *The Wall Street Journal*. Information on debarments were also obtained from *The Wall Street Journal*.

Table 9.5:   Dollar changes in common stock market value by type of fraud and event date.[a]

Type of Fraud	Type of Press Announcement			
	Allegations or Investigations Date Type 1	Charges or Law-suit Filed Date Type 2	Settlement or Verdict Date Type 3	All Initial Press Announcements Date Type 4
Fraud of stakeholders:				
Number of events	19	25	13	57
Median change in value ($1,000s)	−5,540	−3,237	−6,572	−4,477
Mean change in value ($1,000s)	−60,800	−25,483	−28,079	−37,847
t-statistic	−1.41	−1.68	−1.38	−2.32
Fraud of government:				
Number of events	13	17	10	40
Median change in value ($1,000s)	−40,377	9,887	2,192	−9,457
Mean change in value ($1,000s)	−39,993	23,318	14,166	29
t-statistic	−1.29	0.34	0.44	0.00
Financial reporting fraud:				
Number of events	4	7	0	11
Median change in value ($1,000s)	−27,548	−9,524	—	−10,984
Mean change in value ($1,000s)	23,700	−5,247	—	5,280
t-statistic	0.38	−0.57	—	0.24
Violation of regulations:				
Number of events	11	6	7	24
Median change in value ($1,000s)	−5,348	−552	5,578	−552
Mean change in value ($1,000s)	108,273	9,311	579	52,122
t-statistic	0.90	0.20	0.07	0.94

Table 9.5: *(contd)*

Type of Fraud	Type of Press Announcement			
	Allegations or Investigations Date Type 1	Charges or Law-suit Filed Date Type 2	Settlement or Verdict Date Type 3	All Initial Press Announcements Date Type 4
All fraud types aggregated:				
Number of events	47	55	30	132
Median change in value ($1,000s)	−9,457	−924	−3,510	−5,540
Mean change in value ($1,000s)	−8,283	−4,337	−7,310	−6,418
t-statistic	−0.24	−0.20	−0.52	−0.41

Note: (a) Average changes in market values for the two-day interval consisting of the day the first report of corporate fraud or alleged corporate fraud appears in *The Wall Street Journal* and the immediately preceding day for 132 events from 71 firms, 1978–87, are given.

Table 9.6: Comparisons of actual and predicted court-imposed penalties with changes in market value

Firm	First WSJ Report	Type of Fraud	Predicted Criminal Fine	Actual Criminal Fine	Actual Criminal Restitution or Civil Penalties	Actual Court Costs
A) Cases for which *Wall Street Journal* announcements are about investigations or charges filed.						
Chrysler Motor	870625	Stake	$3,147	$7,600,000	$19,500,000	0
Dynalectric Co.	860922	Govt	$115,243	0	0	0
E. F. Hutton	850503	Reg	$86,248	$2,000,000	$6,700,000	0
General Electric	850327	Govt	$31,683	$1,040,000	$2,000,000	0
Litton Systems	860716	Govt	$120,769	$3,000,000	$6,100,000	0
Martin Marietta	850829	Govt	$54,890	$12,000	0	$250,000
Paradyne Corp	850313	Govt	$109,287	$1,000,000	$1,000,000	$200,000
Rockwell International	850429	Govt	$54,516	0	$1,500,000	0
TRW Electronic Products	860603	Govt	$15,672	$100,000	$17,000,000	0
			$591,455	$14,752,000	$53,800,000	$450,000
B) Cases for which *Wall Street Journal* announcements are about the settlement of the verdict.						
Emerson Electric	850222	Govt	$80,722	0	$325,000	0
General Foods	850327	Stake	$50,531	0	0	0
Gould	851004	Govt	$23,107	0	$3,700,000	0
GTE Gov't Systems	850916	Govt	$3,009	$10,000	?	?
Merrill Lynch	850314	Stake	$77,902	0	$300,000	0
Merrill Lynch	870505	Stake	$54,698	0	$2,700,000	0
				$10,000	$7,250,000	0

Estimated Victims' Loss	2-day Forecast Error	z-statistic ($=z_{-1,0}$)	Debarment from Government Contracts	Market Value	Change in Market Value
?	−0.69	−0.29	none	$7,367,562,000	−$51,160,820
$500,000	−6.31	−2.57	none	$153,344,000	−$9,677,289
?	−4.33	−1.70	none	$872,165,000	−$37,699,594
$800,000	−2.78	−2.35	Full 3/29/85–4/19/85 Partial 4/19/85–9/16/85	$28,838,528,000	−$802,491,437
$6.3m	−4.37	−2.28	7/17/86–8/22/86	$2,203,767,000	−$96,192,687
$6,000	−1.84	−0.92	none	$2,296,310,000	−$42,202,074
?	−11.40	−2.20	none	$354,265,000	−$40,376,770
$600,000	2.35	1.11	none	$5,359,200,000	$125,809,812
$2.5m	−3.52	−1.33	none	$2,924,671,000	−$102,948,687
				$50,359,814,000	−$1,056,939,546
$325,000	−1.17	−1.06	none	$5,218,521,000	−$61,175,594
?	−0.57	−0.51	none	$2,996,777,000	−$16,956,090
?	19.77	6.40	8/31/85–9/16/85	$1,353,992,000	$267,662,562
?	0.83	0.62	none	$8,315,241,000	$68,865,187
?	0.57	0.29	none	$3,168,698,000	$18,077,961
?	−0.17	−0.07	none	$3,853,701,000	−$6,572,461
				$24,906,930,000	$269,901,565

The data in Table 9.6 are divided into two groups. Panel A contains nine cases for which the first Press dates were of investigations or filed charges of fraud (date types 1 and 2), and panel B contains six cases for which the first Press dates reported a settlement or verdict (date type 3). The results reported in Table 9.3 indicate that the average stock price reaction to date type 3 is not significantly different from zero, presumably because market prices reflect unbiased estimates of the terms of settlement of the fraud even if *The Wall Street Journal* had not reported the case earlier. Consistent with this hypothesis, half of the stock return forecast errors for the six firms with date type 3 are positive and half are negative.

The two-day stock return forecast error is negative for eight of the nine cases in Panel A, and is significantly different from zero at the 0.10 level using a one-tailed hypothesis test in five of the nine cases. The loss in market value for these nine firms averages 3.65 per cent of firm value and totals $1,057 million. Actual criminal fines, however, total $14.752 million, which is 1.4 per cent of the total loss in firm value. Even when criminal restitution, civil penalties and court costs are included, the total legal penalties sum to $68.552 million, which is still only 6.5 per cent of the loss in firm value. Clearly, the legal penalties imposed on these firms do not explain the observed losses in their market values.

We interpret these results as indicating that most of the loss incurred by a firm accused or found guilty of fraud is its lost reputation. For the nine cases in Panel A of Table 9.6, approximately 93.5 per cent of the reduction in stock market value could be due to the reputational loss suffered by the firm. Even if one assumes that a firm's legal expenses equals the entire amount of its penalties, the reputational loss is still roughly 87 per cent.

There is anecdotal evidence that firms facing debarment have particularly large losses. General Electric was either completely or partially restricted from bidding on government contracts for almost six months, and it has by far the largest market value loss in Panel A. Litton Systems, the other company in Panel A of Table 9.6 to face debarment, suffered the third-largest market value loss. These anecdotes suggest that the firms' market value losses are related to actual reductions in demand.[23]

Of course, the stock price forecast errors reported in Table 9.6 reflect the legal penalties expected at the time, not the actual penalties eventually imposed. A more appropriate breakdown would compare the total loss in market value with the *expected* legal costs. To estimate the expected legal costs for the firms in our sample, we collected data on 1,437 corporate criminal code violations where firms were eventually convicted during 1981–7 from the FPSSIS data set. Using ordinary least squares, the actual criminal fine was regressed on dummy variables that represent the type of criminal activity, the circuit court district in which the case was tried, the year of the criminal activity, and whether the crime was a felony or a misdemeanour. The estimated coefficients from this regression are reported in Appendix 2, and were used to predict the levels of the criminal fines for the firms in our sample. As reported in column 4 of Table 9.6, the predicted criminal fines, on average, are smaller than the actual fines imposed on the nine firms in Panel A.

These predicted values undoubtedly overestimate the expected penalty, since the FPSSIS sample contains just those firms that are eventually convicted, while not all the firms in Table 9.6 were convicted. It seems reasonable to assume that the expected penalty was higher for those firms that are eventually convicted. None the less, the predicted criminal fines still account for only 0.056 per cent of the loss in market value.[24] These results are consistent with the overall picture portrayed when the actual criminal fines are used. The prospective legal penalties account for a small portion of the total loss in firm value when firms are accused or charged with fraud.

5.2   Other possible explanations for the loss in market value

Factors other than lost reputation could explain the large market value losses we observe. In this section we consider – and reject – three alternative explanations of the data: (i) the losses represent market reactions to unfavourable information about firms' earnings or their managers' skills; (ii) the losses represent increases in the firms' expected *future* criminal penalties; and (iii) the losses represent forgone profits from perpetuating the frauds.

5.2.1 Unfavourable information   Maksimovic and Titman (1991) argue that firms whose managers expect low future earnings are more likely to engage in fraud than managers of financially healthy firms. The announcement of a fraud may therefore reveal managers' unfavourable information about the firm's prospects. A related hypothesis is that the announcement of a fraud reveals both that the firm (may have) committed fraud and that the firm's managers were incompetent enough to get caught.[25] The decrease in firm value may therefore reflect a decrease in the market's assessment of managerial ability that is independent of the reputational loss.

The market value losses we attribute to lost reputation also reflect unfavourable information about the firm's earnings and managers – lost reputation means lower expected net profits. However, several findings yield insights into the source of the market value loss. The findings indicate that fraud announcements convey information primarily about the firm's reputation, not about the general state of the firm's financial condition or managerial ability.

The first indication that the loss is due to reputation is the pattern of cross-sectional differences in stock price reactions to fraud announcements. As reported in Table 9.3, the mean stock price response to regulatory violations is small and statistically insignificant. If a fraud announcement conveyed information primarily about the firm's prospects or its managers' abilities, there should be no difference in the stock price reactions to different types of fraud. If, however, the fraud announcement conveys information primarily about the firm's reputation, that is, its future costs and benefits in dealing with customers, investors, suppliers and so forth, then the stock price reaction should be largest where reputational effects are most important. We have argued throughout this study that regulatory violations are likely to have small reputational effects because it is not evident that any private party with whom the firm does business is hurt by the violation. For example, the firm's customers are not much affected by, and conceivably benefit from, regulatory violations such as cheque kiting or failures to report currency transactions.

A second finding that suggests the losses are due to reputation is that criminal fines and other penalties tend to be much higher for regulatory violations than for consumer and government frauds.[26] This suggests that the drop in market value would tend to be the greatest for regulatory violations. We find just the opposite, suggesting once again that reputational penalties play a large role in explaining the market value losses.

Third, we could uncover no evidence that investors or analysts tend to anticipate bad news about the firm before the fraud announcement. Frauds are typically committed weeks, months or years before any Press announcements about the frauds. If a fraud is committed because managers have unfavourable information about the firm, the unfavourable information would surely become evident to investors and analysts by the time the fraud is uncovered and publicised. It is reasonable to expect investors to uncover some of the unfavourable information after managers learn of it but before the fraud is publicised.[27]

None the less, we have found no evidence of systematically poor performance or expectations of poor performance in the period before the fraud is publicised. There is no evidence of a negative stock price drift before the first announcement. For example, the cumulative average forecast error $CAFE_{-230,-2}$ (using market model parameters estimated over days $+31$ through $+230$ relative to the last fraud announcement for each event) is *positive*, 0.28 per cent, with $z_{-230,-2} = 0.05$. This finding is inconsistent with the notion that information effects explain the stock price reactions to fraud announcements.

There is also no evidence that market analysts had acquired information on the possibility of future problems in these firms. Using the Institutional Brokers Estimate System (IBES) data tapes, we regressed the ratio of each firm's median analyst's four-quarter-in-advance forecast to the average of the median forecasts for all the industry's firms on a quarterly time-trend variable for the eight quarters before first announcement of the fraud. The data reveal no clear trend in analysts' forecasts. Forecasts were not available for all the firms in our sample nor for the full eight-quarter period. Using the 15 cases where we had 6–8 quarterly forecasts preceding the first fraud announcement, the average coefficient of the time-trend variable was *positive*, 0.0197, with a standard deviation across coefficients of 0.1272.

Overall, the data are consistent with the interpretation that the losses primarily reflect lost reputation, not unfavourable information about other aspects of the firm or its managers. The data do not support the conjecture that the sample firms committed fraud because they were in financial trouble.[28]

5.2.2 Increased future criminal penalties   It is possible that our numbers understate the total legal costs for firms accused of fraud. Perhaps a charge of fraud provides information about the conditional probability that the firm will be accused of fraud again. The reduction in market value may then reflect both the expected penalties from the current charges and the higher probability of being charged again in the future.

61 of the 132 fraud events in our sample involve repeat offenders. The other 71 cases represent first-time offenders *within this sample*.[29] The probability a firm has a subsequent fraud event in any given year from 1981 to 1987, conditional on having a first fraud event, is 12.45 per cent. Suppose that being accused once with a fraud offence raises the probability of being accused again in each future year from 0 to 12.45 per cent. Assume further that the real discount factor is 5 per cent and that the actual legal cost for each fraud is double our estimate of 6.5 per cent of the change in market value. Even under these extreme assumptions, current and expected future criminal penalties still account for no more than 45.4 per cent of the total reduction in market value.[30]

5.2.3 Lost future fraud profits   It is also possible that the change in market value reflects the fact that an apprehended firm will no longer be able to acquire profits by perpetuating the fraud. One measure of a firm's earnings from the fraud is the loss imposed upon the victims, which equals 1.15 per cent of the change in market value for the six firms in Panel A of Table 9.6 for which we have data on losses. If we assume that a firm's investors anticipated earning this premium every year in the future, and that the real discount factor is 5 per cent, the lost perpetual profit stream from the fraud could account for 23.1 per cent (which equals 1.15 per cent/0.05) of the reduction in market value. This figure undoubtedly overestimates the portion of the change in market value attributable to reduced criminal earnings, because our assumptions imply that no costs were borne by the firm in committing the fraud and that stockholders had assigned a zero probability to the chance that the firm would lose these ill-gotten profits.

It would be double-counting simply to add together the 45.4 per cent of the reduction in market value due to higher expected criminal fines and the 23.1 per cent reduction from reduced criminal earnings. If 23.1 per cent of the firm's market value loss occurs because the firm will not cheat again in the future, it is very unlikely that the firm's expected future penalties will be as high as 45.4 per cent of the loss. Adding together the two numbers would make sense only if a firm stops committing frauds after it is apprehended, and the government none the less keeps on imposing new criminal sanctions in future years. Yet, even if we were to add together the 45.4 per cent and 23.1 per cent figures, reduced reputation still explains 31.5 per cent of the decline in market value. Multiplying the mean market value reductions for allegations or investigations of fraud (reported in Table 9.5) by 0.315, the mean estimates of lost reputation are $19,152,000 for stakeholder fraud and $12,597,795 for government fraud.[31] Even these greatly understated figures for stakeholder fraud exceed Mitchell and Maloney's (1989, p. 353) and Borenstein and Zimmerman's (1988, p. 931) estimates of the reputational loss airlines suffer from airplane crashes.[32]

6   Comparing the expected penalty to the cost of the crime

Another way of looking at our results is that they can be used to compute the implied average probability of fraud detection. This probability equates the expected total penalty to the loss imposed on the fraud victims. In making the computation, we subtract the 23.1 per cent reduction in market value due to reduced criminal earnings (admittedly a high estimate) in determining the total penalty from conviction because the firm would not obtain those extra profits if it had remained honest. However, the 45.4 per cent of the reduction in market value that is possibly due to higher expected future criminal fines is included in the measure of the total penalty from conviction. For the six cases in Panel A of Table 9.6 on which loss estimates are available, the total losses are $10.71 million. If the frauds were committed every year in perpetuity, the present value of victims' losses (at a 5 per cent real rate) would be $214.12 million. After subtracting 23.1 per cent as an estimate of the lost fraud profits, the reduction in market value for these six firms is $713.6 million. Therefore, the expected total penalty equals the value of victims' losses if the probability of detection is 30.0 per cent (equal to $214.12/ $713.60).

This estimate is consistent with prosecutors' beliefs about the probability of detecting criminal fraud. In a Sentencing Commission survey, 95 per cent of the Department of Justice's Criminal Division prosecutors estimated the probability of conviction for consumer fraud at between 38.5 and 57.2 per cent, and the probability for commercial fraud at between 20 and 47.2 per cent (US Sentencing Commission, 1988a).

The simple optimal penalty rule provides a useful first approximation for determining whether current penalties are too high or too low. However, it is really necessary to know the elasticity of supply of the crimes and how enforcement costs vary with the penalty before determining if current penalties differ from optimal penalties (Friedman, 1981). To our knowledge, no such evidence currently exists on either of these questions for firms. Our evidence implies, however, that fraudulent firms do not escape significant expected penalties.

7 Earnings changes around corporate fraud announcements

We have interpreted the returns data as indicating that investors expect corporate fraud announcements to precipitate substantial reputational penalties for the suspected firms. If true, corporate fraud announcements should be followed by earnings decreases, on average, as firms lose sales, incur higher input costs, and/or make additional investments in brand name capital. To test this hypothesis we examined several measures of annual earnings changes for each year from five years before through five years after the fiscal year of the initial announcement of investigated, charged or settled fraud. Date $T = 0$ is defined as the fiscal year in which the corporate fraud event is announced. Using the annual and research files of the 1991 Compustat tapes, we obtained data on 60 of the sample firms representing 112 of the 132 fraud events. For the results presented here we treat each fraud as an independent event, an assumption that is violated slightly by the presence of some firms more than once in the sample. Results obtained when firms with multiple fraud events are excluded are essentially identical to those reported here.

We report results using two measures of earnings changes, although tests using slightly different definitions of the earnings change yielded similar results. The *raw annual earnings change* for firm j in year t, ΔE_{jT}, is defined as:

$$\Delta E_{jT} = (E_{jT} - E_{j,T-1})/P_j \tag{4}$$

where E_{jT} is earnings per share before extraordinary items and discontinued operations (Compustat item number 18) for firm j in year T, and P_j is price per share at the beginning of the fiscal year.[33] The *industry-adjusted annual earnings change* for firm j in year T, ΔE^I_{jT}, is defined as:

$$\Delta E^I_{jT} = \Delta E_{jT} - \Delta E^I_T \tag{5}$$

where ΔE^I_T is the median raw earnings change of all firms listed on the Compustat file with the same two-digit SIC code as that of the sample firm on the date of the fraud announcement.

The mean and median raw annual earnings change for years -5 to $+5$ are reported in Panel A of Table 9.7, along with the associated probability values based on two-tailed tests. The mean and median industry-adjusted annual earnings change are reported in panel B.

The probability levels for the means are computed from the following test statistic:

$$\tau = \frac{\overline{\Delta E_T}}{s_{\Delta E}/n_T} \tag{6}$$

where $\overline{\Delta E_T}$ and $s_{\Delta E}$ are the cross-sectional mean and standard deviation of the earnings changes and n_T is the number of firms with sufficient data to calculate the earnings change for year T. To the extent earnings changes are cross-sectionally independent and normally distributed, the null hypothesis of no earnings change implies that τ in equation (6) has a t-distribution with $n_T - 1$ degrees of freedom. Inspection of the data reveals that some of the annual distributions of earnings changes for firms in our sample are skewed. We therefore include the results of Wilcoxon signed-ranks tests in our interpretation of the data. The probability levels constructed from the Wilcoxon statistic are used to test the null hypothesis that the average earnings change is zero against the alternate hypothesis that the average change is not zero.

Table 9.7:   Earnings changes around fraud announcement[a]

Year in Relation to First Fraud Press Date	Number of Events	Mean Earnings Growth (%)	Student t p-value[b]	Median Earnings Growth (%)	Wilcoxon p-value[b]
A Raw Earnings Changes					
−5	109	8.48	0.032	1.91	0.000
−4	111	3.68	0.000	0.51	0.000
−3	112	0.79	0.267	0.75	0.078
−2	112	−2.28	0.233	0.70	0.132
−1	112	1.10	0.249	1.22	0.054
0	112	0.44	0.824	0.89	0.598
1	108	3.39	0.607	0.22	0.131
2	106	−18.77	0.143	0.40	0.125
3	99	−4.61	0.651	0.66	0.136
4	74	−0.13	0.959	0.81	0.283
5	53	6.17	0.294	0.79	0.379
B Industry-Adjusted Earnings Changes[c]					
−5	109	6.31	0.108	0.83	0.013
−4	111	1.66	0.049	0.02	0.324
−3	112	−0.82	0.223	−0.81	0.014
−2	112	−3.34	0.077	−0.28	0.139
−1	112	0.03	0.977	0.02	0.885
0	112	−0.59	0.764	−0.42	0.180
1	108	2.65	0.687	−0.52	0.012
2	106	−19.47	0.129	−1.60	0.017
3	99	−5.17	0.611	−0.08	0.693
4	74	−0.71	0.782	0.25	0.683
5	53	6.16	0.294	0.38	0.476

Notes: (a) Cross-sectional mean and median measures of earnings growth rates for each of the eleven fiscal years surrounding each firm's first fraud announcement are reported. Earnings growth is defined as the change in earnings per share before extraordinary items and discontinued operations (Compustat item no. 18) divided by the firm's stock price at the beginning of the fiscal year. Year 0 represents the fiscal year of the fraud announcement. The sample, drawn from 1978 to 1987, consists of the 112 events for which data are available on the 1991 annual and research files of Compustat.

(b) Student t and Wilcoxon statistics test the hypothesis that the average earnings change is different from zero. The probability levels reported are for two-tailed tests of significance.

(c) Industry-adjusted earnings changes are defined as the difference between raw earnings changes and the median raw earnings change for all firms in the same two-digit industry.

The results in Panel A reveal evidence of earnings growth in the five years before the year of the fraud announcement. The mean earnings growth rate is positive in four of the five years before the year of a fraud announcement, with a mean over all five years of 2.35 per cent. In contrast, three of the six years from $T=0$ through $T=+5$ have negative mean annual growth rates, and the mean over these six years is -2.25 per cent. The t-statistic on the difference in means between the pre-announcement and post-announcement period is 1.03 (although the assumption of independence is slightly violated by the inclusion of multiple events from some firms). These results provide weak evidence of a decrease in earnings growth in the period after a fraud announcement.

The median raw earnings changes yield a similar inference. The median annual earnings change is positive in each of the five years before the year of the fraud announcement; in four of these five years the Wilcoxon probability levels are less than 10 per cent. In the year of the announcement and the five years after it the median earnings growth is still positive, but is smaller. None of the median percentage changes in these six years is greater than 1 per cent, and none of the Wilcoxon probability values is less than 10 per cent using a two-tailed test.

The industry-adjusted earnings change measure yields somewhat similar but weaker results. As reflected in Table 9.7, Panel B, the mean change over the five-year period $T=-5$ through $T=-1$ is 0.77 per cent. Over the six-year period $T=0$ through $T=+5$, the mean change is -2.855 per cent. This is weak evidence of a decrease in industry-adjusted earnings growth during the period following a fraud announcement. (The t-statistic for the difference in means is 0.80.)

The median industry-adjusted earnings changes produce results that are also weak, but which are broadly consistent with our hypothesis about the reputational effects of a fraud announcement. In particular, the median industry-adjusted earnings change is negative in years $T=0$ through $T=+2$, and the Wilcoxon probability value is less than 5 per cent in years $T=+1$ and $T=+2$.

8   Aggregate wealth effects of the Sentencing Commission's guidelines

On one hand, we argued in Section 2 that reputation is a particularly effective deterrent to frauds of private parties and that increased criminal penalties for private fraud are likely to impose net costs on firms and consumers. On the other hand, our findings indicate that criminal fines represent a small portion of the total penalty imposed on firms committing fraud (1.4 per cent, or 2.1 per cent of the minimum estimate of the average reputational penalty we calculated in Section 5.2.2). If criminal fines are so insignificant compared with reputational penalties, will the Sentencing Commission's new guidelines have much effect on firms?

The magnitude of the penalty increases suggests that the effects are substantial. Cohen (1991b) estimates that fines may increase 50–100 times past practice (see also Cohen, 1991a). A 22.5-fold increase in fines equals our minimum estimate of the average reputational penalty where we subtract the reduction in market value resulting from both higher expected criminal fines and reduced criminal earnings. The aggregate wealth effects of the Commission's corporate penalty guidelines are therefore potentially large.

Searching *The Wall Street Journal, The New York Times* and *The Washington Post*, we identified nine Press dates from 1988 to 1990 on which articles appeared indicating significant changes in the likelihood that the Commission would adopt increased penalties for corporate crimes, including fraud. Table 9.8 presents the CRSP value-weighted and equal-weighted index abnormal stock returns for each of the nine event periods. For each day, the abnormal return is calculated as the difference between the raw index return and the mean index return from 1 January 1988 through 31 December 1990. For articles that report on events that had recently transpired, we define the event period to consist of the Press day and the prior day. For the two editorial articles, the event period is simply the day the article appeared. The two editorials are included because they each contained information leaked from the Commission that made the first public mention of proposed penalty increases. Panel A lists three articles indicating a decreased likelihood that the Commission would adopt high penalties, and Panel B lists six articles indicating an increased likelihood of high penalties.

For the three articles indicating lower prospective penalties, the mean abnormal value-weighted market return is 0.18 per cent. For the six articles indicating higher penalties, the mean abnormal market return is 0.90 per cent. This is weak evidence that investors interpreted higher criminal penalties to be wealth reducing for firms in general. To test for statistical significance, we multiply each of the three returns in Panel A by −1. The resulting mean abnormal return for all nine events is −0.66 per cent, with a z-statistic of −1.68.[34] Using the equal-weighted index, the mean abnormal return is −0.56 per cent with a z-statistic of −2.05.

Our discussion in Section 2 implies that the Sentencing Commission's plans to increase criminal penalties for frauds should not affect all firms equally. Public utility companies, for example, typically face regulation and monitoring by state public utility commissions that substitute for both reputation and criminal penalties in deterring fraud. Because

Table 9.8:   Market-wide effects of the Sentencing Commission guidelines[a]

Date	Title and Description of Press Article	CRSP Index Return (in %):	
		Value-Weighted	Equal-Weighted
A Press Articles Indicating a Likely Decrease in Corporate Penalties			
10 October 1988	'Corporate Penalty Plan Stirs Debate' – *New York Times* article on optimal penalty approach to guidelines and how it would lower many penalties.	1.84 (1.52)	0.76 (0.88)
30 March 1990	'Proposal on Corporate Sentencing Softened' – *Wall Street Journal* article on prospective decreases in corporate penalties.	−0.57 (−0.47)	−0.16 (−0.19)
28 April 1990	'Justice Department Shifts on Corporate Sentencing' – *Washington Post* (also *Wall Street Journal* and *New York Times*) article on Justice Department's retraction of its support for the corporate penalty guidelines.	−0.73 (−0.60)	−0.68 (−0.79)
B Press Articles Indicating a Likely Increase in Corporate Penalties			
10 December 1988	'Be Tough on Corporate Criminals – but Justify It' – *Wall Street Journal* op-ed article on how the Sentencing Commission's proposed guidelines would substantially increase penalties.	−0.19 (−0.22)	−0.28 (−0.45)
8 November 1989	'Corporate Lawbreakers Face Stiffer Penalties' – *Washington Post* article on the impending release of the Commission's new proposed guidelines, which substantially increase penalties.	1.39 (1.14)	0.80 (0.93)
15 January 1990	'Sentencing Plan Likely to Upset Business Lobby' – *Wall Street Journal* article on how stiff corporate guidelines will likely attract many businesses' opposition.	−3.30 (−2.72)	−2.50 (−2.89)
16 May 1990	'Justice and the Unified Executive' – *Wall Street Journal* editorial article on how the Commission's guidelines result in large increases in corporate penalties.	−0.15 (−0.18)	−0.16 (−0.26)

Table 9.8:   *contd)*

| | | CRSP Index Return (in %): | |
| | | Value-Weighted | Equal-Weighted |
Date	Title and Description of Press Article		
16 October 1990	'Thornburg Again Supports Stiffer Corporate Sentences' – *New York Times* article on US Attorney General's support for stiffer corporate penalties.	-0.58 (-0.47)	-0.94 (-1.08)
29 October 1990	'Tough New Guidelines Proposed for Corporate Criminal Sentencing' – *Wall Street Journal* (also *New York Times*) article on Sentencing Commission's new release of proposed corporate guidelines.	-2.58 (-2.13)	-2.13 (-2.48)
Mean (calculated after multiplying each of the three returns in Panel A by -1)		-0.66	-0.56
t-statistic for the mean abnormal return		(-1.68)	(-2.05)

Note: (a) Table contains aggregate stock market reactions to nine Press articles from *The Wall Street Journal, The New York Times*, and *The Washington Post* that reported significant changes in the likelihood the US Sentencing Commission would adopt sentencing guidelines to increase substantially the penalties for corporate crimes, including fraud. The market returns are measured using the Center for Research in Security Prices (CRSP) value-weighted and equal-weighted indices, both with dividends. Abnormal returns are calculated as the difference between the raw return and the mean index daily return during 1 January 1988 through 31 December 1990. For Press dates other than editorial articles, returns are measured over the two-day interval consisting of the (trading) day before and the day of the Press article. For the two editorial articles, returns are measured over only the Press day. z-statistics, which are reported in parentheses, are calculated as in equation (A1) substituting the daily return variance for each market index from 1 January 1988 through 31 December 1990 for the variance of the cumulated forecast error.

criminal penalties probably represent a small portion of the total penalty faced by such firms for committing fraud, reports of increased criminal penalties should have relatively small effects on the values of utilities. This conjecture is weakly supported by the data: over all nine events (reversing the sign for the three events in Panel A), the average abnormal return for the firms in the Standard and Poor's Utility Index is -0.39 per cent, with a z-statistic of -1.32.

Overall, the data indicate that announcements regarding prospective changes in the Sentencing Commission's organisational guidelines are associated systematically with market-wide returns. It is tempting to conclude that the prospect of increased penalties imposes net costs on society. But we cannot rule out the possibility that shareholders' wealth losses were offset by other gains we have not measured.[35]

9   Conclusion

On average, alleged or actual corporate fraud announcements of stakeholders or the government correspond to economically and statistically significant losses in the accused firm's common stock market value. Very little of this loss, of the order of 6.5 per cent, can be attributed to the firm's expected legal fees and penalties. It is possible to compute larger portions of the loss that could reflect higher expected penalties for future frauds and the lost value of the cheating firm's profits from committing fraud. But even under extremely unrealistic assumptions, one-third of the loss remains. We argue that the remaining portion represents lost reputation, that is, the present value of lower output prices or higher input prices. Furthermore, consistent with this interpretation, there is some evidence that firms' earnings decline after a fraud announcement. Anecdotal evidence suggests that firms suffering the largest reputational losses experience reductions in market demand in the form of debarment. Overall, the evidence indicates that reputational effects play an important role in disciplining firms that commit fraud.

We find large reputational penalties associated with frauds of stakeholders, government agencies and investors. The reputational loss for frauds involving regulatory violations, in which firms have not violated an implicit or explicit contract with a stakeholder or investor, is negligible. The market penalty for fraud appears to be systematically related to the cost imposed on parties with whom the firm does business.[36]

Our measure of the average decrease in common stock value exceeds the US Sentencing Commission's estimates of the losses imposed on victims of frauds by more than 100 times. The Sentencing Commission (1988a) reports that Department of Justice prosecutors believe the probability of convicting a corporate fraud is between 20 and 57 per cent, implying an optimal ratio of actual penalty to social costs of between 1.75 and 5. Our findings imply that the expected *total* penalty is greater than the Commission's estimated loss borne by the victims of the fraud, even at 1980s levels of criminal fines.

These findings imply that efforts to increase criminal penalties for corporate fraud substantially, as reflected in the positions of the US

Sentencing Commission and the US Department of Justice, are mis-
guided. Optimal criminal penalties require that the total expected penalty
equals the social costs of the fraud. Expected *legal* penalties for corporate
fraud are currently lower than estimates of the social costs. But total
penalties, which include reputational effects, are much higher. Increases
in legal penalties will reduce the incidence of fraud, but at a cost of
economic efficiency. In particular, increased legal penalties will increase
all firms' costs and force out suppliers of low quality assurance.

We emphasise that our arguments and most of our findings address
cases where the corporate fraud has small or negligible external effects,
such as frauds involving the firm's customers, suppliers, employees,
franchisees and investors. Many other crimes, such as polluting, impose
substantial costs on third parties that are not internalised by the market
mechanism we call reputation. Even in these cases, however, reputational
effects can play some role. It is unlikely that market mechanisms exist to
internalise the costs of reduced ozone from fluorocarbons, but firms may
internalise some of the localised costs of toxic spills as they find it more
costly to locate new or maintain existing plants amidst increased local
opposition.

Appendix 1 Test statistics

Test statistics for average and cumulated average forecast errors for event days k
through t are calculated as:

$$z_{kt} = \frac{1}{\sqrt{N}} \sum_{j=1}^{N} \left(\frac{\sum_{\tau=k}^{t} FE_{j\tau}}{\sqrt{\operatorname{var} \sum_{\tau=k}^{t} FE_{j\tau}}} \right), \tag{A1}$$

where N is the number of firms in the sample. The term in braces represents the
cumulated forecast error for firm j divided by the square root of its variance. The
variance is defined as :

$$\operatorname{var} \sum_{\tau=k}^{t} FE_{j\tau} = s_j^2 \left(T + \frac{T^2}{ED_j} + \frac{\left(\sum_{\tau=k}^{t} r_{m\tau} - T\bar{r}_m(j) \right)^2}{\sum_{i=1}^{ED_j} (r_{mi} - \bar{r}_m(j))^2} \right). \tag{A2}$$

Here, s_j^2 is the variance of the residual from firm j's market model regression, T is
the number of days in the cumulation interval and equals $t-k+1$, ED_j is the

number of observations in the period used to estimate the market model for firm j, and $\bar{r}_m(j)$ is the mean market return during firm j's estimation period.[37]
The test statistics in Table 9.4 are computed as

$$
t = \frac{\sum_{j=1}^{n}\sum_{p=1}^{q} CAFE_{-1,0,jp}}{\sqrt{\sum_{j=1}^{n}\sum_{p=1}^{q}\sum_{t=-1}^{0} s_{jtp}^{2}}}
\tag{A3}
$$

where n is the number of firms over which the average is taken and q is the number of available event dates over which two-day forecast errors are summed. Under the null hypothesis of a zero forecast error, the test statistic is distributed approximately unit normal.[38]

Appendix 2 Estimation of expected criminal fines using the data from the Federal Probation and Parole Sentencing and Supervision Research File

This Appendix presents our method for estimating the predicted criminal fines presented in Table 9.6 and discussed in Section 5.1. Our intent is to provide estimates of the portion in lost market value that can be attributed to expectations of the forthcoming criminal penalty at the time a firm is investigated, charged or found guilty of criminal fraud.

To calculate the expected criminal penalties, we first estimated the relation between actual criminal penalties and a set of dummy variables that represent characteristics of the crimes using ordinary least squares regression. The data consist of 1,437 corporate criminal fine violations from 1981 through 1987, and are taken from the Administrative Office of the US Courts' data set entitled the Federal Probation and Parole Sentencing and Supervision Research File (FPSSIS). The estimators from the regression were then used to calculate the predicted criminal fines for the cases summarised in Table 9.6.

The following table reports the estimated coefficients. The actual criminal fine is the dependent variable. Year dummies are included in the regression for the years 1981, 1983, 1984, 1986 and 1987. The intercept term reflects the effect of cases in 1985. The data for 1982 were excluded because of the presence of two very large outliers. Inclusion of the data for 1982 does not qualitatively affect our results. Dummy variables for the Federal District Courts were also included. The first US District Court includes Maine, New Hampshire, Massachusetts and Rhode Island; the second includes New York, Connecticut and Vermont; the third, Pennsylvania, New Jersey and Delaware; the fourth, Maryland, Virginia, West Virginia, North Carolina and South Carolina; the fifth, Texas, Louisiana and Mississippi; the sixth, Michigan, Ohio, Kentucky and Tennessee; the seventh, Wisconsin and Illinois; the eighth, North and South Dakota, Nebraska, Minnesota, Iowa, Missouri and Arkansas; the tenth, Utah, Wyoming, Colorado, Kansas, New Mexico and Oklahoma; and the ninth, the remaining states in the west. The intercept is for when the individual lives in the Eleventh Court District which includes Alabama, Florida and Georgia. Offense Levels 3 and 4 are

Table 9A2.1:   Explaining the criminal fines firms face from conviction

Exogenous Variables	Coefficient	t-statistic
Year 1981	−86,167	−1.042
Year 1983	−22,173	−1.022
Year 1984	−24,150	−1.456
Year 1986	34,521	2.106
Year 1987	13,669	0.730
Court District DC	374,329	6.128
Court District 1	41,121	1.182
Court District 2	−7,770	−0.302
Court District 3	5,526	0.234
Court District 4	−32,388	−1.193
Court District 5	10,603	0.385
Court District 6	−20,806	−0.814
Court District 7	6,618	0.171
Court District 8	−26,270	−0.910
Court District 9	−41,803	−1.677
Court District 10	−41,901	−1.280
Offense Level 3	−10,469	−0.209
Offense Level 4	17,756	0.342
Offense Code 4200	−45,476	−0.297
Offense Code 4601	−67,190	−0.441
Offense Code 4700	7,113	0.210
Offense Code 4920	−6,310	−0.050
Offense Code 4911	−29,696	−0.905
Intercept	55,853	0.905

$R^2 = 0.12395$ Adjusted $R^2 = 0.06188$ F-statistic $= 1.997$ $N = 1.437$

dummy variables that indicate whether the crime was classified as a misdemeanour or a felony. Dummy variables for 77 different types of criminal offences were also included, where these categories were defined by the Administrative Office of the United States Courts. Only the five coefficients that are used in computing Table 9.6 are listed in the regression results reported above. Offense code 4200 refers to postal embezzlement, 4601 is for bank fraud, 4700 is for postal and interstate wire fraud, 4920 is for securities fraud, and 4911 is for making false claims. Unfortunately, estimates of the loss from the crimes were available for only a very small portion of the cases in the sample. We suspect that their inclusion would have increased the explanatory power of the regression used to predict the criminal fines.

NOTES

*   This paper is a slightly revised version of a paper with the same title in the October 1993 issue of the *Journal of Law and Economics* (Vol. 36, No. 2). Jonathan M. Karpoff is Professor of Finance at the University of Washington

School of Business, and John R. Lott is John M. Olin Visiting Professor at the Graduate School of Business of the University of Chicago. We would specially like to thank Graeme Rankine for his assistance with the paper. We would also like to thank John Byrd, Gertrud Fremling, Marilyn Johnson, Scott Lee, Paul Malatesta, Linda McDaniel, Mark Mitchell, Rob Neal, Jeff Parker, Sam Peltzman, Dick Roll, Ed Rice, D. Shores, Dan Siegel, Sheridan Titman, an anonymous referee, and the seminar participants at Arizona State University, Brigham Young University, Commodities Futures Trading Commission, Federal Trade Commission, George Mason University Law School, North Carolina State University, US Office of Management and Budget, Santa Clara University, Simon Fraser University, University of Arizona, University of Alberta, University of British Columbia, University of California, Los Angeles (Business and Law Schools), University of Pennsylvania (Law School and Wharton), University of Texas, University of Washington, Washington State University, York University, the fourth annual Pacific-Basin Capital Markets Research Center Finance Conference, the CEPR/STEP/Università di Bologna conference on 'The Economics of Organized Crime', the 1990 meeting of the Western Economic Association, and York University for helpful comments. The data used in this paper were collected while Lott was Chief Economist for the United States Sentencing Commission during 1988 and 1989. We thank John Daley, Scott Lyden, Mike Smolens and Geoffrey Waring for providing valuable research assistance. Our views and conclusions do not reflect those of the US Sentencing Commission nor those of any of its Commissioners.

1 While Block and Lott (1991) estimate that the sentencing guidelines will increase criminal penalties by at least twentyfold, a *Wall Street Journal* editorial ('Justice and the Unified Executive', May 16, 1990, p. A16) and testimony before the US Sentencing Commission (1990) claimed increases of fiftyfold. The actual magnitude of the penalty increases is difficult to estimate because of vagueness in the sentencing rules. Cohen (1991b) argues that the penalty increases for frauds by organisations 'involve increase of 20, 30, or 40 times current levels', and he points out that increases of fraud of 50–100 times over past practice are possible. A discussion of the earliest proposed versions of the corporate guidelines is provided by Lott (1988a).

2 These papers examine the stock price effects of product recalls (for example, Jarrell and Peltzman, 1985; Rubin, Murphy and Jarrell, 1988; Reilly and Hoffer, 1983; and Hoffer, Pruitt and Reilly, 1988) airline crashes (for example, Chalk, 1986; Mitchell and Maloney, 1989; and Borenstein and Zimmerman, 1988), product tampering as in the Tylenol case (Mitchell, 1989) changes in product quality (Mitchell and Benjamin, 1989), and Federal Trade Commission findings of deceptive advertising (Peltzman, 1981). The overall findings are mixed, however, with some researchers finding reputational losses of several per cent of a firm's value and others finding no or very small reputational losses. See also Sauer (1990) and Strachan, Smith and Beedles (1983).

3 Government safety requirements may be designed to promote wealth transfers, not efficiency. For example, high-income consumers who desire a high level of quality assurance can end up paying less for such assurance if

regulations force producers to provide high-quality assurance for all consumers. Such regulations may also reduce search costs for politically influential groups that place high value on additional quality assurance.

4 Common law prohibits privately negotiated penalty clauses in civil cases. Lott (1988b) criticises several efficiency arguments for such restrictions. But even if these arguments are valid, they would apply to government-determined criminal penalties as well. That is, if frauds are not published sufficiently because civil fines are restricted, the efficient reform is to change the common-law prohibition, not to increase criminal penalties.

We also distinguish between two issues: the mix of fines and reputation to police fraud, and whether private parties or government agents are better suited to determine the fine levels through civil or criminal procedures. To address the latter issue, one must examine whether the government has lower costs of determining the fine levels than do parties directly involved in the transactions. Block (1991) has argued that criminal fines involve a much more costly process than that involved with civilly imposed fines.

5 In the Klein–Leffler (1981) model, firms either cheat or do not cheat with certainty. Lott (1988b) extends this model by admitting the stochastic nature of the firm's decision to cheat. The size of the reputational bond is set so that the marginal value consumers obtain from a lower probability of fraud is equal to the marginal cost of increasing the bond. See also Darby and Karni (1973).

6 Consumers also value learning about potential frauds sooner if it is costly for firms to change quickly their investments in reputation.

7 For simplicity, this discussion assumes that the probabilities of detection and punishment are the same for criminal fines and lost reputation.

8 For discussions of this see Darby and Lott (1989) and Klein and Leffler (1981).

9 The fact that many business people actively oppose increases in criminal penalties for corporate fraud, as indicated by the intense lobbying by the Business Roundtable on this issue, implies that these people expect their firms to be guilty of fraud, or they expect their firms' expected costs of defending against charges of fraud to increase with the criminal penalties even when the firms are innocent. This latter possibility provides anecdotal evidence that type II errors (accusing innocent firms) are important for these firms. See Epstein (1990).

10 Quoted in *Time*, October 28, 1991, p. 18.

11 One third-party role we do not rule out is the role of a governing body to enforce agreements, as privately arbitrated decisions can be turned over to the public legal system to enforce. But it does not follow that governments have a comparative advantage in determining the penalty level upon conviction (see Lott, 1988b). Individuals are likely to have better information than a government about how much they value higher levels of quality assurance.

Our argument can also be viewed as an application of Posner's (1977) proposition that economic institutions can more efficiently discourage dissipative behaviours than legal institutions. The empirical tests reported below are joint tests of market efficiency and the hypothesis that reputational penalties are important.

12 *Wall Street Journal*, June 25, 1987, p. 3, col. 1.

13 *Wall Street Journal*, September 5, 1985, p. 41, col. 2.

14 *Wall Street Journal*, March 8, 1985, p. 19, col. 1.

15 *Wall Street Journal*, April 13, 1984, p. 21, col. 4.

16 *Wall Street Journal*, September 2, 1986, p. 22, col. 2.

17 In examining the data, an outlier appeared: the stock return forecast error for Professional Care Inc. on the day *The Wall Street Journal* reported that the firm's president was indicted for submitting $1.8 million in fraudulent medical bills to Medicaid was −47 per cent. This firm is omitted from the results reported below. The average loss is larger when the firm is included.

18 Note that our empirical method does not use a control group of matching firms. Instead, we calculate market value losses for the sample firms using the estimators from a market model, as presented in equation (1).

19 Stakeholder frauds are associated with three-day forecast errors over 14 events of −3.05 per cent (with a z-statistic of −1.84), roughly 2.5 times that found in the main sample. The forecast error of −7.73 (with a z-statistic of −3.36) for five government frauds is 4.6 times that for the main sample. The forecast error of −1.20 (with a z-statistic of 1.05) is smaller in the DJNRS sample for the nine financial frauds. The result from the one case of a regulatory fraud is consistent with the previous finding that such events tend to be associated with negligible stock price effects. When we disaggregate by event date type, the only result that substantially differs from its main-sample counterpart is for announcements that fraud charges had been settled (date type 3), which suggests that such announcements convey substantial information about firm value, on average, for this small sample of events.

We examined the average and cumulated average forecast errors for the three-day period centred on the date assigned to the story by DJNRS (i.e. $CAFE_{-1,+1}$) because many of the DJNRS stories are carried late in the trading day. Results are qualitatively the same using two-day and one-day event windows where the event day $t=0$ is defined as the day following the DJNRS date for cases identified as coming across the Broad Tape later than 4.00 p.m. Eastern Time.

20 Excluding Gould, Inc., for which a rumoured take-over was publicised on the same day as a fraud settlement was announced, the mean market value change for government frauds is −$6.833 million.

21 The large positive mean value for regulatory violations results from a single outlier. Excluding the outlier, the mean change in market value for regulatory violations is −$2.25 million.

22 See US Sentencing Commission (1988b, Chs. 8.9–8.13) for a discussion of how these losses were calculated.

23 Section 7 below reports on tests for changes in earnings in the years surrounding the fraud announcement period.

24 The difference between the average actual fine and the average predicted fine may be due to differences in the types and sizes of firms considered. Most of the cases in the FPSSIS data set are privately held firms or firms that are smaller than those listed on the New York or American Stock Exchange, unlike the firms in our sample.

25 We thank the referee at the *Journal of Law and Economics* for suggesting this hypothesis.

26 See Cohen (1991b) and US Sentencing Commission (1991), Appendix C.

27 For example, earnings announcements tend to be partially anticipated by analysts and investors (for example, see Dempsey, 1989).

28 In Section 7 below, we report evidence that, if anything, the firms' earnings

tended to increase during the five-year period before the year the fraud received Press attention. This finding is consistent with the stock return and analysts' forecast data reported here.

29 The mean two-day forecast error for the 61 cases from repeat offenders is smaller ($CAFE_{-1,0} = -0.91$ per cent with $z_{-1,0} = -1.73$) than for the 71 first-timer cases ($CAFE_{-1,0} = 2.00$ per cent with $z_{-1,0} = 4.38$), suggesting that the informational content is smaller for repeat offences.

30 The proportion of the drop in market value that can be explained by current and expected future court-imposed sanctions equals:

$$\frac{0.1245\,(2 \times 6.5 \text{ per cent})}{r} + (2 \times 6.5 \text{ per cent})$$

where r is the real interest rate. This formula overestimates the reduction in market value that can be explained by future penalties because the probability of being charged with fraud is unlikely to change from 0 to 12.45 per cent. The probability of being charged is positive for nearly all firms even before their first offences. In addition, some of the firms in our sample had previously been charged with frauds, indicating that the change in the conditional probability of being accused changed by a smaller amount than 12.45 per cent.

31 The estimates in this section are sensitive to the choice of discount factor. For example, a 3.5 per cent discount rate changes the estimates of lost reputation to $4.9 million for stakeholder fraud and $3.2 million for government fraud. We believe, however, that the assumption of a 5 per cent rate is a conservative estimate of firms' real average cost of capital during this period.

32 The reputational losses that firms suffer from committing fraud compose a similar portion of their total monetary penalty as that borne by individuals in the commission of crimes. Lott (1992b) finds that criminals earning the mean pre-conviction legitimate incomes suffer a reduction in legitimate earnings between the last twelve months before conviction and the last twelve months of probation or parole equal to 66 per cent of their total monetary penalty for those convicted of bank embezzlement and 49 per cent of the total for bank larcenists. For different types of drug convictions the same percentages range from 35 to 96 per cent. See Lott (1992a); also Lott (1990), Mitchell and Maloney (1989, p. 353) and Borenstein and Zimmerman (1988, p. 931). The nine firms in panel A of Table 9.6 averaged market declines of 3.65 per cent compared to 2.2–2.3 per cent for Mitchell and Maloney's (1989, p. 342) sample of airline crashes and the less than one per cent drop in market value reported by Borenstein and Zimmerman (1988, p. 924).

33 We also scaled earnings by the previous year's earnings and obtained results that are consistent with the results reported below.

34 The z-statistic is calculated as in equation (A1), using the variance of the index daily return from 1 January 1988 to 31 December 1990, to estimate the variance of the daily abnormal return.

35 The new Sentencing Guidelines came into effect on 1 November 1991 and apply to crimes committed after that date. If lost reputation is a substitute for criminal penalties (although an imperfect one), the increased criminal penalties should lead to greater total losses for crimes committed after 1 November 1991, but the increase in loss should be less than the increase in criminal penalties.

244   Jonathan Karpoff and John Lott Jr

36 This finding suggests that market penalties deter frauds at the margin, which differs from previous findings about product recalls (for example, Jarrell and Peltzman, 1985) that find no relation between the market value loss and the seriousness of the deception. If there was no relation, we would have been left with a peculiar system of deterrence: the market would in effect be telling firms that, if they are going to commit fraud, they should make it as large as possible.

37 The expression for the variance in equation (A1) adjusts for serial correlation in AFE_t that arises from a common estimation error in a single firm's prediction errors across different days, which comes from using the same market model parameters to calculate prediction errors. See Salinger (1992) for a general description, and Mikkelson and Partch (1988) for an early use of equation (A2).

38 The t-statistics reported in Table 9.4 are biased upward slightly because the standard errors in equation (A3) are not adjusted for slight serial correlation in the daily average forecast errors. With a 200-day estimation period and a two-day forecast period, the bias in the standard errors is approximately 0.5 per cent. (See Salinger, 1992, p. 41, n. 3.)

REFERENCES

Becker, G. S. (1968), 'Crime and Punishment: An Economic Approach', *Journal of Political Economy*, 76(2), March/April, pp. 169–217.
Block, M. K. (1991), 'Optimal Penalties, Criminal Law, and the Control of Corporate Behavior', *Boston University Law Review*, 71(2), March, pp. 395–419.
Block, M. K. and J. R. Lott Jr (1991), 'Is Curbing Crime Worth the Cost?', *The New York Times*, Sunday, May 4, p. F13.
Borenstein, S. and M. B. Zimmerman (1988), 'Market Incentives for Safe Commercial Airline Operation', *American Economic Review*, 78(5), December, pp. 913–35.
Chalk, A. (1986), 'Market Forces and Aircraft Safety: The Case of the DC-10', *Economic Inquiry*, 24(1), January, pp. 43–60.
Cohen, M. (1991a), 'Corporate Crime and Punishment: An Update on Sentencing Practice in the Federal Courts, 1988–1990', *Boston University Law Review*, 71(2), March, pp. 247–79.
Cohen, M. (1991b), 'The New Corporate Sentencing Guidelines: The Beginning or the End of the Controversy?', in J. R. Lott Jr and R. Pilon (eds.), *Corporate Sentencing: The Guidelines Take Hold*.
Darby, M. R. and E. Karni (1973), 'Free Competition and the Optimal Amount of Fraud', *Journal of Law and Economics*, 16(1), April, pp. 67–88.
Darby, M. R. and J. R. Lott Jr (1989), 'Qualitative Information, Reputation, and Monopolistic Competition', *International Review of Law and Economics*, 8(2), June, pp. 87–103.
Dempsey, S. J. (1989), 'Predisclosure Information Search Incentives, Analyst Following, and Earnings Announcement Price Response', *Accounting Review*, 64, pp. 748–57.
Epstein, A. (1990), 'Companies Resist Having Punishment Fit Big-Ticket Crimes', *Seattle Times and Seattle Post-Intelligencer*, April 22, p. A3.

Friedman, D. (1981), 'Reflections on Optimal Punishment, Or: Should the Rich Pay Higher Fines?', in R. O. Zerbe Jr (ed.), *Research in Law and Economics*, Vol. 3, Greenwich CT: JAI Press.

Hoffer, G. E., S. Pruitt and R. J. Reilly (1988), 'The Impact of Product Recalls on the Wealth of Sellers: A Reexamination', *Journal of Political Economy*, 96(3), June, pp. 663–70.

Jarrell, G. and S. Peltzman (1985), 'The Impact of Product Recalls on the Wealth of Sellers', *Journal of Political Economy*, 93(3), June, pp. 512–36.

Klein, B. and K. B. Leffler (1981), 'The Role of Market Forces in Assuring Contractual Performance', *Journal of Political Economy*, 93(3), June, pp. 512–36.

Leffler, K. B. and R. D. Sauer (1990), 'Did the Federal Trade Commission's Advertising Substantiation Program Promote More Credible Advertising?', *American Economic Review*, 80, March, pp. 191–203.

Lott, J. R. Jr (1988a), 'Let the Punishment Fit the Crime', *Regulation*, 1, pp. 5–8.

Lott, J. R. Jr (1988b), 'The Optimal Level of Criminal Fines in the Presence of Reputation', Working Paper, Washington DC; US Sentencing Commission, August.

Lott, J. R. Jr (1990), 'The Effect of Conviction on the Legitimate Income of Criminals', *Economic Letters*, 34, pp. 381–5.

Lott, J. R. Jr (1992a), 'An Attempt at Measuring the Total Monetary Penalty from Drug Convictions: The Importance of an Individual's Reputation', *Journal of Legal Studies*, 21(1), January, pp. 159–87.

Lott, J. R. Jr (1992b), 'Do We Punish High Income Criminals Too Heavily?', *Economic Inquiry*, 30(4), October, pp. 583–608.

Maksimovic, V. and S. Titman (1991), 'Financial Policy and Reputation for Product Quality', *Review of Financial Studies*, 4(4), pp. 175–200.

Malatesta, P. H. (1986), 'Measuring Abnormal Performance: The Even Parameter Approach using Joint Generalized Least Squares', *Journal of Finance and Quantitative Analysis*, 21, March, pp. 27–38.

Mikkelson, W. H. and M. M. Partch (1988), 'Withdrawn Security Offerings', *Journal of Finance and Quantitative Analysis*, 23(2), June, pp. 119–33.

Mitchell, M. L. (1989), 'The Impact of External Parties on Brand-Name Capital: The 1982 Tylenol Poisonings and Subsequent Cases', *Economic Inquiry*, 27(4), October, pp. 601–18.

Mitchell, M. L. and D. Benjamin (1989), 'Quality-assuring Price Premium: Classic Evidence from the Real Thing', Working Paper, Washington DC: US Securities and Exchange Commission.

Mitchell, M. L. and M. T. Maloney (1989), 'The Role of Market Forces in Promoting Air Travel Safety', *Journal of Law and Economics*, 32, October, pp. 329–55.

Peltzman, S. (1981), 'The Effects of FTC Advertising Regulation', *Journal of Law and Economics*, 24, December, pp. 403–48.

Posner, R. (1977), *Economic Analysis of Law*, Chicago: University of Chicago Press.

Reilly, R. J. and G. E. Hoffer (1983), 'Testing the Impact of Recalls on the Demand for Automobiles', *Economic Inquiry*, 21, July, pp. 444–7.

Rubin, P. H., R. D. Murphy and G. Jarrell (1988), 'Risky Products, Risky Stocks', *Regulation*, 1, pp. 35–9.

Salinger, M. (1992), 'Standard Errors in Event Studies', *Journal of Financial and Quantitative Analysis*, 24(1), March, pp. 39–53.

Sheer, A. and Ch-Ch. Ho (1989), 'Preliminary Review of Sentences Imposed on Organizations in 1988', Memorandum, Washington DC: US Sentencing Commission, August 16.

Strachan, J. L., D. B. Smith and W. L. Beedles (1983), 'The Price Reaction to (Alleged) Corporate Crimes', *Financial Review*, 18(2), May, pp. 121–32.

US Sentencing Commission (1988a), 'Department of Justice Corporate Fraud Survey', Memorandum, Washington DC: US Sentencing Commission, April 6.

US Sentencing Commission (1988b), 'Chapter Eight – Sentencing of Organizations', Proposed Addition to the Sentencing Guidelines, Washington DC; US Sentencing Commission, July.

US Sentencing Commission (1990), 'Public Hearing: Sentencing Guidelines for Organizational Defendants', Washington DC; US Sentencing Commission, February 14.

US Sentencing Commission (1991), 'Supplementary Report on Sentencing Guidelines for Organizations', Washington DC; US Sentencing Commission, August 30.

Discussion

MICHELE POLO

Karpoff and Lott's paper considers the incentives firms face to abstain from opportunistic behaviour, comparing the effectiveness of the legal fines with that of the market mechanism and analysing the trade-off between the two instruments. The authors develop initially at a qualitative level a theoretical model, but the focus of the paper is on the empirical evidence they present on the issue.

The market mechanism works through the usual repeated purchase story: a stakeholder – an employee, a customer, a supplier, an investor – who is hurt by the firm's behaviour refuses to conduct economic transactions with the firm in the future. Hence, when committing a fraud, the firm has to compare the short-run benefit with the long-run losses due to a reduction in the economic activity. Then, a firm may invest in reputation – abstaining from these short-run gains – to preserve its long-run profits. The authors claim that legal fines act as imperfect substitutes for the investment in reputation, and that the optimal level of criminal penalties should be evaluated by considering how the investments in reputation are adjusted to a marginal increase in the penalties.

Applying this framework of analysis, the authors criticise the conventional wisdom that penalties for corporate frauds are too low. First, they claim that in most cases the external effects of a fraud are negligible, and the market mechanism is therefore sufficient to discipline the firms. Secondly, since fines and reputation are imperfect substitutes, an increase in penalties increases the total social cost of fraud control.

The article presents a very detailed empirical analysis of this issue considering 132 fraud events referred to different types of frauds. The first point examined is whether abnormal stock returns can be observed when the information on the fraud becomes public. If this is the case, the result can be interpreted as suggesting that the market value of the firm decreases when a fraud is discovered. Secondly, the authors estimate the loss imposed by the market mechanism by comparing the estimated loss in the firm's market value with the expected legal penalties.

The main findings are consistent with the qualitative model proposed in the paper. The forecast errors of the returns are negative and significant after the information becomes public, showing that the market reacts to the announcement of a fraud. Moreover, the estimates of the market punishment are extremely large when compared with the expected legal penalties faced by an accused firm.

The paper is interesting and deals with a problem which appears to be crucial when we try to combine market and legal incentives in the design of regulatory interventions. I will discuss two major points, one referred to the model and the other to the empirical analysis.

The theoretical discussion is built upon a crucial assumption, that criminal penalties and losses from lost reputation act as substitutes in the firm's decision on committing a fraud. It is certainly true that the total cost suffered by a cheating firm is the sum of the fine and the market punishment. However, it is not entirely convincing that the firm is able to choose the desired mix of legal penalty and market punishment, as the authors suggest by referring to a rather vague *investment in reputation* that could be reduced in response to an increase in penalties. More to the point, one can imagine several situations in which the firm can control whether or not to suffer the total expected cost from punishment but cannot control its composition.

Consider the following example: the good supplied to the customers can be produced at different levels of quality. If the firm can perfectly control the quality, an opportunistic behaviour could be that of selling a poor-quality product as a high-quality one. Notice that a consumer is cheated if there is no correspondence between the promised and the effective quality: hence it is not a problem of goods of poor quality but that of lemons. If the firm chooses this cheating strategy, it faces a criminal penalty *and* a reduction in future sales. Comparing the discounted profits from an honest behaviour with those of a cheating one, the quality of the product will not be secretly reduced if:

$$\frac{\Pi^h}{1-\delta} \geq \Pi^c + \frac{\delta\Pi^p}{1-\delta} - \delta f$$

where Π^h, Π^c and Π^p are respectively the per period profits when a high-quality product is supplied, when cheating and when the market punishment is at work, δ is the discount factor and f is the fine. The above expression helps us to understand the interplay between the criminal penalty and the market punishment: first of all, the fine could be insufficient to prevent a fraud even when coupled with the market punishment; in other cases f can help to meet the above condition, for a given level of the discount factor δ, in cases where the market punishment is insufficient to prevent a fraud; finally, in some cases f can be excessively severe as a disincentive device, increasing only the expected cost of punishment.

The effectiveness of the criminal penalty is therefore non-monotonic, and is redundant only when the market punishment is sufficiently high. But in all cases it is rather difficult to imagine a relationship between the amount of the fine and the loss induced by the market punishment. The latter is in fact a consequence of consumers' reaction to the opportunistic behaviour of the firm. Even when penalties are very high, if a low-quality product is marketed as a precious one, a reduction in sales must be expected, since this contraction is triggered only if the firm's opportunism has not been discouraged by the fine, i.e. if the penalty is not sufficiently high. Finally, notice that fines and market punishment have the same time-pattern in a world of certainty, i.e. they occur if and only if the firm misbehaves, and begin immediately after the criminal episode.

Hence, we conclude that the loss due to the market punishment does not depend on the level of the fine. Moreover, the firm can simply control whether to incur the threat of a (legal and market) punishment or not. The welfare effects of an increase in penalties must therefore be added to that of the market mechanism, with no relevant substitution between the two. Whether the legal fines are too high or too low to satisfy the condition above is an empirical problem that has no uniform answer but depends upon the specific cases examined.

In a world of certainty, the cost of the incentive device should be irrelevant from a welfare point of view, since in equilibrium no cheating behaviour – and no punishment – occurs. The point is less clear if we admit, realistically, imperfect monitoring of the firm's behaviour. In this case customers are not sure of the quality of the good purchased, and the court needs to investigate the issue before sentencing. However, in this second situation the time-pattern of the legal penalty and that of the market mechanism need not be the same. The former must fulfil a predetermined procedure that can take time before the final sentence is issued, while typically the market reaction can work in a much more rapid, rough and unbalanced way. For instance, the firm could be punished by the market before a final assessment is reached, with no possibility of a future reimbursement.

The welfare evaluation of fraud controls must take into account that one of the instruments, the market one, can inflict severe losses even to innocent firms.

Moving now to comment on the empirical results, the analysis of the forecast errors after the information of the fraud becomes public is certainly consistent with a fall in the market value of the firm. However, the adjustment is extremely low: while we have an initial forecast error of -1.04 per cent, the cumulative forecast error continues to grow, reaching -2.51% after 10 days, -3.55 per cent after 20 days and -4.01 per cent after a month. This pattern seems rather inconsistent with the implicit assumption of a very rational market usually adopted in the event studies. Moreover, the authors recognise that the post-announcement drift is sensitive to the model specification.

These observations make the reader cautious in interpreting the results not only at a qualitative level, but also as a first step to construct a quantitative estimation of the fall in the market value of the firm. The authors use a two-period forecast error referred to days -1 and 0, without an explicit motivation of their choice. When compared with the very lengthy adjustment and with the instability of the predictions, their specification leaves some doubts concerning their quantitative estimates.

A point that I find very interesting in the results is the time-path of the market punishment: the authors consider many types of announcements, referring to the initial allegation or to the date the charges were filed, or to the final settlement. The forecast errors result is less significant when moving from the initial allegation to the final settlement. The authors claim, and I agree with them, that if the first Press announcement is a settlement one it is very likely that the market already knows about the criminal episode and that the firm's returns were already adjusted. There is however a second point that is relevant. The market reacts when the episode has not yet been evaluated by the court. In the analytical results presented in Table 9.6 it can be observed that in some cases the firm was not found guilty but a market punishment occurred anyhow.

The asymmetry between the legal procedure and the punishment triggered by the market is therefore confirmed: in the latter case the firm is punished even if innocent, resembling the kind of strategies that are adopted in the literature on repeated games with imperfect monitoring. As suggested above, this raises serious doubts about the ability of the repeated purchase story to internalise the effects of firms' opportunistic behaviour.

Part V
Deterrence policies against organised crime

10 Regulating the organised crime sector

MARCO CELENTANI, MASSIMO MARRELLI and RICCARDO MARTINA

1 Introduction

The economic analysis of criminal activity, with the notable exceptions of Beccaria and Bentham, came to the attention of the economics profession in the late 1960s. Becker (1968) interpreted individual criminal behaviour as the solution to a portfolio choice problem and studied the normative question of the optimal punishments to be used to enforce a given legislation. In his own words, the main contribution of his work 'is to demonstrate that optimal policies to combat illegal behavior are part of an optimal allocation of resources'. From this point of view the 'economic framework becomes applicable to, and helps enrich, the analysis of illegal behavior' (Becker, 1968, p. 209).

Motivated by the casual observation that the externalities imposed by the criminal sector are much larger when cooperation among individuals active in that sector increases its efficiency, Schelling (1967, 1971) turned attention to organised crime and to the issue of collusion of organisations dedicated to illegal activities.

Schelling (1967) raises the point that victimless activities, i.e. activities for which there is a demand, such as the sale of narcotics or arms and illegal gambling, generate enough profits for large-scale criminal organisations to come into being and to maintain themselves: 'It may be ... that without these important black markets, crime would be substantially decentralized, lacking the kind of organization that makes it enterprising, safe, and able to corrupt public officials. In economic development terms, these black markets may provide the central core (or 'infrastructure') of underworld business' (Schelling, 1967, p. 177).

Schelling's argument becomes much more compelling when it is recognised that large-scale organisations may actually collude in these black markets so as to maximise total profit.

253

The purpose of the present paper is to pursue this idea to study how a government might 'regulate' the sector of victimless activities, so as to keep down aggregate profits of criminal organisations, and in turn control the expansion of organised crime and of the externalities that it imposes on the rest of the economy.

The first question that arises is: What is organised crime? Schelling (1971) defines organised crime as an organisation that has monopoly power over illegal activities. Recent experience indicates that, normally, organised crime is conducted by several organisations that can and often do gain from cooperative behaviour. For this reason we will refer to a more general definition of organised crime, describing it as a set of agents (criminal firms) that have market power and recognise the mutual influence of their activities and are therefore possibly in a position to exploit some sort of cooperation.

Regulation theory, and in particular the 'New Regulatory Economics', examines the economic rationale for a government agency to control an industry and identifies a menu of instruments, in the form of legally enforceable contracts, which can provide an optimal solution to the problem for a given set of political, informational and transactional constraints. It is clear, however, that the very essence of the problem of controlling criminal activities is that no enforceable contract can be written. In this sense the goal of this paper is to show that a government agency *can* devise strategies that may succeed in regulating the organised crime sector without assuming the existence of rules (laws) that ensure some degree of cooperation on the part of the agents being regulated.

In this paper we will assume that the goal of the 'regulator' is to minimise the aggregate profit of criminal firms. Such a goal should not, however, be taken for granted. Buchanan (1973) raises the interesting point that if the good sold in an illegal market is actually a bad, allowing collusion and the resulting monopoly outcome minimises the amount of the bad traded in equilibrium.

While simplifying the analysis, concentrating on aggregate profit minimisation can be justified mainly on the ground that it pursues the intuitive idea that long-run negative effects of large profits generated by collusion in black markets (such as investing in sectors which are not traditionally affected by criminal activities) can outweigh the short-run positive effects of a lower supply of bads.

In a previous paper (Celentani, Marrelli and Martina, 1993) we studied the repeated strategic interaction between the government and two criminal firms as an infinitely repeated game with discounting. In such a situation a collusive agreement is a possible sub-game perfect equilibrium outcome only if it is supported by off-equilibrium punishment paths that are themselves equilibrium strategies. Even though a fixed strategy of the government (i.e. a history-independent strategy) fails to guarantee that the equilibrium outcome will not be the collusive one, we show that if the government uses a particular history-dependent strategy then any punishment path that might support a collusive equilibrium outcome will fail to be an equilibrium path, so that collusion is no longer a sub-game perfect equilibrium outcome.

The main idea of Celentani, Marrelli and Martina (1993) is that the government can profit from using a strategy that affects the discount factors of criminal firms following different histories in different ways. By increasing the termination probability of one firm on a given punishment path, thereby decreasing its *effective* discount factor, the government guarantees that no punishment threat that could sustain a collusive outcome can be sub-game perfect.

The main point of the present paper is that if it is true that good outcomes for the firms (i.e. high profits) are possible only if the discount factor is high enough, it is also true that the government can ensure bad outcomes (i.e. low profits) to the firms in equilibrium only if the discount factor is likewise sufficiently high. Only if firms are sufficiently patient would they accept pay-offs that are lower than the static Nash equilibrium pay-offs out of fear of a future punishment.

This suggests that, in order to keep profits in the organised crime sector low, the government has to devise a strategy that threatens intervention if a deviation is observed but at the same time guarantees that the discount factor on the equilibrium path is as high as possible. This is to say that the government has to reward criminal firms with no intervention as long as they play in the prescribed way.

In the following some simplifying assumptions will be made in order to concentrate on a specific aspect of the problem. In particular we will assume that there is free entry to the criminal sector once one firm is destroyed, and that the probability of destroying a criminal firm with a given amount of resources is the same irrespective of its size (or in other words we dispense with relative size as a relevant variable).

These assumptions might be unrealistic but they are made in order to be able to look at a simple setting that allows one to study some strategic elements in the fight against organised crime.

The structure of the paper is the following. In Section 2 we give a description of the setting we want to study. Section 3 introduces notation and pay-off functions in the stage game and the repeated game. Section 4 gives the main result. Section 5 provides conclusions.

2   Description of the setting

In order to keep things as simple as possible, we will consider a setting in which the government opposes two criminal firms.[1] These three agents play repeatedly a fixed stage game. The objective of the criminal firms is to maximise their discounted profits, whereas the government aims at minimising the sum of the discounted profits of the two criminal firms. The implication of this particular objective function for the government is that the utility of individuals belonging to criminal organisations does not enter the social welfare function, so that the government is only concerned about the externalities such organisations might impose on the rest of the economy.

We assume that the government has a fixed amount of resources to be employed in the fight against criminal firms.[2] The way it allocates these resources affects the probabilities of survival of the two firms at the end of each period. To describe this situation we will assume that the government has a fixed amount of *termination probability* to distribute between the two criminal firms. For example, the government has sufficient resources to inflict a 20 per cent probability of termination on the two firms at the end of each period and this probability can be 'allocated' in any way – (0, 20), (5, 15), (10, 10), (20, 0) etc. As a consequence, the discount factor for a criminal firm is equal to the factor of time preference multiplied by the probability of survival, and, therefore, 'effective' discount factors depend on the strategy of the government as will be explained below.

The game is played in the following way. At time $t = 0$, the government has a fixed amount of resources and commits to a given, possibly history-dependent strategy. Starting at time $t = 1$, a fixed *stage game* is repeated an infinite number of times. The stage game is simultaneous in this sense: the two firms choose their actions and simultaneously the government chooses an action (the proportions of resources it allocates to the fight against each firm) which depends on the strategy it committed to at $t = 0$ and the past play (the history of the game).

After players choose their actions, it is revealed whether the government's fight against the firms was successful (i.e. whether any of the firms was terminated). Finally, non-terminated criminal firms receive their pay-off (profit), while terminated firms get a zero pay-off and the government suffers a disutility equal to the sum of profits of the non-terminated firms.

If a firm is terminated it is replaced in the following period by a new one.

To illustrate the setting, suppose that the strategy the government committed to at $t = 0$ and the play of the game up until time τ call for the government to fight each of the two criminal firms with $1/2$ of the resources available, and suppose that the (fixed) resources the government has decided to allocate to fight criminality are such that the total probability of termination is 0.2 (as above), so that the probability of termination of each of the two firms is equal to 0.1.

Suppose now that the time-preference factor for both firms is equal to 0.9. Then the firms will get the pay-offs implied by their play in the current stage with probability 0.9, 0 with probability 0.1, and, since they will not be terminated with probability 0.9, they will discount future pay-offs with a discount factor equal to $0.9 \times 0.9 = 0.81$.

Given a particular strategy for the government, the infinitely repeated game between the two firms can have a whole set of equilibrium outcomes. The goal of the paper is to find a strategy for the government that satisfies a particular condition and that maximises the government's pay-off in the infinitely repeated game. In particular, the strategy will be required to be *simple* in the sense that it can be described with reference to only one *desired path* and to three *phases*: one equilibrium phase and two punishment phases (one for each firm).

3   The model

At each point in time there are three active players: two criminal firms, A and B, and the government, G. Pure actions and action spaces are denoted respectively by $a^A \in A^A$, $a^B \in A^B$, $a^G \in A^G$.

The pure action spaces for the two firms are assumed to be compact sub-sets of a Euclidean space. We will make the assumption that the resources of the government are such that γ, the total termination probability, is less than or equal to 1,[3] and that the government's pure strategy space is $A^G = \{0, A, B\}$, where 0 is to be interpreted as the government attacking no firm, and A and B are to be interpreted as the government attacking firm A or B respectively with all its resources, thereby imposing a termination probability equal to the total termination probability.

As will be shown, the assumption concerning the particular form of the government's pure action space implies no loss of generality since the optimal commitment for the government calls for it to use all its resources against one firm or none at all.[4]

In the stage game players choose their actions simultaneously and actions are perfectly observed.[5]

Define β^i to be the survival probability of firm i at the end of the current stage; obviously:

$$\beta^A = \begin{cases} 1 - \gamma \text{ if } a^G = A \\ 1 \quad\quad \text{ if } a^G = 0, B \end{cases} \tag{1}$$

$$\beta^B = \begin{cases} 1 - \gamma \text{ if } a^G = B \\ 1 \quad\quad \text{ if } a^G = 0, A \end{cases} \tag{2}$$

After actions are played (and observed) it is observed whether the action of the government was successful, i.e. if A or B were terminated. If $i = A, B$ is not terminated, it gets a pay-off to be specified below; if it is terminated, it receives a pay-off of 0. The government gets a pay-off which is equal to the negative of the sum of the pay-offs of the criminal firms.

As we said above we will consider only pure strategy equilibria. The results we will discuss, however, are in general valid for action spaces that are compact sub-sets of finite-dimensional Euclidean spaces. For this reason our results would also hold for mixed strategy equilibria, *provided* that players randomise using a public randomising device. This is to say that for our analysis it is crucial that *deviations* be observed with certainty and without a lag, even though, as stated above, qualitatively similar results could be obtained by introducing noisy observation of the play.

3.1   Pay-offs

Pay-off functions are common knowledge. Let $v^i : A^A \times A^B \times A^G \to R$ be player i's pay-off function ($i = A, B, G$).

Let x^i be a random variable that assumes value 0 when firm i is not terminated and value 1 when it is terminated. Then, the pay-off to firm $i = A, B$, conditional on the realisation of x^i, will be:

$$v^i(a^A, a^B | x^i) = \begin{cases} \pi^i(a^A, a^B) \text{ if } x^i = 0 \, (i \text{ is not terminated}) \\ 0 \quad\quad\quad\quad \text{ if } x^i = 1 \, (i \text{ is terminated}) \end{cases}$$

and its expected pay-off:

$$v^i(a^A, a^B, a^G) = \beta^i \cdot \pi^i(a^A, a^B) \tag{3}$$

where β^A and β^B are the functions of a^G defined in (1) and (2). The pay-off to the government, conditional on the realisation of x^A and x^B is:

$$v^G(a^A, a^B | x^A, x^B) = -v^A(a^A, a^B | x^A) - v^B(a^A, a^B | x^B) \qquad (4)$$

and its expected pay-off is:

$$v^G(a^A, a^B, a^G) = -v^A(a^A, a^B, a^G) - v^B(a^A, a^B, a^G) \qquad (5)$$

We will make the following assumption concerning the pay-off functions:

Assumption 1 π *is continuous and concave on* $A^A \times A^B$ *and* $0 \leq \pi \leq \bar{\pi}$.
Let $\Pi = \{(\pi^A, \pi^B) | \exists (a^A, a^B) \in A^A \times A^B : \pi^A(a^A, a^B) = \pi^A, \pi^B(a^A, a^B) = \pi^B\}$ denote the socially feasible set. Let m be the minmax pay-off (reservation utility):

$$m = \min_{a^B \in A^B} \max_{a^A \in A^A} \pi^A(a^A, a^B).$$

Finally define $\Pi^* = \{(\pi^A, \pi^B) \in \Pi | \pi^A \geq m, \pi^B \geq m\}$ as the *socially feasible individually rational set*, i.e. the set of socially feasible pay-off pairs that are larger than the minmax pay-off. Then Assumption 1 together with compactness of the pure action spaces guarantees that Π^* is convex.

3.2 Repeated game

If a firm is terminated at time t, it will be replaced at time $t+1$ by another criminal firm with the same pay-off function, drawn from the infinite set N (in the following we will refer to $n \in N$ as the *name* of a criminal firm). A *history* of the game at time t is therefore the sequence of observed actions of the players together with the names of the criminal firms active at each point in time.

Since we assume that the government commits to a strategy at time 0 and never changes it, a given play up to time t also induces a unique sequence of actions of the government until t. Since the government's commitment strategy is known, we can exclude it from the history of the game for notational purposes:

$$h_1 = (a_0^A, a_0^B, n^A, n^B) \in H_1 = A^A \times A^B \times N \times N$$
$$h_t \in H_t = (A^A \times A^B \times N \times N)^t$$
$$h_t = (h_{t-1}; a_t^A, a_t^B, n_t^A, n_t^B)$$
$$H = H_\infty$$

A pure strategy for player $i = A, B, G$ at time t is a mapping $s_t^i : H_t \to A^i$. (Notice that a criminal firm is also allowed to condition its play on the history of the game before it became active.) Infinite strategies are $s^i = (s_1^i, s_2^i, \ldots) \in S^i$, $i = A, B, G$, where S^i denotes the space of infinite strategies for player i.

All players (A, B, G) have a common *time-preference* factor $\delta \in (0,1)$, so that the discount factor for firm $i = A, B$ will be equal to $\delta \cdot \beta^i$. The usual assumption that criminal agents have a lower discount factor is here interpreted to be a consequence of the probability of being terminated, and it is therefore incorporated into β^i, the probability of survival in each period (and hence it is a function of the action of the government).

With an abuse of notation we denote by $V^i : S^A \times S^B \times S^G \to [0, \bar{\pi}]$ the normalised infinite discounted pay-off of firm $i = A, B$ that arises from the infinite history induced by (s^A, s^B, s^G):

$$V^i(s^A, s^B, s^G) = (1 - \delta) \sum_{i=1}^{\infty} \delta^{t-1} \prod_{\tau=1}^{t} \beta_\tau^i \pi^i(a_t^A, a_t^B) \tag{6}$$

$i = A, B$, where $a_t^i = s_t^i(h_t)$, $i = A, B$ and β_τ^i is defined as a function of $s_t^G(h_t)$ as in (1) and (2). The normalising factor $(1 - \delta)$ is used in order to express the infinite game discounted pay-offs in the same unit as the stage game.

As we said above, we will make the assumption that the government suffers a disutility which is equal to the sum of the pay-offs (profits) of the criminal firms. It should be noted, however, that equation (6) gives the normalised discounted pay-off for the two firms that are alive at time 1, so that in particular the discounted pay-off to firm i in period t is equal to $\Pi_{\tau=1}^{t} \beta_\tau^i \pi^i(a_t^A, a_t^B)$ since firm i will be alive at time t with probability $\Pi_{\tau=1}^{t-1} \beta_\tau^i$ and will have pay-off $\pi^i(a_t^A, a_t^B)$ with probability β_t^i and 0 with probability $1 - \beta_t^i$. If a given firm is terminated at time $t - 1$, however, it will be replaced by a new firm at time t so that the normalised discounted pay-off to the government at time 1 will be:

$$V^G(s^A, s^B, s^G) = (1 - \delta) \sum_{t=1}^{\infty} \delta^{t-1} [\beta_t^A \pi^A(a_t^A, a_t^B) + \beta_t^B \pi^B(a_t^A, a_t^B)] \tag{7}$$

where, with an abuse of notation, it is understood that, if a given firm is terminated, the continuation of its strategy is replaced by the continuation of the strategy of the firm that replaces it.

4   Government commitment strategies

The goal of this section is to find an *optimal commitment strategy* for the government in a set of appropriate commitment strategies.

As we said above, we will impose a condition on the commitment strategy the government can choose. In particular we will require such a strategy to be simple.

4.1   Simple commitment strategies

Given a path of play for the firms (the path of play desired by the government, Q^D), and following the spirit of Abreu (1988), we will define a strategy for the government to be *simple* if it has the following structure:

(i)   At each point in time one of three possible *phases* (the equilibrium phase, the phase of punishment for firm A, and the phase of punishment for firm B) is *in force*;

(ii)   At the beginning of the game, the equilibrium phase is in force and it stays in force as long as no firm deviates from Q^D;

(iii)   If firm i unilaterally deviates from the desired path Q^D, then the punishment phase for firm i will be in force until firm i is terminated (a firm is punished for unilaterally deviating from the desired path);

(iv)   Once a firm is terminated, the equilibrium phase is in force again;

(v)   If the equilibrium phase is in force and both firms deviate, then the punishment phase that will be in force depends on the play in the last period only;

(vi)   The government strategy (i.e. which firm to attack) depends only on which phase is currently in force.

To define a simple commitment strategy more formally, it is convenient to introduce the indicator variable $\theta_t \in \{E, A, B\}$. θ_t is defined by the desired path Q^D, by (P^A, P^B), a partition on the firms' strategy profiles that differ from the desired path, $A^A \times A^B - \{(a_A^D, a_B^D)\}$, by an initial value, $\theta_1 = E$, and by the following law of motion, which is valid as long as no firm was terminated in the previous period:

$$\theta_{t+1} = \begin{cases} j & \text{if } \theta_t = E \text{ and either } a_t^i = a_t^D, d_t^j \neq a_t^D, \text{ or } (a_t^A, a_t^B) \in P^j \\ \theta_t & \text{otherwise} \end{cases} \quad (8)$$

If a firm was terminated at time t, then $\theta_{t+1} = E$.[6]

Clearly θ just indicates which phase is in force at time t. With this notation we can now give a formal definition of a *simple commitment strategy*:

Definition 1   *A commitment strategy for the government, s, is said to be simple if there is a path Q^D and a partition of the firms' strategy profiles different from the desired path (P^A, P^B), such that $a_t^G = a_{\theta_t}^G$ for all t.*

The main goal of this section is to show how the use of a strategy that depends in a simple way on the past play of the criminal firms can dramatically improve the effectiveness of the resources used in the fight against organised crime as compared to the case in which the government always allocates half of its resources to the fight against each of the two criminal firms.

To do this we will exploit the idea that a firm that values future profit is probably willing to trade today's profit in exchange for future profit, and in particular in exchange for the possibility of earning profits in the future, that is to say for being alive at future dates. This observation suggests that it should be possible to devise a strategy for the government that rewards firms with zero termination probability as long as they do not deviate from a low-profit path, and that punishes them with high termination probabilities if they deviate from such a path.

An important point is that the fact that a criminal firm is willing to exchange today's profit for future profit does not mean that the government is promising higher profits in the future. We assumed that there would always be two firms in the market, so that even if the firms that are currently in the market will be terminated, there will be other firms (with new *names*, in the terminology we introduced above) that will make profit and impose externalities. The government is just exploiting its ability to influence the survival probabilities of criminal firms by promising them that they will be the firms in the market in the future provided that they conform to a low-profit profile today.

In other words, the criminal firms accept lower profits today in exchange for the possibility of making profits tomorrow, while the government experiences a net gain both today and in the future, since the level of aggregate profits of criminal firms decreases.

4.2   Optimal commitment strategy

The purpose of the remainder of this section is to make the previous observations precise and to show that the government can devise a strategy of the type described above in a very wide range of examples.

To do this we will propose a particular simple commitment strategy and show that such a strategy succeeds in inducing the desired play on the part of the criminal firms independently of the fine structure of the pay-off function. This is to say that we will employ only the bounds on the pay-off function (0 and $\bar{\pi}$), the highest symmetric pay-off, and the minmax pay-off (m).

In the following we will let π^M denote the highest symmetric pay-off ($0 \leq \pi^M \leq \bar{\pi}$). Moreover, remember that $m = \min_{a^j \in A^j} \max_{a^i \in A^i} \pi^i(a^i, a^j)$. In words, m is the minimum pay-off firm j can hold firm i to if firm i correctly foresees a^j and plays a best response to it.

Suppose the government tries to induce the criminal firms to play according to Q^D, the desired path, and assume that this is stationary, i.e. $Q^D = ((a_A^D, a_B^D), (a_A^D, a_B^D), \ldots).$[7]

Suppose that the government commits to the following strategy:

(i) At the beginning of the game the equilibrium phase is in force;

(ii) If the equilibrium phase was in force and firm i unilaterally deviated from the desired path, then punishment phase i will be in force;

(iii) If the equilibrium phase was in force and both firms deviated from the desired path, then the punishment phase for firm i will be in force if firm i made a profit which is no higher than the profit of firm j; or the punishment phase for firm j will be in force if firm j made a (strictly) lower profit than firm i.

(iv) Do not attack any firm as long as it does not deviate from the desired path (as long as the equilibrium phase is in force);

(v) Attack with all resources the firm that is being punished (attack firm i when punishment phase i is in force);

Let this commitment strategy for the government be denoted by $s^* = s^* (Q^D, (P^A, P^B))$, since it is defined by Q^D, by $(P^A, P^B) \in A^A \times A^B - \{(a_A^D, a_B^D)\}$ such that $P^A = \{(a^A, a^B) \in A^A \times A^B - [(a_A^D, a_B^D)] | \pi^A(a^A, a^B) \leq \pi^B(a^A, a^B)\}$ (which implies $P^B = A^A \times A^B - [\{(a_A^D, a_B^D)\} \cup P^A]$), and by the law of motion for θ described in (8).

Let $V^D = (V_A^D, V_B^D)$, $V^A = (V_A^A, V_B^A)$, and $V^B = (V_A^B, V_B^B)$ denote the normalised discounted pay-offs to the two firms on the desired path and in the two punishment phases.

We are now in a position to state our first result:

Proposition 1 *Sufficient conditions for s^* to have Q^D as the unique best response outcome are:*

$$\delta m(1 - \delta\gamma) > \frac{1 - \delta}{1 - \delta(1 - \gamma)} \pi^M \qquad (9)$$

$$V_A^D \geq (1 - \delta)\bar{\pi} + \delta V_A^A \qquad (10)$$

$$V_B^D \geq (1 - \delta)\bar{\pi} + \delta V_B^B \qquad (11)$$

Proof: First we want to show that no strategy profile for the firms giving rise to an outcome different from Q^D can be an equilibrium together with s^* if condition (9) is satisfied.

Suppose that the criminal firms are following a strategy profile whose path is different from Q^D. We want to show that for any strategy profile whose path is different from Q^D there is at least one firm that has an incentive to deviate and play according to the desired path whenever the equilibrium phase is in force. The right-hand side of inequality (9) is an upper bound on the pay-off to the firm that gets the lowest pay-off when the government plays s^*. This is the case since the firm that gets the lower pay-off will get at most π^M at time $t = 1$ and will get at most $(1 - \gamma)^t \pi^M$ for $t > 1$.

Suppose that the firm that gets the lowest pay-off (firm i without loss of generality) deviates from the proposed strategy profile at time t and plays a_t^D (the action that the government expects firm i to play in the equilibrium phase).

By doing so the lowest pay-off to firm i will be 0 at time t, m at time $t + 1$, $m(1 - \gamma)$ at time $t + 2, t + 3, \ldots$, since for $\tau = t + 2, t + 3, \ldots$, at time τ it will get m if the firm that was alive at time $\tau - 1$ is still alive, an event that under strategy s^* happens with probability $1 - \gamma$, and a minimum of 0 if the firm that was alive at time $\tau - 1$ has been destroyed and has been replaced by a new firm, an event that under strategy s^* happens with probability γ.[8]

Condition (9) then guarantees that the lowest pay-off a firm could get by deviating and conforming to the strategy desired by the government is higher than the highest pay-off a firm could get by conforming to any alternative strategy profile.

Now we want to show that the strategies for the firms, which give rise to Q^D, form a Nash equilibrium together with s^* if conditions (10) and (11) are satisfied.

Conditions (10) and (11) guarantee that no firm wants to deviate from the desired path when the equilibrium phase is in force, since the left-hand side gives the pay-off from the desired path and the right-hand side gives an upper bound from deviation from the desired path (remember that after deviating from the desired path a firm will be punished).

No condition is imposed on the firms' pay-offs in the punishment phases, since they cannot affect the enforced phase.

Remark: Condition (9) might be counterintuitive since the left-hand side of the inequality (the pay-off to a firm that deviates from a candidate strategy profile that gives rise to a path different from the desired one) is decreasing in γ, the amount of resources used by the government to fight against its opponent. This is the case since we considered the possibility that this firm deviates to play according to the desired path when the equilibrium phase is in force.

Whenever this happens the firm that deviates might get a pay-off of zero, whereas during the punishment phase (since the government places no restrictions on the way firms should play) the firm that deviated will get at least the minmax pay-off. m. Since we want to show that the candidate strategy profile does not constitute a Nash equilibrium together with s^*, we have to consider unilateral deviations of one firm. However, if the government has a high γ, a large portion of the game will be spent in the equilibrium phases following the frequent terminations of the firms that did not deviate.

The next proposition uses Proposition 1 to find a desired path that gives normalised discounted pay-offs that satisfy conditions (10) and (11) and that, at the same time, maximises the government's pay-off provided that condition (9) is satisfied.

Proposition 2 *If condition (9) is satisfied, the equilibrium pay-off to the government from strategy s^* $(Q^D, (P^A, P^B))$ is maximised if Q^D is such that:*

$$V_A^D = V_B^D = V^* = \frac{1-\delta}{1-\delta(1-\gamma)}\bar{\pi} \tag{12}$$

Proof: Equation (12) easily follows from minimisation of $V_A^D + V_B^D$ subject to inequalities (10) and (11) once we recognise that:

$$V_i^I \leq (1-\delta)(1-\gamma)\sum_{t=0}^{\infty}(\delta(1-\gamma))^t\bar{\pi} = \frac{(1-\delta)(1-\gamma)}{1-\delta(1-\gamma)}\bar{\pi} \tag{13}$$

$$V^D = (1-\delta)\sum_{t=0}^{\infty}\delta^t\pi(a^D, a^D) = \pi(a^D, a^D) \tag{14}$$

and once we substitute the upper bound on V_i^l to V_i^l in inequalities (10) and (11) and we satisfy them both with equality.

Proposition 2 says that provided that condition (9) is satisfied (which excludes the possibility of other equilibria with a path different from Q^D) the government maximises its pay-off by imposing a desired path Q^D that gives each criminal firm a pay-off of exactly $V^* = \bar{\pi}(1 - \delta)/[1 - \delta(1 - \gamma)]$. Proposition 2 also implies that the simple strategy of the government with a desired path that gives pay-off V^* is also the strategy that maximises the government pay-off in the set of simple strategies whose desired path depends only on the bounds on the criminal firms' pay-off functions (0 and $\bar{\pi}$).

We now want to compare the pay-off to the government from playing s^* with the pay-off it would get by playing s, a fixed strategy that prescribes allocating half of the resources to fighting each of the two firms independently of the history of the game. Since there does not need to be only one equilibrium when the government plays the fixed strategy s, we can only give bounds on this difference.

Proposition 3   *Lower and upper bounds on the difference between the pay-off to the government from playing s^* and the pay-off from playing s, $D(\gamma, \delta)$, are:*

$$- 2\frac{1 - \delta}{1 - \delta(1 - \gamma)}\bar{\pi} + 2m\left(1 - \frac{1}{2}\gamma\right) \leq D(\gamma, \delta) \leq \gamma\frac{3\delta - \delta\gamma - 1}{1 - \delta(1 - \gamma)}\bar{\pi} \quad (15)$$

Proof: The pay-off to the government from playing s^* is $-2V^D$. The lower bound on the pay-off to the government from playing the fixed strategy is $-2(1 - \frac{1}{2}\gamma)\bar{\pi}$, since this is the pay-off the government gets if, with the fixed strategy, a strategy profile giving the maximum pay-off $(1 - \frac{1}{2}\gamma)\bar{\pi}$ in every period to the firms that are alive in that period is an equilibrium strategy profile. Similarly, an upper bound on the government's pay-off from the fixed strategy s is $-2(1 - \frac{1}{2}\gamma)m$.

Thus Proposition 3 gives a measure of the gain to the government from using a history-dependent strategy rather than a history-independent one. In particular, it should be noted that if δ is sufficiently large, then the lower bound is positive for any value of γ. This shows that the intuition that, if the firms are sufficiently patient, they will play as the government desires, that is to say they will accept a lower average pay-off in order to be sure to be alive in the future, is actually true in a very wide range of situations of strategic interaction.

More importantly, however, Proposition 3 shows the extent to which criminal firms are willing to accept a lower average pay-off. Surprisingly, if the criminal firms are patient enough they will accept a pay-off which is even lower than their minmax pay-off in the stage game and which actually tends to zero as their discount factor tends to 1 (see equation (12)).

5   Conclusion

This paper provides a framework to analyse important strategic elements of the government's policy in the fight against organised crime (or the government's 'regulation' of the organised crime sector). The objective of the government has been assumed to be the minimisation of profits in the criminal sector with the implicit goal of controlling the expansion of the criminal sector and thus of the externalities it imposes on the rest of the economy.

The minimisation of the aggregate profit of the criminal sector is achieved by employing a strategy that rewards criminal firms for following a low-profit path and threatens the use of resources in such a way as to impose a non-negligible probability of termination if the criminal firms deviate from such a low-profit path. We have shown that such a goal can be accomplished in a very wide range of situations describing a strategy that attains this result and that depends only on the bounds on the criminal firms' pay-off functions.

The description of the model can be enriched in several ways. The first possible generalisation involves relaxing the assumption that the actions of the criminal firms must be perfectly observable. In such a case a similar result can be expected to hold, even though it is reasonable to expect that the equilibrium pay-off to the government may be decreasing with the amount of noise.

More importantly, the fact that the criminal firms can use past profits in order to accumulate 'capital' could be explicitly taken into account and could further justify the assumption that the government's objective is to minimise aggregate profits. This would introduce a 'size' state variable and would complicate the analysis because it would no longer be possible to assume that the probability of termination is independent of the firm's past decisions (i.e. of its size). On the other hand, this could even reinforce our result because it would give additional incentives to the government to destroy a firm that had large profits in the past. An important policy implication of the analysis is that the state, in designing its deterrence policy, should take advantage of the nature of the organised crime sector; the state should recognise and take advantage of the repeated nature of the strategic interaction among criminal firms by using history-dependent strategies which allow the government to pursue fully its objective with a given amount of resources.

NOTES

* The financial support of the Consiglio Nazionale delle Ricerche is gratefully acknowledged. We wish to thank Jean Tirole for useful comments and suggestions. All remaining errors are of course ours.

1 The results we will discuss easily generalise to the case of n criminal firms.

2 This assumption is needed for the sake of simplicity; it can be justified if one believes that deterrence costs are to some degree sunk because of their human capital component.

3 The purpose of the assumption is to simplify notation. The same kind of result can be obtained with $\gamma \in [0, 2]$.

4 Defining the government's action space as the set of convex combinations of 0, A and B would lead to the same results.

5 The assumption of perfect observability of actions only simplifies notation and the derivation of the result. Assuming that there is imperfect observability gives a lower equilibrium pay-off to the government but modifies the government's strategy in a way that gives no additional intuition to the result.

6 The intuitive interpretation of (8) is that, if we are in P^j, firm j is being 'punished', since θ_t is the indicator variable of which phase is in force at time t.

7 Since the set of socially feasible, individually rational pay-offs is convex, there is no loss of generality in requiring the desired path to be stationary.

8 Remember that the government strategy calls for firm i to revert to a_i^p when the competing firm is terminated and is replaced by a new firm. If this new firm carries out the punishment implicit in the proposed strategy profile, firm i might get 0 in the first period in which a new firm is alive.

REFERENCES

Abreu, D. (1988), 'On the Theory of Infinitely Repeated Games with Discounting', *Econometrica*, 56(2), pp. 383–96.
Becker, G. S. (1968), 'Crime and Punishment: An Economic Approach', *Journal of Political Economy*, 76(2), March/April, pp. 169–217.
Buchanan, J. (1973), 'A Defense of Organized Crime?', in S. Rottemberg (ed.), *The Economics of Crime and Punishment*, Washington DC: American Enterprise Institute for Public Policy Research, pp. 119–32.
Celentani, M., M. Marrelli and R. Martina (1993), 'La rottura di accordi collusivi nel settore criminale', in S. Zamagni (ed.), *Mercati illegali e mafie*, Bologna: Il Mulino, pp. 153–64.
Schelling, T. C. (1967), 'Economics and Criminal Enterprise', *The Public Interest*, 7, pp. 61–78, reprinted in R. Andreano and J. Sigfried (eds.) (1980), *The*

Economics of Crime, Cambridge MA: Schenkmann, and in Schelling, T. C. (ed.) (1984), pp. 158–78.

Schelling, T. C. (1971), 'What is the Business of Organized Crime?', *Journal of Public Law*, 20, pp. 71–84, reprinted in T. C. Schelling (ed.) (1984), pp. 179–94.

Schelling, T. C. (ed.) (1984), *Choice and Consequence*, Cambridge MA: Harvard University Press.

Discussion

CARLO SCARPA

'All punishment is mischief: all punishment in itself is evil.'
Jeremy Bentham, *Principles of Morals and Legislation*

In 'Economics and Criminal Enterprise', now a chapter in his *Choice and Consequence* (1984), Tom Schelling suggested that 'a good many economics and business principles that operate in the "upperworld" must, with suitable modification for change in environment, operate in the underworld as well'. The paper by Celentani, Marrelli and Martina (CMM, for short), like most of the recent literature on the subject, shows how one of these principles can be applied to the economics of criminal activity. In particular, they try to show how the idea of achieving a pseudo-cooperative outcome through non-cooperative behaviour can be usefully introduced in this field. It is indeed well known that, thanks to the repeated interaction among rational agents – modelled through supergames – the Pareto-inefficiency of Nash equilibria can be overcome, and this intelligent paper shows how crime repression can be improved by explicitly considering this possibility.

The supergame this paper considers is one between the government and two criminal organisations operating in a 'victimless' sector. The government aims at minimising the aggregate profits of the firms, and pursues its goal by spending in each period either nothing, or a given sum of money to attack one of the two firms. In each period, no more than one firm can be attacked by the government, and this determines the probability (either 0 or γ) that a firm is 'terminated' in that period. Notice that the government really never 'wins', as it is assumed that, whenever a firm is 'terminated' another (identical) one appears on the scene; otherwise, no entry is considered.

Each firm's objective (v^i) is named profit, but it is actually a black box that depends on the actions undertaken by both firms. The relevance of this interdependence is never clearly discussed. It depends on the government strategy only in that: (i) if the firm is 'terminated' the pay-off is zero; and (ii) the probability of being terminated affects a firm's *expected* pay-off. In other words, crime deterrence cannot directly affect actual pay-offs, unless a firm is destroyed. Each firm's strategy is an action that, given the other firm's behaviour and the government's decisions, determines each period's expected pay-off. No action undertaken by the firms has a direct effect on the government, except through profit levels.

This paper proves that there exists an equilibrium for this repeated game in which the government spends nothing on crime deterrence as long as the firms' pay-offs are low enough, and then devotes all its resources to punish the firm that – deviating from the equilibrium path – earns excessive profits. Therefore, criminal organisations that are willing not to earn 'too much' are rewarded by the government with a guarantee of their survival. Furthermore, it is shown that the government gains using such a strategy, rather than devoting one-half of its resources to fight each organisation in each period.

The discussion of the paper might start from a list of criticisms of the above assumptions, but that would be too easy an exercise, and not a particularly interesting one. The modelling strategy the authors had to follow has necessarily led to some simplifications, but that as such should not be reason for excessive concern. However, a few remarks are in order.

First of all: what are 'victimless' activities? Typically, we are in the field of illegal trade of, say, arms or drugs, where the 'victim' is the community as such, rather than individuals. Apart from a possible discussion of the foundations of this concept, it should be clear that these activities are often at the very core of the most important criminal organisations in the world. In this respect, the strategy space of criminal organisations seems a bit too narrow, at least as it is assumed that the only way they can affect the government is *via* their profit levels, and not by controlling significant parts of a state's territory, murdering and so on. In other words, criminal organisations are typically multi-product firms, and isolating one part of their activities does not seem appropriate; moreover, the government's objective function is defined in such a narrow way, that many significant interactions are simply assumed away. Although it is far from obvious how a model could handle these issues, one should be very cautious in interpreting these results.

More generally, the interdependence between the government and the criminal organisations is extremely stylised. The assumption that the repressive activity can be effective only if the organisation is terminated is quite extreme, and far from obvious. For instance, it seems that the recent wave of anti-corruption investigations in Italy has decreased the number of criminal events, while increasing the risk that corruption entails; this has apparently increased the profit on each transaction, i.e. the level of each bribe. Although the global effect is far from obvious, it might be interesting to develop an analysis in which the relationship between government interventions and the pay-offs of criminal organisations is less simplified.

This is also true for the assumption that crime repression is firm-specific: it is possible to increase the probability of destroying one criminal organisation only by decreasing the effort against the other one. Although this captures one aspect of the story, it neglects the fact that there are several pre-emptive activities that are of a general nature, in that they hit all organisations. One example might be controlling passengers in airports, or patrolling the coasts: these are interventions that are not against a specific organisation, but against whoever tries to commit certain crimes. It would be interesting to see whether the equilibrium of the supergame would necessarily require these general expenditures to be cut, or whether it is only firm-specific activities that 'should' disappear.

One of the most debatable points is the government's objective function. The government aims at minimising firms' profits, and this assumption might be criticised in two respects. The first, minor remark is that the cost of public funds is implicitly assumed to be zero, as the resources spent on crime deterrence are not included in this objective function. Probably including it in the government's objective might render the occurrence of the no-punishment equilibrium even more likely.

Furthermore, and more importantly, the authors correctly point out that the objective function they assign to the government is far from obvious. In particular, they remind the reader of Buchanan's objection, according to which a better assumption would be that the government minimises the *volume* of transactions: after all what the government is concerned about is the volume of criminal activity *per se* (for instance, the quantity of illegal weapons exchanged in the black market), and not so much how profitable it is. The authors defend their choice by referring to the idea that 'in the long run' the negative effect of large profits on the volume of criminal activity might be a more serious problem, as large profits can attract more criminals, or because profits can be used to finance other criminal activities.

This defence leaves me a bit perplexed. The analysis CMM develop is one of a supergame with an infinite time horizon, so that one might wonder what 'long run' can come after a period of infinite length. On the one hand, it seems that this assumption rests on features that remain outside the model (e.g. how the profits can be used elsewhere). On the other hand, however, it is probably true that several criminal activities exhibit relevant economies of scale, and in this case profit would be an increasing function of output, so that concentrating on reducing profit and on reducing the volume of transactions might not necessarily make a substantial difference. However, it would have been useful if the authors had indicated the conditions on the profit function of criminal firms under which Buchanan's objection does not apply, and when – instead – some caution in interpreting the results is in order.

Now, let us turn to the conclusions the paper reaches. One of the obvious problems of supergames is the plethora of possible equilibria to which they typically lead, and this paper tackles this issue by concentrating on 'simple' strategies of the government, and showing under what conditions a situation in which the government never fights criminal organisations is an equilibrium. Of course, we know that this is only one of the infinite equilibria that exist in such a supergame, and thus the correct interpretation of the result should probably be that, if we observe a government that does not lift a finger against organised criminals, there is a chance that this behaviour is part of an optimal strategy to repress crime in a supergame context.

Although the conclusion seems formally impeccable, and not surprising either if one thinks of the general features of supergames, I must admit that I find it quite unpalatable, at least when applied to large and powerful criminal organisations. It is hard to take this indication seriously as a normative statement, or else it might be accepted only if it has to do with 'secondary' criminal activities (e.g. cigarette smuggling). However, in this case, the reasons why crime is not always repressed have more to do with the cost of repression and the social cost of destroying an economic (although illegal) activity which produces income for the people, rather than with a supergame strategy, i.e. with the fact that smugglers know that they cannot go beyond certain limits.

When it comes to large criminal organisations dealing in drugs, arms, uranium or the like, the conclusion that it might be optimal not to do a thing seems less acceptable. The objective function of the government should definitely be enriched, if we want to tackle these problems. Unless one really accepts that the government should find a middle point, an 'agreement' with the mafia, an idea that apparently has been quite popular with some politicians in Italy and elsewhere, and that has led to a substantial loss of credibility of the state in several fields. If we want to invoke 'externalities' to explain why the state wants to reduce the profits of criminal organisations, one should also consider the reputational externality that exists within the state sector, where a no-fight situation might destroy the credibility of public policies. Quite obviously, the relevance given to these issues might be considered a matter of taste, or of 'sensitivity' to certain problems, but it seems to me that here we also have an ethical problem that cannot be easily bypassed.

Last, but not least, the 'philosophy' of the paper. The layman would probably be puzzled by the idea of regulating something that in theory should not exist (i.e. criminal activity). Economists (cynical as we are!) are instead quite used to this idea, at least since Schelling's path-breaking 'Economics and Criminal Enterprise'. Of course some might think that this realism is really excessive and unethical, and it would probably be hard to discard such criticism completely.

However, it is interesting to point out that one might push this view even further, by considering explicit (maybe cooperative) bargaining between the government and criminal organisations. The idea is less absurd and empirically ill founded than it might seem at first glance. A few years ago, an Italian Minister of Finance proposed to guarantee public sector employment (as civil servants?!) to cigarette smugglers who agreed to surrender their boats, giving up their illegal trade. But the proposal was never transformed into a proper law, and the reason is that in the political debate 'general equilibrium' considerations came into play. Basically, some people argued that incentives to become criminals might have become excessive, with unpredictable consequences.

This banal political debate raises the final question, which I will try to translate into economic terms: to what extent can we take seriously conclusions based only on partial equilibrium analyses? The tendency to forget this question is obviously a common 'vice' of economists, who always have to struggle to find the optimum in a trade-off between the manageability of the models and their generality. The choice of CMM is certainly legitimate, and has allowed them to write a very interesting paper; *hic et semper*, some caution in interpreting the results as normative suggestions is required.

11 Oligopolistic competition in illegal markets

GIANLUCA FIORENTINI

1   Introduction

One of the better-known features of criminal organisations is that they
need to invest resources in activities which reduce the effectiveness of
deterrence against them. Such activities can take the shape of investments
in violence, or the threat of violence, corruption, protection of secrecy
and so on.[1] For this reason, in this paper we analyse how different
strategies of deterrence affect the interaction between criminal organisations which not only produce an illegal commodity but also invest in
anti-deterrence activities in order to reduce the costs of completing
transactions in the output market. This interaction between criminal
organisations is framed in an oligopolistic market structure because of
the growing body of evidence indicating that oligopolistic market
structures are prevalent in most core illegal industries such as large-scale
drug trafficking, illegal trade in military equipment and money laundering.[2]

Apart from the empirical evidence, we also focus on models of
oligopolistic competition for theoretical reasons. Indeed, we do not find
convincing the arguments that core illegal industries tend to be either
competitive or monopolistic. As for the assumption of monopolistic
markets in the core illegal industries, we object to it for the following
reasons.[3] First, illegal contracts can be enforced only at relatively high
cost and a small scale of activity reduces the risks arising from disputes
over contracts. Second, the degree of secrecy needed to manage an illegal
organisation implies that agency problems represent a severe constraint
on the increase of the scale of operation. Third, the need to build a
hierarchical structure for large organisations represents a further risk due
to larger information sets at the disposal of some members of the
organisation.[4] Nor do we regard the assumption of competitive markets
for the core illegal industries as convincing.[5] First, in such markets, there

are significant sunk costs, especially in running the core activities. Second, there is the possibility of imposing price discrimination. Third, management of a portfolio of risky activities may be improved by increasing the scale of operation.

If one believes in the efficiency of law in general and, more specifically, of the deterrence regulation, one can find further support for the assumption that oligopolistic market structures are prevalent in core illegal industries. Indeed, several Western countries have recently introduced deterrence rules which can only be rationalised under the implicit assumption of oligopolistic illegal industries. In fact, such legislation is not aimed at increasing the costs of undertaking illegal activities through heavier sanctions, but it is strictly targeted to decreasing the profits of criminal organisations. Of course such an objective would be not very significant if the illegal industries were mainly competitive.[6]

In recent years, building on a rather widespread consensus on the analysis of oligopolistic structures, and with special reference to the operations of Sicilian organisations affiliated to the Cosa Nostra, most authors claim that criminal organisations active in the same illegal industries succeed in undertaking collusive agreements aimed at maximising their joint profits.[7] Such cartels can be limited to agreements on how much to invest in anti-deterrence activities or they may also include agreements on how to operate in the output market. The alleged advantages (different from those that also exist in legal industries) for the organisations joining such cartels are two: first, it is possible to internalise the negative externalities arising from conflicts between different organisations; second, it is possible to centralise the corruption and lobbying activities so as to avoid wasteful dissipation. On similar lines, in a pioneering contribution, Buchanan (1973) argues that a cartel controlling an illegal industry has the effect of reducing the equilibrium output of the illegal commodity with respect to the competitive equilibrium. Analogously, Schelling (1967) argues that a similar cartel is likely to have the further effect of reducing the amount of violence and corruption needed to enforce transactions in such an illegal industry.

In this paper, we deal with a modified version of the two aforesaid classic propositions in the economics of illegal markets. More precisely, we analyse such propositions in a formal model by comparing the equilibrium levels of investment in violence (corruption) and the output (price) levels in an oligopolistic equilibrium in which symmetric criminal organisations are faced by different types of deterrence strategy. We focus on three settings.[8] In the first setting, the two criminal organisations act non-cooperatively in both their investment and their decisions concerning the output market. In the second setting, the criminal organisations collude over their investment in anti-deterrence activities, but they act non-cooperatively in the definition of their strategies in the output market. In the third setting, the criminal organisations collude over both their investment in anti-deterrence activities and their decisions concerning the output market. In the analysis of these settings we always assume that there is no possibility for the incumbent criminal organisations to exit or for new organisations to enter the illegal output market. This is for two reasons already mentioned in presenting the evidence on the permanence of oligopolistic market structures. First, in order to operate in the illegal output market, the organisations need to invest in anti-deterrence activities. Second, the investment in such activities is sunk in that it cannot be used in order to reduce the costs of completing transactions in any other market, be it legal or illegal.

Our main general result is that the two classic propositions must be qualified with respect to the type of deterrence policy faced by criminal organisations, and with respect to the mechanism through which an equilibrium is reached in the output market. For instance, Schelling's (1967) suggestion that cartels of criminal organisations lead to a decrease in violence depends strictly on the assumption that an increase in the use of violence by one organisation spurs an increase in deterrence activity even against the other organisations active in the same industry. However, as we will show, if deterrence is mainly targeted against more active organisations, an increase in the use of violence may well give rise to a positive externality for the other organisations, Schelling's proposition no longer holds. Following similar lines, we try to characterise which settings entail larger investments in violence and corruption and larger outputs of illegal commodities.

2   Competition in outputs

In this section, we build a model in which two organisations interact in a two-stage game. In the second stage, the two organisations compete in a Cournot duopoly where the output, for which there is a voluntary demand, can be either legal or illegal. In the first stage, the two organisations invest in anti-deterrence activities aimed at decreasing the costs of producing the second-stage output. We also assume that the investment in anti-deterrence activities directly affects the cost function of the rival organisation via the deterrence policy chosen by an enforcement agency. More specifically, a negative externality arises when one organisation's investment in violence and corruption also has the effect of increasing the deterrence against the rival organisation. On the contrary, a positive externality arises when one organisation's increase in anti-deterrence investment has the effect of reducing the deterrence effort against the rival organisation.

The idea which we want to capture using a Cournot model is that of two organisations working in isolation and determining the quantity of output which they bring to the market. Each organisation has a knowledge of the market structure, the characteristics of demand and cost structures and the deterrence technology, but neither organisation knows how much output the other is bringing to the market. When the output reaches the market-place the price is fixed by agents who specialise in trading such output and set the price at a level which equates demand and supply. The latter, which act as commissioners, have strong incentives to equate demand and supply because they face high costs in storing illegal commodities. Some scholars have noticed that similar market-clearing mechanisms can be observed in those industries in which the suppliers incur relatively high costs in varying their output levels so as to accommodate the demand conditions.[9] Such a situation often occurs in those industries in which the production technology calls for significant sunk costs. Among the illegal activities which seem to share such features one can list large-scale dealing in drugs, illegal trade in military equipment, international trade in body organs and so on.

The two organisations know that the enforcement agency has a budget which is proportional to the overall investment in anti-deterrence activities. This is because the agency is under the control of elected decision-makers who are not interested in minimising violence and/or corruption. Indeed, having crime reduced to a minimum is not electorally productive because the general public may believe that this is due to exogenous reasons. On the other hand, what is electorally productive – because clearly visible to the general public – is to show that the enforcement agency is capable of responding successfully to active criminal organisations. Moreover, elected decision-makers seem to believe that effective deterrence activity against larger criminal organisations is more electorally productive than that against smaller groups.[10] Accordingly we assume that the agency produces the following amount of deterrence activity against the organisation i:

$$D^i = \frac{\beta(g^i + g^j)}{(1 - \theta)} \left[\frac{g^i}{g^i + g^j} - \frac{\theta g^j}{g^i + g^j} \right] = \alpha(g^i - \theta g^j) \text{ where}$$

$$\alpha = \frac{\beta}{(1 - \theta)} \ i \neq j = 1, 2 \tag{1}$$

where g^i is the investment in violence and corruption of the organisation i, β is a measure of the productivity of the deterrence activity ($\beta < 1 - \theta$), and $\mid \theta \mid < 1$ is a measure of the selectivity of the deterrence activity against the activities of the larger organisation. Indeed, from (1) it is easy to see that $\partial D^i / \partial \theta > 0 \Leftrightarrow g^i > g^j$. The rationale behind (1) is that, when $\theta = 0$, each organisation faces a proportion of the deterrence activity which is equal to its proportion of the overall investment in violence and corruption. On the other hand, when $\theta > 0$ (< 0) the organisation which is the larger producer of violence and corruption faces a proportion of the deterrence activity which is larger (smaller) than its share of the overall investment in violence and corruption.

In the second stage, each organisation produces the output q^i with the cost function $C^i = c^i(G^i)q^i$ which includes all costs except that for the production or the purchase of the anti-deterrence activities which is assumed to be quadratic.[11] The costs of the production of the output are assumed to depend on the difference between the anti-deterrence investment of the organisation and the deterrence activity produced by the agency:

$$G^i = g^i - D^i = (1 - \alpha)g^i + \alpha\theta g^j \qquad i = 1, 2$$

where we further assume that $c^i_G < 0$ and that $c^i_{GG} > 0$, using subscripts to indicate derivatives. Defining the revenue function of the organisation i as r^i, its profit π^i can be written as:

$$\pi^i(q^i, q^j, G^i) = r^i(q^i, q^j) - c^i(G^i)q^i - v\left(\frac{g^{i2}}{2}\right) \qquad i \neq j = 1, 2 \qquad (2)$$

We assume that the outputs of the two organisations are strategic substitutes.[12] This can be expressed as: $r^i_j < 0$ and $r^i_{ij} < 0$. The Nash equilibrium in the second stage is characterised by the following first-order conditions:

$$\pi^i_i = r^i_i(q^i, q^j) - c^i(G^i) = 0 \qquad i = 1, 2 \qquad (3)$$

and second-order conditions: $\pi^i_{ii} = r^i_{ii} < 0$. Following Dixit (1986), we also assume that own effects of output on marginal profits dominate cross effects. This gives rise to the following condition:

$$S = r^i_{ii}r^j_{jj} - r^i_{ij}r^j_{ji} > 0$$

which has been shown to hold for most demand and cost structures and is fairly standard in non-cooperative models. If it holds globally, in fact, it ensures not only uniqueness, but also global stability of the equilibrium.[13] The implicit solution for the output levels in (3) depends on g^i and g^j and can be expressed as:

$$q^i = h^i(g^i, g^j); \quad q^j = h^j(g^i, g^j) \quad i \neq j = 1, 2 \tag{4}$$

which can be used in order to derive comparative static results. Totally differentiating (3) with respect to q^i and q^j, holding g^i and g^j constant, we obtain the slope of the reaction function:

$$\frac{dq^j}{dq^i} = -\frac{r^i_{ii}}{r^i_{ij}} \quad i \neq j = 1, 2$$

which is negative because the two outputs are strategic substitutes. To see what happens when g^i is increased, we totally differentiate (3) with respect to g^i. Using (4), and defining for symmetry $r_{ij} = r^i_{ij} = r^j_{ji}$ and $r_{ii} = r^i_{ii} = r^j_{jj}$, we end up with the following expressions:

$$q^i_i = \frac{\partial q^i}{\partial g^i} = \frac{c_G[(1 - \alpha)r_{ii} - \alpha\theta r_{ij}]}{S} \tag{5}$$

$$q^j_i = \frac{\partial q^j}{\partial g^i} = \frac{c_G[\alpha\theta r_{ii} - (1 - \alpha)r_{ij}]}{S} \tag{6}$$

which allow some comments on the comparative static effects of the investment in violence and corruption on the competition between the two organisations. When $\theta \leq 0$, the Cournot–Nash equilibrium level of output is strictly increasing (decreasing) in the level of the own (rival) investment in violence or corruption. On the contrary, when $\theta > 0$, the sign of the effect of an increase in the own or rival's investment in violence and corruption depends on the productivity of the deterrence effort (α). More precisely, (5) can become negative, for $\theta > 0$, when:

$$\frac{1 - \theta - \beta}{\beta\theta} < \frac{r_{ij}}{r_{ii}} \tag{7}$$

while (6) can become positive, again for $\theta > 0$, when:

$$\frac{\beta\theta}{1-\beta-\theta} > \frac{r_{ij}}{r_{ii}} \tag{7'}$$

In order to better understand (7) and (7'), recall that r_{ij}/r_{ii} is the absolute value of the slope of the reaction functions. It measures how much change in the rival organisation's output is induced by a unit of change in its own output. As it becomes larger, a change in an organisation's behaviour induces greater responses from the rival organisation and the amount of profit shifting becomes larger. In the present context, if there is a positive externality due to an aggressive deterrence activity against the larger producer of violence and corruption, and if such deterrence is sufficiently efficient (β is large), an increase in investment in violence and corruption shifts the reaction function of the other organisation outward to such an extent as to increase its equilibrium output. The economic intuition behind it is as follows. The less sloped are the reaction functions and the higher is the effect of the positive externality brought about by an increase in the rival's investment in violence and corruption, the greater is the incentive for the two organisations to increase their investment in g. This is because such investment is used to increase the output share in the second-stage competition.

In the first stage, both organisations realise the dependence of the output levels on the choice of the optimal g. This brings us to analyse only sub-game perfect equilibria where profits can be written as functions of g^i and g^j. If we indicate with k^i the profits of the organisation i in the first stage, we can write the objective function for the organisation i as:

$$\max_{g^i} \ k^i = r^i(q^i(g^i,g^j),q^j(g^i,g^j)) - c^i(G^i)q^i - v\left(\frac{g^{i2}}{2}\right)$$
$$i = 1,2 \tag{8}$$

The Cournot–Nash equilibrium in anti-deterrence activity levels, using (2), (3) and (8) is characterised by the first-order conditions:[14]

$$k_i^i = r_j^i q_i^j - c_G^i(1-\alpha)q^i - vg^i = 0 \qquad i \neq j = 1,2 \tag{9}$$

Some interesting implications of the above model can now be introduced. From (9) one can obtain the non-cooperative investment in violence and corruption for i:

$$g_*^i = \frac{-c_G^i(1-\alpha)q^i + r_j^i q_i^j}{v} \qquad i \neq j = 1,2 \tag{12}$$

Expression (12) tells us that the investment in violence and corruption is smaller, the greater the productivity of the deterrence agency. Moreover, a shift from a deterrence activity biased against large producers of violence and corruption to small producers (θ from positive becomes negative) has the effect of increasing investment in violence and corruption. This is because such investment imposes a negative externality on the rival organisation only when $\theta < 0$, giving a further incentive to invest in g.[15] Accordingly, (12) tells us that, *ceteris paribus*, a lower selectivity in the deterrence against large producers of violence and corruption can lead to the undesirable consequence of increasing investment in such activities.

A relevant bench-mark to understand the anti-deterrence behaviour of the two organisations can be obtained by comparing their non-cooperative behaviour with the case in which such organisations collude in order to determine their investment in violence and corruption. The analysis of this case is greatly simplified by assuming that the second-stage competition does not change, and that the collusive behaviour is strictly limited to the investment in anti-deterrence activities.[16] When the two organisations jointly maximise, their objective function in the first stage becomes:

$$\max_{g^1, g^2} k = \sum_{i=1}^{2} r^i(q^1(.), q^2(.)) - \sum_{i=1}^{2} c^i(G^i)q^i - v\sum_{i=1}^{2}\left(\frac{g^{i2}}{2}\right)$$

from which, after some algebraic manipulations, the first-order conditions can be written as:

$$r_j^i q_i^j + r_i^j q_i^i - c_G^i(1-\alpha)q^i - c_G^j\alpha\theta q^j - vg_i = 0 \qquad i \neq j = 1,2$$

Using symmetry, the expression above can be rewritten as:

$$g_c^i = \frac{-c_G^i[(1-\alpha)q^i + \alpha\theta q^j] + r_j^i(q_i^j + q_i^i)}{v} \qquad i \neq j = 1,2 \tag{13}$$

for which most of the comments concerning the comparative statics performed on (12) still hold. Comparing (12) and (13) one can see that:

$$g_c^i \geq g_*^i \quad \Leftrightarrow \quad -c_G \alpha \theta q^j + r_j^i q_i^i \geq 0$$

that is, when $\theta \leq 0$ (low selectivity in deterrence policy), the two criminal organisations, operating as a profit-maximising cartel, always reduce their investment in violence and corruption with respect to the non-cooperative solution. On the other hand, when $\theta > 0$, the cartel can bring about an increase in anti-deterrence activities, especially for high levels of α. This means that when the deterrence activity is mostly concentrated on the larger producer of violence and corruption, the creation of a cartel between criminal organisations can even increase the overall investment in violence and corruption with respect to the case in which such organisations compete non-cooperatively.

Let us now compare (12) with the equilibrium level of g obtained when the two organisations jointly maximise their profits in both stages. In such circumstances, in order to find out the equilibrium level of g, one needs to substitute in (13) the values of q_i^i and q_i^j obtained from a modified second stage in which the two organisations jointly maximise their profits. The first-order conditions equivalent to (3) are the following:

$$\pi_i^i = r_i^i(q^i, q^j) + r_i^j(q^i, q^j) - c^i(G^i) = 0 \qquad i = 1, 2 \tag{2'}$$

Following the same steps which have led to expressions (5) and (6) it is easy to show that in this case $q_i^i + q_i^j = 0$. It follows that the equilibrium investment in violence and corruption when the two organisations collude at both stages is:

$$g_m^i = \frac{-c_G^i[(1-\alpha)q^i + \alpha\theta q^j)]}{v} \qquad i = 1, 2 \tag{13'}$$

Comparing (13) and (13') one can see that, when the two organisations collude in both stages, they further reduce their investment in violence and corruption with respect to the case in which they collude only in the first stage. This is because the two organisations now fully take into account the profit-reducing effect of increasing their investment in violence and corruption via larger equilibrium outputs. This reduction in the equilibrium level of g holds irrespective of the degree of selectivity of the deterrence activity. On the other hand, comparing (12) and (13'), it is easy to show that even in this case $\theta \leq 0$ ensures that the creation of a cartel in both stages has the effect of lowering the equilibrium investment in violence and corruption. This result may be reversed only under the same circumstances in which q_i^j becomes positive, that is when the deterrence activity is strongly biased against larger producers of violence and corruption.

We can now summarise the main results obtained from the positive analysis of those industries in which the Cournot conjectures can be seen as an approximate description of how the market-clearing mechanism works, such as large-scale drug trafficking or dealings in military equipment. The above analysis has shown that one needs to distinguish between two polar cases according to the degree of concern about the level of violence and corruption originating in the industry at stake.

In the case of a deterrence activity which does not focus on larger producers of violence and corruption, the creation of a cartel (with binding agreements on either one or two decision variables) decreases the investment in violence and corruption with respect to the non-cooperative equilibrium. This is because at the collusive equilibrium the two organisations take into account the negative externalities which they are inflicting on each other by investing in violence and corruption. Due to the fact that the aforesaid reduction in g has a cost-increasing effect, in a Cournot environment the creation of a cartel also has the further implication of reducing the equilibrium output of the illegal commodity.

On the contrary, in the case of a deterrence activity biased against larger producers of violence and corruption it can happen, especially when the deterrence activity is highly productive, that the creation of a cartel (again with binding agreements on either one or two decision variables) increases the investment in g with respect to the non-cooperative equilibrium. This is because, when the investment in violence and corruption creates a positive externality for the rival organisation, the two organisations under-invest in g at the non-cooperative equilibrium in order not to give a competitive advantage to the rival organisation.

Finally, at the non-cooperative equilibrium, a decrease in the bias towards larger producers of violence and corruption increases the overall investment in such activities. This is due to the fact that such a shift transforms what was before a positive externality into a negative one, which gives greater incentives for non-cooperative organisations to invest in violence and corruption.

3   Competition in prices

A natural extension of the analysis pursued so far is to focus on a two-stage game in which the second-period competition is in prices rather than in outputs. In order to allow for a comparison between the two cases, the assumption of homogeneity of outputs is kept. The idea we want to capture using a Bertrand model is that of two organisations which independently call some commissioners and give them a price at which they are willing to sell. The commissioners investigate the market demand at those prices and then call back the two producers telling them how much output they are asked to bring to the market.[17] A similar mechanism by which the price is set and demand is filled is likely to be observed in those industries in which the two organisations can costlessly vary their output levels to accommodate the demand conditions. Such a situation often occurs in those lines of business which do not involve significant sunk costs. Among the illegal activities which share such features one can list the laundering of dirty money, loan-sharking, illegal lotteries and so on.

The Bertrand competition can be characterised in the second stage by output functions such as $q^i = d^i(p^i(g^i, g^j), p^j(g^i, g^j))$ where $d^i_i < 0$, $d^i_j > 0$, $d^i_{ii} < 0$ and $d^i_{ij} > 0$ because they are assumed to be strategic complements. The other assumptions on the cost-reducing effects of g and on its own costs of production still hold. The organisation i maximises its profits π^i:

$$\max_{p^i} \pi^i(q^i, q^j, G^i) = p^i d^i(p^i, p^j) - c^i(G^i)d^i(p^i, p^j) - v\left(\frac{g^{i2}}{2}\right)$$
$$i \neq j = 1, 2 \tag{14}$$

The Bertrand–Nash equilibrium is then defined by the following first-order conditions:

$$\pi^i = d^i + [p^i - c^i(G^i)]d^i_i = 0 \qquad i = 1, 2 \tag{15}$$

and second-order conditions:

$$\pi^i_{ii} = (1 + p)d^i_i + [p - c^i(G^i)]d^i_{ii} < 0 \qquad i = 1, 2 \tag{16}$$

where the parentheses for the arguments have been dropped. The same conditions as in Cournot are assumed to hold in order to ensure local stability and uniqueness of the equilibrium. Totally differentiating (15) with respect to p^i and p^j, holding g^i and g^j constant, we obtain the slope of the reaction function:

$$\frac{dp^j}{dp^i} = -\frac{2d^i_i + (p^i - c^i)d^i_{ii}}{d^i_j + (p^i - c^i)d^i_{ij}} \qquad i \neq j = 1, 2$$

which is positive because of the assumptions made on the function d^i. To see what happens when g^i is increased – *ceteris paribus* – we totally differentiate (15) with respect to g^i. Using (15) and (16) we end up with the following expressions:

$$p_i^i = \frac{\partial p^i}{\partial g^i} = \frac{c_G^i d_i^i \{[2(1 - \alpha)d_i^i - \alpha\theta d_j^i] + (p^i - c^i)[(1 - \alpha)d_{ii}^i - \alpha\theta d_{ij}^i]\}}{S'} \quad (17)$$

and

$$p_i^j = \frac{\partial p^j}{\partial g^i} = \frac{c_G^i d_i^i \{[2\alpha\theta d_i^i - (1 - \alpha)d_j^i] + (p^j - c^j)[\alpha\theta d_{ii}^i - (1 - \alpha)d_{ij}^i]\}}{S'} \quad (18)$$

where S' is the determinant of the relevant comparative statics' matrix. Given our assumptions on d^i, when $\theta \geq 0$, that is when the enforcement agency's budget constraint is binding, both (17) and (18) are negative. This is due to the fact that in Bertrand competition, and without externalities via deterrence activity, a decrease in the marginal cost brings about a reduction in the equilibrium price which is followed by the rival organisation. Such an effect is reinforced by the positive externality for which an increase in one organisation's g also has the direct effect of reducing the rival's operating costs. On the other hand, when $\theta < 0$, an increase in one organisation's investment in violence and corruption imposes a negative externality on the rival organisation whose costs also increase. This has the effect of raising the rival's equilibrium price which, in its turn, induces an increase in the own price due to the positive slope of the reaction functions.

If we indicate with k^i the profits of the organisation i in the first stage, its objective function becomes:

$$\max_{g^i} k^i = p^i(g^i, g^j)d^i(p^i(g^i, g^j), p^j(g^i, g^j))$$

$$- c^i[(1 - \alpha)g^i + \alpha\theta g^j]d^i(p^i(g^i, g^j), p^j(g^i, g^j)) \quad (19)$$

$$- v\left(\frac{g^{i2}}{2}\right) i \neq j = 1, 2$$

The Bertrand–Nash equilibrium in the investment in violence and deterrence is characterised by the following first-order conditions:

$$(p^i - c^i)d_j^i p_i^j - c_G^i(1 - \alpha)d^i - vg^i = 0 \quad i \neq j = 1, 2 \quad (20)$$

which allow us to write:

$$g_*^i = \frac{(p^i - c^i)d_j^i p_i^j - c_G^i(1 - \alpha)d^i}{v} \qquad i \neq j = 1, 2 \tag{21}$$

From (21) one can notice – in analogy with the observation on (12) in Section 2 – that the investment in violence and corruption is smaller the greater is the productivity of the enforcement agency. Moreover, even in this case, a shift from a high to a low level of selectivity of the deterrence activity against the larger producer increases the overall investment in violence and corruption. In Section 2 we observed that this is due to the fact that such investment imposes a negative externality on the rival organisations only when $\theta < 0$, giving a further incentive to invest in g.

Let us now assume that the second-stage competition does not change, and that the two organisations collude only for their investment in the anti-deterrence activity. Given that, when the two organisations jointly maximise, their objective function in the first stage becomes:

$$\max_{g^i} \; k = \sum_{i=1}^{2} d^i(p^i(.), p^j(.))p^i(.) - \sum_{i=1}^{2} c^i(G^i)d^i(p^i(.), p^j(.))$$

$$- v\sum_{i=1}^{2}\left(\frac{g^{i2}}{2}\right) \qquad i \neq j = 1, 2$$

after some algebraic manipulations, the equilibrium level of the investment in violence and corruption for the colluding organisations can be written as:

$$g_c^i = \frac{(p^i - c^i)d_j^i(p_j^i + p_i^i) - c_G^i[(1 - \alpha)d^i + \alpha\theta d^j]}{v} \qquad i \neq j = 1, 2 \tag{22}$$

Comparing (21) and (22), we can show that:

$$g_c^i \geq g_*^i \qquad \Leftrightarrow \qquad (p^i - c^i)d_j^i p_i^i - c_G^i \alpha\theta d^j \geq 0 \tag{23}$$

In this case it is not possible to obtain clear-cut results. Indeed, when $\theta < 0$ ($\theta \geq 0$) p_i^i becomes positive because α is large (negative), so that the two terms in the LHS of the second inequality in (23) tend to have opposite signs. The only result which can be stated is that for $\theta < 0$ (low selectivity in the deterrence policy), and relatively low efficiency of the enforcement agency, the two organisations operating as a cartel invest less in violence and corruption than at the non-cooperative equilibrium. Unlike the case examined in Section 2, however, for $\theta < 0$ the opposite can also hold.

Let us now compare (21) with the equilibrium level of g obtained when the two organisations jointly maximise their profits in both stages. In such circumstances, in order to find out the equilibrium level of g, one needs to substitute in (22) the value of $\partial p / \partial g^i$ obtained from the modified second stage in which the two organisations jointly maximise their profits. The first-order condition equivalent to (15) for the jointly-maximising cartel which chooses a unique price level is the following:

$$d^i + pd_i^i - c^i(G^i)d_i^i = 0 \tag{15'}$$

Following the same steps which have led to expressions (5) and (6), it can be shown that in this case:

$$\frac{\partial p}{\partial g^i} = \frac{c_G d_i^i (1 - \alpha - \alpha\theta)}{2d_i^i + (p^i - c^i)d_{ii}^i}$$

It follows that the equilibrium investment in violence and corruption when the two organisations collude at both stages is:

$$g_m^i = \frac{(p^i - c^i)d_j^i[c_G^i d_i^i(1 - \alpha - \alpha\theta)]}{v(2d_i^i + (p^i - c^i)d_{ii}^i)} - \frac{c_G^i[(1 - \alpha)d^i + \alpha\theta d^j]}{v}$$
$$i \neq j = 1, 2 \tag{22'}$$

Comparing (22) and (22') one can see that, irrespective of the value taken by $\theta, g_m^i < g_c^i$. This is in line with what we have observed in Section 2, since the two organisations now fully take into account the profit-reducing effect of increasing the investment in violence and corruption via lower equilibrium prices. On the other hand, comparing (21) and (22') we again find it impossible to obtain definite results, as we observed comparing the equilibrium investment in violence and corruption at the non-cooperative equilibrium (21) and in presence of a cartel in the first stage only (22).

When the two organisations compete in prices at the second stage, the effects of the creation of cartels between criminal organisations on both the investment in violence and corruption and on the equilibrium outputs of the illegal commodities are not clear.[18] With respect to the Cournot model analysed in Section 2, in the Bertrand model, even when the deterrence activity is not biased against larger producers of violence and corruption, the creation of a cartel may not reduce the investment in violence and corruption. This is because at the collusive equilibrium the two organisations can try to increase their partners' costs in order to induce them to set higher price levels. When the two organisations compete non-cooperatively they do not consider the implications of such externalities for the equilibrium profits.

A relevant implication of this result is that at the non-cooperative equilibrium in Bertrand competition the criminal organisations are not necessarily over-investing in violence with respect to the collusive equilibrium. From this result it follows that, differently from the Cournot model, at the non-cooperative equilibrium costs and therefore prices are not necessarily lower than at the collusive equilibrium. Let us try to be more detailed on this point. In a one-stage Bertrand model the organisations are characterised by an individual demand curve that is more elastic than in the Cournot model. In fact, with price competition, each organisation realises that lowering its price makes it possible to take all the market from its rivals. In one-stage models this leads to an equilibrium outcome characterised by higher outputs and a lower price than in the Cournot case. However in a two-stage model some limited strategic reaction can be analysed and this changes the outcome of the two games. In fact, as in most models of this type, the environments that in a one-stage framework would lead to lower profits become those where the implicit coordination among organisations is higher. In our case, for instance, it is in the Cournot model that the non-cooperative equilibrium implies over-investment in g and therefore high equilibrium output and low profits. This is due to the fact that in a two-stage game the criminal organisations can be credibly punished if they do not implicitly coordinate their decisions in the first stage. As Shapiro (1989) properly notices, in these models 'anything that makes more competitive behavior credible or feasible actually promotes collusion'.

4   Conclusions

The positive analysis undertaken in Sections 2 and 3 has shown that the aggregate resources invested in violence and corruption – as well as the output of the illegal commodity – are not related in a simple way to the existence of collusion or competition among the criminal organisations. Two analytical elements play crucial roles in determining the equilibrium level of violence and corruption: the type of response which the criminal organisations expect as a reaction to an increase in investment in violence and corruption on the part of the enforcement agency, and the mechanism through which an equilibrium is reached in a given market.

In this respect, we have shown that a deterrence activity highly (moderately) concentrated against the organisations investing more heavily in violence and corruption gives rise to a positive (negative) externality when one organisation increases its investment in such activities. Accordingly, when deterrence is highly selective under Cournot competition, an increase in g^i shifts both reaction functions inward, that of j to an extent proportional to the scale of the externality. In these circumstances it is profitable for the organisation i to lower its investment in violence and corruption to increase its market share. In the Bertrand case, when such investment increases, both reaction functions shift outward, again that of the organisation j proportionally to the scale of the externality. This increases the price that both organisations face in the second-stage competition and the latter may therefore have a direct incentive to over-invest in violence and corruption. However, this is less likely to be so the more efficient is the deterrence agency. The opposite holds when the deterrence activity is not heavily biased with respect to the relative investment in violence and corruption. Indeed, in the presence of a negative externality, over-investment with respect to the collusive equilibrium can also occur under Cournot competition.

These results show that in our framework Schelling (1967) and Buchanan's (1973) propositions according to which cartels in core illegal markets tend to reduce the investment in violence and corruption must be qualified in the two aforesaid directions. Given these qualifications, we have restricted the settings in which this proposition holds to the case in which deterrence activity is highly concentrated on the larger producers of violence and corruption and in which the criminal organisations engage in Cournot competition in the illegal output market.

NOTES

1 Notice that criminal organisations do not need to become direct producers of such activities as they can be provided by other criminal organisations which specialise in such lines of business.

2 Schelling (1971) defines these as *core* activities because criminal organisations need to have complete control over the economic transactions taking place in the underworld to enter these markets.

3 See Anderson (1979) and Rubin (1973) for a thorough discussion of this point.

4 The most complete exposition of this line can be found in Reuter (1983), but see also Jennings (1984).

5 The following arguments have been suggested by Martin and Romano (1992) and Ehrenfeld (1992).

6 The main instances of such deterrence legislation are: restriction of the patrimonial assets; international agreements against money laundering and for stricter regulation of banking firms; public intervention in legal markets monopolised by criminal organisations; introduction of more competitive forms of public procurement; lower enforcement against illegal activities regarded as mildly harmful, but which are relevant sources of profits for the criminal organisations. See Savona (1992) for more on this issue.

7 On this point see Catanzaro (1989) and Arlacchi (1983).

8 We do not focus on the analysis of the stability of cartel agreements between criminal organisations. For a similar analysis focusing on the links between different deterrence policies and cartel stability see Celentani, Marrelli and Martina (1993).

9 See Catanzaro (1989).

10 This description of the objective function of elected decision-makers for deterrence policies against organised crime is the fruit of several discussions with members of the Italian Anti-Mafia Parliamentary Commission during the preparations for a conference held under the auspices of the Italian Parliament on 'The Economics of Organized Crime', held in Rome, May 1993.

11 The sunkness of the investment g^i comes from its own specification, since the structure of the game does not allow for disinvestments during the second stage.

12 This definition of strategic substitutes is given by Bulow, Geanakoplos and Klemperer (1985).

13 This is the Routh-Hurwitz condition for stability of the standard adjustment mechanism. See Nikaido (1968), Ch. 7.

14 The second-order conditions are:

$$k_{ii}^i = r_j^i \frac{\partial^2 q^j}{\partial g^{i2}} - c_{GG}^i q^i - c_G^i \frac{\partial q^i}{\partial g^i} < 0 \quad i \neq j = 1, 2 \tag{10}$$

and we also assume the following stability assumptions analogous to (4):

$$R - k_{ii}^i k_{jj}^j - k_{ij}^i k_\chi^j > 0 \quad i \neq j = 1, 2 \tag{11}$$

where

$$k_{ij}^i = r_j^i \frac{\partial^2 q^j}{\partial g^i \partial g^j} - c_G^i \frac{\partial q^i}{\partial g^j} - c_{GG}^i \theta q^i$$

Condition (11) still ensures stability with the standard adjustment mechanism and ensures uniqueness provided that it holds globally. However from (10) and (11) it can be seen that the existence and uniqueness of the equilibrium can be a problem in this two-stage model. In fact, at least one term in k_{ii}^i is positive, making it uncertain whether the second-order conditions for an interior profit maximum hold. Nevertheless (10) and (11) will hold if c_{GG} is

large enough, that is if the cost-reducing effect of anti-deterrence activities declines rapidly.
15 To check the latter relation one should substitute in (12) the expression for q^j_i given in (6).
16 This assumption seems to be supported by some empirical evidence concerning the cartels formed by different Sicilian mafia families at a regional level. See Santino and La Fiura (1990).
17 The commissioners have no incentives to report quantities which are not market clearing: if they provoke an excess supply they incur costs in storing illegal commodities, and if they induce an excess demand they give up part of their commissions.
18 Recall that Bertrand conjectures can be seen as an approximate description of how the market-clearing mechanism works, such as the laundering of dirty money or loan-sharking.

REFERENCES

Anderson, A. G. (1979), *The Business of Organized Crime*, Stanford CA: The Hoover Institution.
Arlacchi, P. (1983), *La mafia imprenditrice*, Bologna: Il Mulino.
Becker, G. S. and G. J. Stigler (1974), 'Law Enforcement. Malfeasance, and Compensation of Enforcers', *Journal of Legal Studies*, 3(1), pp. 21–35.
Bulow, J., J. Geanakoplos and P. Klemperer (1985), 'Multimarket Oligopoly: Strategic Substitutes and Complements', *Journal of Political Economy*, 93, pp. 488–511.
Buchanan, J. (1973), 'A Defense of Organized Crime?', in S. Rottemberg (ed.) (1973).
Catanzaro, R. (1989), *Il delitto come impresa. Storia sociale della mafia*, Padova: Liviana.
Celentani, M., M. Marrelli and R. Martina (1993), 'Cartel Stability and Deterrence Policies', mimeo, Department of Public Economics, Università di Napoli.
Dixit, A. K. (1986), 'Comparative Statics for Oligopoly', *International Economic Review*, 27, pp. 107–22.
Ehrenfeld, R. (1992), *Evil Money: Encounters Along the Money Trail*, New York: Harper Business.
Jennings, W. P. (1984), 'A Note on the Economics of Organized Crime', *Eastern Economic Journal*, 10(3), July–September, pp. 315–19.
Martin, J. and A. Romano (1992), *Multinational Crime*, Newbery Park CA: Sage.
Nikaido, H. (1968), *Convex Structures and Economic Theory*, San Diego CA: Academic Press.
Reuter, P. (1983), *Disorganized Crime: The Economics of the Visible Hand*, Cambridge MA: MIT Press.
Rottemberg, S. (ed.) (1973), *The Economics of Crime and Punishment*, Washington DC: American Enterprise Institute for Public Policy Research.
Rubin, P. (1973), 'The Economic Theory of the Criminal Firm', in S. Rottemberg (ed.) (1973).
Santino, U. and G. La Fiura (1990), *L'impresa mafiosa*, Milano: Franco Angeli.
Savona, E. (1992), 'La regolazione del mercato della criminalità', mimeo, Roma.

Schelling, T. C. (1967), 'Economics and Criminal Enterprise', *The Public Interest*, 7, pp. 61–78, reprinted in R. Andreano and J. Sigfried (eds.) (1980), *The Economics of Crime*, Cambridge MA: Schenkmann, and in Schelling, T. C. (ed.) (1984), pp. 158–78.

Shapiro, C. (1989), 'Theories of Oligopoly Behavior', in R. Schmalensee and R. D. Willig (eds.), *Handbook of Industrial Organization*, Amsterdam and New York: Elsevier Science Publishers.

Discussion

SAM PELTZMAN

Fiorentini's paper models criminal activity as a game with two stages. In the first stage, criminal groups invest in violence which negatively affects the cost of producing output. In the second stage the criminal group picks output. In each of these stages criminals either compete or cooperate. In the first stage the police choose one of two reactions to violence. Already we have eight possible states-of-the-world, and the paper has more possibilities than those I have mentioned. As is typical of this genre, the paper generates more possibilities than it does clean behavioural implications.

It would be unproductive to go through the catalogue of possible states-of-the-world and the equilibria resulting therefrom. Instead I will focus on some of the paper's more interesting results.

Fiorentini addresses two main questions about the equilibrium level of criminal violence: first, how is it affected by the degree of competition among criminal firms; second, does the police reaction to violence affect this equilibrium? Consider first the case where criminals are competing and total police resources do not respond to changes in criminal violence; the police have 'low concern' in Fiorentini's terminology. In this case, if one firm increases violence it confers a benefit on other criminals, because resources, being fixed in total, are drawn away from enforcement against other firms. The first firm ignores this external benefit, so it underproduces violence from the standpoint of the group. If police do respond to more crime with more total resources (the 'high-concern' case), there would instead be an external cost imposed by one firm's violence. The extra police resources thereby drawn to fighting crime would raise the costs of the other firms. Because the firm initiating violence ignores this external cost, it overproduces violence when viewed from the group's perspective. These externalities can be internalised by collusion or mergers among criminal firms.

From this analysis Fiorentini draws two important conclusions. First, collusion among firms does not necessarily decrease violence. Specifically, in the low-concern case where competition leads to underproduction of violence, cooperation would increase violence. This possibility had been ignored in the previous literature. The second conclusion is even more intriguing. Increased social concern about crime can have the paradoxical effect of inducing the criminals to increase their investment in violence. Recall that violence is underproduced when there is low concern (fixed budgets) and overproduced when there is high concern. So, if politicians respond to a crime wave by shifting from a passive to a reactive stance, the criminals will respond by stepping up their investment in violence.

Fiorentini stops short of giving us empirical implications of the analysis. To do so would require operational counterparts of the level of concern and of criminal investment in violence. In Fiorentini's model, the observable amount of violence is an equilibrium outcome of a process in which criminals' investment and the police response to that investment are the key decision variables. There is no obvious practical way to measure this underlying investment. Nor does Fiorentini provide implications about the 'reduced form' variables like the crime rate or police expenditures.

Until such missing links are provided, I think the important point that emerges from the paper is a suggestion that economic analysis of crime needs to take account of the degree of competition among criminal organisations. We should expect different amounts of crime to accompany production of illegal goods when criminals compete than when their competition is suppressed by cartel-like organisations. The specific results which Fiorentini derives from this intuition are less appealing to me. My main reservation about these results stems from the completely passive, even stupid, role played by police and the political process in his model. Specifically, their choice of response (low or high concern) is arbitrary in the sense of being exogenous. Their objective – is it crime reduction? budget maximisation? political power? – is only discussed lightly. And it is this passive character of the enforcement sector that, I think, produces Fiorentini's specific results.

Consider, for example, the result that a shift from low to high concern raises criminal investment in violence. Now, if the police (or their employers) have as an intermediate or ultimate objective the reduction of this investment in violence, Fiorentini's result has an obvious problem:

the police would always choose low concern. This stance would both save resources and curtail the investment in violence. There may to be sure be better alternatives than maintaining a fixed budget which retain the underproduction-of-violence characteristic of this case. Perhaps for example the police could randomise any response or concentrate any extra resources on expanding firms.

My point is that a more complete story has to say something about the police response that makes sense in the light of some plausible police objectives. Such an approach would permit the police, no less than criminals, to use knowledge of their opponents' actions to help condition policies consistent with their objective. The complement of this is that a fuller model of criminal behaviour should also include the criminals' anticipation of police reactions which are sensible rather than arbitrary. Such an approach would obviously be less tractable than Fiorentini's approach. He has, probably wisely, chosen to pursue an incomplete model for the results its produces. But some caution in interpreting the results is warranted until the gaps are filled.

Another topic that I think demands fuller treatment is the relations between criminals and police. In Fiorentini's model they act independently. The Coase theorem and a casual knowledge of the history of some American cities suggests to me that this not so. Crime is, after all, something of a deadweight loss in the context of this paper, and both sides would gain from reducing it. Whether these gains are exploited or not would depend on factors like the number of firms, the technology of agreement and enforcement when cooperation must be *sub-rosa*, etc. – in short on transactions costs. It seems clear that these costs are not always insuperable. Examples of the resulting agreements include confining criminal violence to targets that are not sensitive politically (e.g. other criminals) and, on the police side, focusing enforcement on recalcitrant firms.

Indeed, it is my sense that the breakdown of this cooperation is behind some of our heightened concern about crime. Part of the apparently reduced ability of criminals and police to reach a *modus vivendi* may be due to a less supportive political climate (the decline of machine politics in the United States, for example). But another part may be the changed competitive environment; there are so many criminal firms that the cost of negotiating and enforcing the *modi vivendi* has become exorbitant.

This example illustrates what I believe the reader can usefully take away from Fiorentini's paper: a general sense that the way criminal markets function is conditioned by the nature of competition or cooperation among criminal actors. I would add that a complementary subject, not touched at all in this paper, may be of even greater importance. This is the state of competition in enforcement. Like most of the literature, Fiorentini assumes a monopoly enforcer. This is highly unrealistic. For example, in the United States the number of privately employed guards and police exceeds those employed by governments by roughly 15 per cent.[1] This is only one indication of how much we miss if we ignore private enforcement. The sort of analysis we see in this paper might usefully be applied to this interaction between public and private enforcement. Consider the externalities from competition which Fiorentini emphasises. They surely exist in enforcement as well as in crime. For example, if a potential target increases deterrent and enforcement efforts, some criminals will be driven to other territories. This negative externality is ignored by the private enforcer, and, in the spirit of this paper, would lead to excessive private enforcement. There are also positive externalities – the private enforcer catches criminals who might have marauded elsewhere and public resources may be diverted elsewhere.[2] Does, on balance, the private response to crime contribute to an efficient overall level of enforcement? This is a subject for future work possibly along the lines of this paper.

NOTES

1 There were 685,000 of the latter in 1991 compared with 601,000 government-employed police, detectives, sheriffs, bailiffs and other law enforcement officers.
2 In the 1970s the University of Chicago (a private institution) established its own police force to patrol the University and the surrounding neighbourhood. Prior to this, eleven police cars from the city's police department patrolled the area. Currently, only three do so.

Index